The Swifts

The Swifts

Printers in the Age of Typesetting Races

WALKER RUMBLE

University of Virginia Press Charlottesville and London

University of Virginia Press
© 2003 by the Rector and Visitors of the University of Virginia
All rights reserved
Printed in the United States of America on acid-free paper

First published 2003

9 8 7 6 5 4 3 2 1

LIBRARY OF CONGRESS CATALOGING-IN-PUBLICATION DATA
Rumble, Walker.
   The swifts : printers in the age of typesetting races / Walker Rumble.
      p.   cm.
   Includes bibliographical references and index.
   ISBN 0-8139-2161-9 (alk. paper)
   1. Typesetting—United States—History—19th century.   2. Typesetting—
Competitions—United States—History—19th century.   3. Printers—United
States—Biography.   4. Printers—Employment—United States—History—
19th century.   5. Printing industry—Employees—Effect of technological
innovations on—United States—History—19th century.   6. Typesetting
machines—United States—History—19th century.   I. Title.

Z253 .R75 2003
686.2′25′097309034—dc21   2002010957

TITLE PAGE: Retired compositors preparing to race at the International Typographical Union's Printers Home in Colorado Springs, Colorado, ca. 1910. (Courtesy, University Archives, University of Colorado at Boulder; ITU Collection, Box
3, Env. 4)

For KD

Contents

Illustrations

Acknowledgments

PORTIONS OF THIS BOOK FIRST APPEARED IN THE FOL-
lowing journals: *Printing History, New England Quarterly, Journal of Popular Culture, Chicago History,* and *American Heritage
of Invention and Technology.* My thanks to each of them. Vincent
Kinane of the Department of Early Printed Book at the Trinity
College Library, Dublin, supplied important Irish printing union
records of the young Joseph W. McCann. McCann's grandson,
Charles Potter of Washington, D.C., provided an archival record
of his grandfather, rare among printers. John McCrillis of the New
Haven (Conn.) Colony Historical Society offered help on Augusta
Lewis. I am especially grateful to Philip Weimerskirch, Special
Collections Librarian at the Providence (R.I.) Public Library. He
opened that institution's splendid Updike Printing Collection to
me. Thanks also to Alice H. R. H. Beckwith, Professor of Art at

Providence College, and Jean Rainwater, Coordinator of Reader Services at Brown University's John Hay Library. The staff of the Barrington, Rhode Island, public library helped throughout.

I learned to print at the firm of Hamilton I. Newell, Inc., in Amherst, Massachusetts, instructed and inspired by many friends, especially Christopher Conley, Steven Durland, and Roxie Mack. Bill Sneeberger's printing life intersected mine at the University of Alabama's Book Arts Program. Coriander Reisbord, printer, friend, and bookbinder, listened to an original draft of the essay that would become this book. Few printers are better than Asa Peavy, proprietor of Bullnettle Press. A long friendship with Michael Grinley surpasses his contribution to this book, itself considerable.

My great debt, the one of longest standing, is to Horace S. Merrill, Professor of History at the University of Maryland and mentor. Sam taught us how to write narrative history. And I would honor an ancient pledge. To Dennis Burton, Pete Daniel, David R. Goldfield, James B. Lane, and Raymond W. Smock: finally, thanks.

Introduction

I T   W A S   A   M A T C H   R A C E   B E T W E E N   T W O   F A M O U S L Y
fast typesetters, a showdown of Swifts. Bill Barnes started quickly
on that wintry December 15, 1885. His first two lines of type were
his fastest, while, at his side, Joe McCann, the betting favorite,
stumbled out of the gate. They would race for four hours, and
McCann would win, but when he fell back early, the crowd, betting on the fly, smelled trouble. They thought they knew McCann;
the young Irishman had beaten Ira Somers six months before in
sensational fashion. Onlookers knew less of Barnes, a *New York
World* journeyman. Barnes's motion, noticed a reporter, was "free
and graceful," while McCann's seemed "stiff." McCann, representing the *New York Herald*, grabbed at his letters, snatching
type "in about the same way that an unsuspecting child would
touch a red hot stove." Then, quickly after his slow start, McCann

found his rhythm. Driving, he pulled abreast of Barnes. The minutes passed, and they "were heard clicking together at the end of each line." Excitement gathered. Cash changed hands. "Oh, boys!" cried the typo Jimmy Hart at the end of every early stickful. "Oh, boys!"[1]

William C. Barnes and Joseph W. McCann were compositors, printers who set type, not printing press operators. In the late nineteenth century, compositors set type by hand, individually, letter following letter. Machines that might do this difficult work—and replace Barnes and McCann—remained fallible and their use visionary. Printing firms necessarily employed multitudes of typesetters. Printers called the fastest and very best of them "Swifts." This book is about the Swifts.

In time, of course, a mechanized workplace replaced the Swifts, but that world left behind the residue of myth. In 1923 the old newspaperman Irvin S. Cobb recalled his youth on the shopfloor: "We had our share of tramp printers," remembered Cobb, "erratic, uncertain, capable chaps, born spellers most of them, men who had been everywhere and had seen everything, and generally men who had read a lot and remembered what they had read; so that, from reading and travel and observation, they were walking mines of information on all manner of subjects—a strangely attractive type who died out as a class when the linotype machines came in."[2]

The Swifts constituted a particular segment of Cobb's late-nineteenth-century compositors, men who became famous by winning typesetting races. Along with their cash prizes and their fame, the brash independence of those fast typesetters impressed others of their trade, and by the 1880s fellow printers acclaimed them as working-class heroes. At the height of their glory, however, Swifts confronted serious threats to their way of life and manner of livelihood. As Irvin Cobb suggested, newly introduced typesetting equipment automated what for centuries printers had done by hand, and contention did not end with shifts in technology. After the American Civil War, women printers pressed traditional claims on male shopfloor legitimacy with renewed vigor.

Subsequently, graphic designers, newly installed in printing plants at the turn of the century, challenged what was left of the Swifts' prized shopfloor expertise. Handsetting journeymen compositors found few remedies for their suddenly endangered existence. Most Swifts simply vanished. By the turn of the twentieth century, their races had already faded to dim memory.

The story of the Swifts revives those memories in a new context. Early twenty-first-century techniques in mass communications have changed remarkably in response to the impact of electronic media, the personal computer, and desktop publishing. We have left an age of print and entered an electronic age, and if we have been told this too often and too emphatically, the changes are real, and they will take getting used to. But there is precedent. Nineteenth-century compositors, exemplified by typeracing Swifts, gave way to machine operators in the same way that phototype compositors have given way to code-writing computer programmers and text formatters. Simply put, the digital present is heir to a long typographic tradition of metal.

Contexts for Change

This is a study of technological dislocation in the printing industry and the shifting power under the feet of a group of elite workers, the Swifts. Four broad social changes underlie the narrative. First, *technological advances.* Machine composition replaced handwork, and thus ended the hegemony of the Swifts. Second, *broadened work opportunities for women.* The advent of women on the printing shopfloor threatened to lower wages, "feminize" male workplace culture, and present a competitive challenge to job performance. Third, *the rise of an entertainment culture.* Dime museums, inexpensive entertainment palaces that combined carnival sideshow and vaudeville comedy, discovered profit in typesetting races and transfigured printing as a public amusement. Fourth, *a redefinition of artisanry.* Stylistic refinement among printers redefined competence, supplanting speed with aesthetics.

When typesetting machines displaced the Swifts after the

mid-1880s, the new technology ended 450 years of setting type Johannes Gutenberg's way: by hand. For the next ninety years, until the mid-1970s, printers depended on versions of Ottmar Mergenthaler's Linotype or Tolbert Lanston's Monotype to compose their type. Both Linotype and Monotype machines used a keystroke triggering mechanism to inject small amounts of hot-lead alloy into a type mould, or matrix. Mergenthaler's machine stacked these matrices into a row and produced an entire line, or "slug," of metal type (a line o' type). The Monotype system, as its name suggests, produced single metal letters. Hot-metal composing machines typified typesetting until the last quarter of the twentieth century.

Then, for roughly fifteen years dating from the mid-1970s, a new technology called phototypesetting swept aside the old. The operator keyboarded text into a computer, which then drove a typesetting machine that photographed letters and characters from photographic filmstrip negatives. In short order, the process of photographing letters evolved to filmsetting from digital impulses. In both cases, the operator developed the resulting positive—the text—in a standard photographic filmbath to produce a proof.

The keyboards of phototypesetting machines differed from the Linotype's original "etaoin shrdlu" configuration.[3] All phototype-setters (Compugraphic, Wang, Mergenthaler, Varitype, several others) used "qwerty" keyboards, keyboards typical of standard clerical typewriters. Predictably, Linotype operators and other old-line printers called the operators of the new machinery—these new compositors—"glorified typists" and did not consider them printers at all.

Hot Type, Cold Type, No Type

Late-nineteenth-century printers had rehearsed much of this history. Compositors who set type by picking up tiny metal letters and manually aligning them into rows could not imagine how machines might replace them. The simplest evidence indicated the contrary. As of the late nineteenth century, no machine had convincingly done it, while sophisticated machinery dominated every other aspect of the printing trades.

At first a printing type had been a discrete piece of metal—the celebrated Gutenberg gift. Even when typesetting became mechanized, the type itself remained metal. Type changed radically when phototype (often called "cold type" to distinguish it from earlier molten metal "hot type") replaced metal letters with photographs of those letters. Still, type remained an entity. If it no longer was something a printer could toss in his hand, it nonetheless continued to be something you could see, an image on a negative film strip. Likewise, the computer manipulation required to drive a phototypesetter remained a compositor's job, one that was performed by typesetting personnel in printing plants.

This, too, changed in the last decade of the twentieth century. Letters of the alphabet, numbers, and all the rest of the symbols of the printed page became congeries of electronic impulses, bits lacking spatial or material existence. Correspondingly, the practice of setting type—on this very page, for instance—an activity that once involved hundreds of thousands of artisans and dominated an industry, also changed completely. By the last years of the twentieth century, most composition was a species of "information processing," a procedure by which typesetting itself became an exchange of information, keyboarded "input" that was forwarded through networked computers or swapped floppy disks. Actual remaining printshop composition fell into generalized "prepress" activity.

According to the printing historian Alexander Lawson, the journeyman Swift "represented the ultimate triumph of the ordinary compositor as a free spirit who could fully control at the frame the design of the printed work, before giving way as a typographic entrepreneur." Swifts raced one another at this, on the edge of momentous change. It was a significant moment in the history of the printed word, "a time," Lawson called it, "of giants."[4]

The Swifts

1   A Gutenberg Legacy

BY THE LAST THIRD OF THE NINETEENTH CENTURY, large cities throughout the United States had matured and factories fed their enterprise. Printers in those industrialized places worked, played, and socialized within the boundaries of a handful of interrelated institutions, typically shopfloors, union halls, and saloons. Earlier in the century, however, most Americans had lived in small towns, isolated villages with complex and interwoven relationships. In these island communities, small printing shops produced an entire range of necessary local literature: deeds, advertising circulars, bills of exchange, church and entertainment programs, contracts. Amid the miscellany, a weekly newspaper was a printshop mainstay. Chances were the shop sat on Main Street, squarely in the center of town. All breezes, foul wind and fair, passed through it.

It followed that the requirements and techniques of communicating with each other were those appropriate to isolated small towns and villages. Printers, for instance, used traditionally accessible equipment and tools: a hand-operated press, paper made from rag pulp, homebrewed ink. Printing had changed very little from its origins, from the tools and materials used by Johannes Gutenberg himself.

The Classic Trade

Printers used hand presses similar in design to the model made famous by Revolutionary-era printer Isaiah Thomas. Indeed, many early-nineteenth-century presses were wooden "screw" presses exactly like those used by the very earliest American printers—Ben Franklin's press, and before it, that of Stephen Day. Day had used a wooden screw press to print the *Bay Psalm Book*, first printed book in the colonies. Ordinarily two men operated such printing presses. Using padded leather balls, one of these men batted ink onto a batch of metal type, a text block situated in the bed of the press. The other selected a sheet of paper, probably dampened in order to receive the best impression, and readied that sheet on the press. He then pulled heavily on the lever arm of the press, and a screw mechanism forced a platen down and into the standing letters. The second person thereupon removed the inked sheet and literally hung it to dry. Press operation, of all printing work, particularly demanded strong arms and a stout back.

One by one, sheet by sheet, through long hours, printers accomplished their press run. Printing was time-consuming, heavily routine work. The people who did that work conformed to a standard shopfloor occupational pattern. A printing shop pressman was a skilled "journeymen" who had learned the trade in just such an establishment. His helper might also be a journeymen, a second printing hand fully prepared to spell the first. Possibly, though, the helper was an apprentice, a youngster not much beyond his twelfth birthday who was indentured to the shop in order to learn the trade. A master printer owned such a shop. He hired

A journeyman compositor at his cases.
(From a nineteenth-century engraving of Willard Poinsette Snyder's drawing)

these persons, boarded and instructed the youngsters, and over-saw the entire operation.

Type, of course, had been set before pressmen fed paper onto the printing press. Village printing shop compositors, as typesetters were called, were likely the same individuals who would subsequently operate the press. A typesetter "composed" a text in tiny pieces of metal arranged to specific measures that formed agreeable patterns. A newspaper column was a simple rectangle of letters, while a business card or letterhead stationery became an adroit combination of large and small letters, tasteful symbols, and helpfully ruled lines.[1]

Before machines arrived to mechanize the task, printers set type by hand with tools of elemental simplicity. An individual faced an elevated case containing an assortment of discrete metal characters: letters of the alphabet, punctuation symbols, numbers. Each of these characters occupied an appropriate cubbyhole in the case, large for a couple hundred of the letter *e* and small for a dozen semicolons. The typesetter reached into the case for each and every letter and then placed that letter, upside down and running backward, in a "typestick" that he held in his left hand. The typestick was a small, traylike receptacle—often called a "pan," one of many nicknames—in which a typesetter's single letters formed words, then lines, and then stacked lines of type that became a block of text perhaps twenty lines deep, depending on the size of the type. When the typesetter had filled his composing stick, he carefully slid the block of type out of the stick and onto a larger metal tray called a "galley." Then he turned back to the case and repeated the process.

Printers had much to know. A master printer, that is to say an employing printer, might assume a range of abilities in all of his journeymen, those workers who had learned their trade after years of apprenticeship. All journeyman printers had learned to choose ink and paper and to compose a page by standard spacing rules of margin, lines, and letters. In the end, they had learned to achieve a readable printed impression of that page on those papers.

Journeymen typesetters were the codebreakers of village America. Before typewriting machines, only handwritten copy arrived at printing shops. In a land of local inflection and neighborhood argot, master printers gave compositors the job of translating scribbled and garbled texts into grammatical prose. Deciphering badly handwritten copy was not merely an occupational nuisance; it was an essential part of a printer's literacy and therefore of his skill. The codes were, of course, local variants of standard English usage expressed in ignorance, jargon, or slang. The compositor became an intermediary between variously literate contributors and their reading public. A compositor's skill combined wide-ranging literacy and deft craftsmanship. More than anything, it suggested prowess.

Prowess, in turn, was the stuff of sport. Printing shopfloors were deadline driven, busy in spurts. The ebb and flow of printing projects as well as the varying time demands of those jobs translated into a work flow of consistent irregularity. At slack moments, shopfloors might be extremely casual places. Printing offered plenty of opportunities for socializing and many occasions for games.

Journeymen might, for instance, "jeff." Jeffing was a dice game, an ancient printing pastime inherited through dim European antecedents. It was a form of craps, printing's version of shooting dice, a game of chance that printers often used to settle shopfloor disputes or priorities. Given a dense Sunday sermon of solid text or a local poet's latest lines, airy and widely spaced, two compositors might jeff for the jobs. Instead of dice, however, they played with metal spacing cubes the trade called quadrats, or "quads." Printers used quads to fill out the ends of partial lines, those that ended paragraphs, for instance, or those that completed all the short lines—the "fat"—of a poet's verse.[2]

Printers also raced at setting type. Although printers might do this in various ways, typesetting races were basically simple affairs. One typesetter thought he was faster at his task than another and offered a challenge. The compositors thereupon selected equivalent portions of a job at hand, set a time limit, and raced. As was true of all shopfloor athletics, compositors without any other bone of contention raced for beer, a shopfloor lubricant in any case.

Occasionally a printing shop employed a prodigy, a compositor so clearly superior to his colleagues as to preclude challenge. Facing dreary prospects, shopmates might offer their speed demon a prize if he could set an impossibly large quantity of type within equally impossible time limits. They bet on his chances. In time, modest printshop contests such as these became the headline events of Swifts.

A Manly Competence

The village printing shop was a basic communications system, and more besides. Within its simple structure, the master-journeyman-apprentice system also defined a labor force and described the way—the only way—a person became a full-fledged printer. From earliest colonial America, such an education governed the entrance of boys into the working world of men. By design, the system socialized its youngsters while it regulated a labor supply. Boys learned a trade and how to behave—and learned to be men.[3]

A nineteenth-century printing education produced tradesmen, workingmen who considered themselves part of a fluid hierarchy of skills. Master printers were proprietors who waited on customers, ordered paper and ink, kept the books, and, most important, supplied printing press and types—the tools of the trade. They also scheduled the work, supervised its flow, and worked along with their employees. Those employees were skilled journeymen who once had been green apprentices, as had been the master printer himself. Masters paid their journeymen "by the piece," by the amount of their daily work. Apprentices, who received no pay whatever, spent three to seven years learning the "art and mystery" of their calling under the stewardship of a master and by the examples of shop journeymen. A master's stewardship included an apprentice's room, board, and various personal necessities. In parental fashion, a master punished small crimes and insubordination, but protected his youngsters from external dangers from sheriff's deputies to village ruffians. At some point between his eighteenth and twenty-first birthday, an apprentice completed his indenture and became a journeyman printer. His master thereupon gave him a suit of clothes, a symbol of arriving manhood, and a set of work tools—perhaps a personal composing stick and a rule—in recognition of his formal entry into the fraternity of the trade.[4]

As important as clothing and tools, a young printer's working equipment by now included a supple, competent literacy. Apprenticeships in all the trades were expected to confer solid bedrock values—hard work, responsibility, competence, sobriety. These characteristics made you a man. A printer's literacy, however, made a young man special. Among urban immigrant enclaves as in rural populations, his literacy meant that the young man sustained a claim on a community elite, townspeople who were widely read and accustomed to grammatical niceties. It was this special literacy that made printing the "aristocracy" of trades, as it always had been. It was the essence of his "manly competence."[5]

No girls shared this preparation; female printing apprentices were nonexistent. This is not to say there were no women printers. There were thousands of them. In village America, wives and daughters and helping girls regularly worked in the shop. Indeed, printers' widows routinely inherited their late husband's shops and successfully maintained those businesses in numbers sufficient to make them virtually a social type.[6] At midcentury, *Finchers' Trades Review* reported that at least half the compositors in American towns were women.

Nonetheless, printing and its journeymen represented a completely gendered occupation. Despite the number of women in the trade, none of them ever completed a printing apprenticeship, and therefore none of them became journeymen compositors, members in good standing of a trade. This meant that thousands of skilled and tireless workers were individually most valuable when relatively little was expected of them as a group. Women often worked at reduced wage levels. Although it was rare enough in rural America, women workers might even replace costlier men—or their presence might so threaten journeymen. As wrenching to shopfloor tranquillity as this may have been, cheap, unapprenticed labor further deprived young women of their full claim to the moral stature of working men. In the fullest sense of the word, women could not possibly achieve a "competence," the skills required to hold up one's head, support a family, be a responsible member of the community. The idea was inculcated in young male printers. In their view, adult women, like apprenticed boys, lacked the credentials that defined a working person's virtue. They were "other" than men, categorically and contingently different.[7]

A Printing Explosion

During the second quarter of the nineteenth century, printing diversified in two interrelated but distinct ways. First, having left Main Street, the nation's printing shops became an "industry." That printing industry specialized, and did so in three general ways. In the cities, large daily newspapers created enormous and specialized printing plants. In the largest of the cities—New York, Boston, Philadelphia—book publishing companies also established their own printing facilities. The multitasked village job shop remained, perhaps much larger, but shorn of its book and newspaper work. By the 1840s, the system matured, and printing subsequently divided into three distinct varieties: miscellaneous jobbing work, book manufacture, and newspaper publishing.

The second kind of change was a simple explosion in trade. All types of printing experienced huge growth, but something very like a revolution happened among newspapers. The village newspaper, ordinarily published weekly, had always been the mainstay of a local printing shop. As the printing trades expanded and diversified throughout the nineteenth century, journeymen often favored newspaper work because it paid particularly well. In 1830 the country had 650 weeklies and 65 daily newspapers. The average circulation of a daily was 1,200, so the total daily circulation was about 78,000. Ten years later there were 1,141 weeklies and

138 dailies. The dailies averaged 2,200 in circulation and a total circulation of 300,000. This was in excess of population growth, which itself was considerable.

Newspapers of the early nineteenth century were either narrowly commercial or frankly political. Commercial newspapers, often with words such as "advertiser" or "mercantile" in their titles, were unadorned announcements of available merchandise and scheduled ship landings. Political sheets frankly supported one party or another, expressed predictably partisan points of view, and made little effort toward "objectivity." These newspapers were expensive, usually costing six cents an issue when local workmen made eighty-five cents a day. Even if a reader were prepared to pay, newspapers were difficult to find. Publishers sold them mainly by subscription, and single issues were available only at the printer's office. The system helps explain low circulation figures of the early nineteenth century.[8]

In the 1830s several newspapers broke with this tradition and introduced what became known as the "penny press." Starting in New York and spreading to the other major American cities, newspaper publishers sold their sheets for a penny, startlingly cheap when most papers cost six cents. Moreover, instead of billing clients for annual subscriptions, publishers hired newsboys to peddle penny papers on city street corners. The *New York Sun,* first published on September 3, 1833, became the first of the penny papers. Within months it claimed a circulation of 5,000, and two years later it was selling 15,000 copies a day. Others followed: James Gordon Bennett's *New York Herald,* the *Boston Daily Times,* the *Philadelphia Public Ledger,* the *Baltimore Sun.* Instead of political partisanship or the ties to a subscribing elite of commerce and society, the penny press relied on market-based income from advertising revenue and street sales. The penny press chased its readers, offering them what they wished to read, from "want ads" and patent medicine cures to the coverage of murder trials. Newspaper business boomed.[9]

Book manufacture in America expanded, as well. More accurately, early-nineteenth-century Americans invented their own book printing industry. Typically, local authors had forwarded their work to London for publication, particularly their longest efforts. What remained were sermons, primers, and miscellaneous tracts meant for local consumption. Early-nineteenth-century printers imported much of the material of book production—paper, type, ink, printing presses, decorated papers, gold leaf for binding—as well as the skilled labor to use these things. By the 1850s everything had changed. Americans continued to import books, of course, and did so cheaply in the absence of copyright laws. By 1856, however, schoolbooks, which made up between 30 and 40 percent of book production, were wholly American, and resident Americans wrote three-quarters of the new novels, romances, and popular reading of most of the population. American book houses profited by reprinting foreign works in the sciences, philosophy, jurisprudence, medicine and surgery, divinity, criticism, and much more. According to the historian Michael Winship, "there can be no doubt that by the 1850s a thriving literary culture had been established in the United States."[10]

The expansion and diversification that occurred in newspaper and book printing also enlarged the tasks of local or neighborhood job shops—the traditional printers. In the early 1840s, for example, the young New York job printing firm of John F. Trow began printing city directories, a new kind of document. Trow's first such effort was a commercial compendium called *Wilson's Business Directory,* and shortly thereafter the Trow firm inaugurated a complete *City Directory of New York,* a listing that accounted for everyone in town and that presaged and resembled the ubiquitous telephone book. Together, these publications made Trow's fortune and reputation. A half-century later, Howard Lockwood's *American Dictionary of Printing and Bookmaking* called Trow "the most considerable printer New York has ever had, taking into view the magnitude of his office and the length of time it has continued."[11]

Over the years, Trow's printing firm became a large version of a small town or neighborhood job shop, akin to the link between Andrew Carnegie's steel business and the village smithy. In the process, jobs such as the city directory became labor-intensive work, work that was also difficult to coordinate under the pressures of deadline. "In years in which there has been competition," said Howard Lockwood, Trow turned out that directory in eleven or twelve days.[12]

To do this, Trow innovated in several ways. He first of all turned to power presses, replacing the old hand-pulled platen models with newer and faster machines called "bed and platen" presses. These presses, first a model introduced by the inventor Otis Tufts and subsequently a press developed by the brothers Isaac and Seth Adams, used a flywheel assembly connected to a central drive shaft. This, in turn, drove the cams and pulleys that advanced paper and raised and lowered the bed of the press at the point of impression. Power other than human muscle drove bed and platen presses. Trow originally used mules to power his Tufts

John F. Trow became wealthy and famous for printing New York's first city directory, the precursor to the modern telephone book. The city directory was an extensive and highly patterned typesetting project that, in 1855, allowed Trow to use Mitchel composing machines, thus becoming the first successfully to replace handsetting journeymen with "automatic" typesetting equipment.

(From *American Dictionary of Printing and Bookmaking,* New York: Howard Lockwood & Co., 1894)

model. Adams models eventually replaced horsepower with the energy produced by steam. Operating at speeds of from five hundred to one thousand impressions an hour, power-driven machines were two to five times faster than traditional hand-pulled presses.[13]

The Trow Printing Company also introduced stereotyping as early as 1840. This process manufactured a single metal plate from a text block of individually set types. Printers (stereotypers quickly became specialists within the trade) made papier-mâché (or plaster or clay) casts of entire pages of handset type. A pressman printed from these stereotype plates, not the originally handset letters, the types themselves being dispersed for further use. Extended press runs quickly wore out type, and stereotype plates naturally alleviated this stress. Further, stereotyping provided Trow and others, especially book manufacturers, the option of shorter press runs of any given title. Should a publication prove popular, printers could reprint it quickly from plates. It saved the printer the expense of standing type (and the concomitant requirement of buying more) or of resetting the job from scratch.

Perfection of these technologies and techniques in the 1830s represented a cost savings, especially on big jobs and jobs that might need reprinting. It also increased a printing firm's productivity. Originally, the Trow Printing Company imported unusual fonts of type—Greek, Hebrew, Arabic, Syriac, Ethiopian, Coptic —and specialized in printing books using these languages. Supplies of these exotic types allowed Trow to print elaborate and voluminous projects such as *Appleton's Cyclopaedia*. Stereotyping allowed Trow to minimize his available supply of highly specialized typefaces by filing and warehousing plates and not the types themselves.[14]

The expansion and diversification in printing mirrored similar changes in all sectors of the nation's economy. An early-nineteenth-century American republic of island communities, liberal, mercantilist, and socially deferential, became an egalitarian, self-interested society that was closely tied to an expanding marketplace. People invested in and consumed goods produced outside the household, and according to media theorist James W. Carey, out of the pattern came a "national commercial middle class."[15] Modern consumer democracy arrived. The historian Michael Schudson called it a "democratic market society."[16]

Technological change accompanied the evolving specializations within the market economy. Printers innovated to cut their costs and boost their production. By midcentury, printing entrepreneurs and inventors introduced new printing presses, experimented with innovative power sources for those presses, and developed a new kind of paper to print on. Printers, in order to work faster, cheaper, and more efficiently, changed everything they could think of—except one. They needed a machine that could set type.

Nineteenth-century technology rarely stood still. Inventors offered a consistent stream of new and improved printing presses. As early as 1814, faster models, many of them employing a revolving cylinder mechanism, began replacing the classic and ancient flatbed press. Frederick Koenig's steam-powered cylinder press produced one thousand sheets per hour per side, roughly ten times faster than the best flatbed hand press. Koenig's press, like other cylinder machines, was difficult to operate compared to flatbed presses, besides which it produced inferior work. Moreover, apart from the largest newspaper and magazine printers, few early-nineteenth-century printers needed its productivity. Still, as early as 1847, the printing press firm of Hoe and Company, a colossus in the field throughout the century, installed the first two-cylinder press at the *Philadelphia Public Ledger*. The "Hoe Type Revolving Machine" and its improvements became standard equipment in newspaper pressrooms. The speed and convenience of rotary cylinder presses increased after midcentury and upon the perfection of curved stereotype plates that could be adapted to the new presses.

The new machines that increased shop capacity required greater power, from more efficient sources. Arm strength alone could not drive the new machines. At his Manhattan printing firm, for example, John F. Trow experimented first with a mule-driven

Tufts press and then introduced an Adams bed-and-platen press driven by steam. And power demands did not cease with printing presses. Beginning in 1825 gas illumined printing establishments, replacing candles. Electricity became a viable shopfloor option only at the end of the century. Before mechanization, printing managers expected high composing room labor costs in any circumstance. As a result, high-volume printers such as book manufacturers and newspapers looked to their pressmen for their profits. Accordingly, pressrooms were wired first. In any event, handsetting compositors disliked electricity. Early lighting systems pulsated.[17]

In addition to equipment and power, printers looked for cheaper paper. Innovations in papermaking techniques and products were crucial to the expansion of printing. The Chinese invented paper, using pulped vegetable fibers, but the technology languished. Thirteenth-century Italians at Fabriano, Italy, opened the first European paper mill, and linen rag paper subsequently became the routine and essential nineteenth-century printing surface. Pounding machines beat rags into pulp. A workman then scooped a wire screen through a vat of pulp, shook that mould, drained away its water, and pressed the residue into a sheet. The process was slow and expensive. Worse, nineteenth-century papermakers were running out of rags. In 1827 the Fourdrinier mechanical papermaking process had arrived in the United States. This speeded the papermaking process but depleted its raw materials. In 1850 American papermakers began producing wood pulp paper, which was cheap but degradable and flimsy. Sixteen years later, papermakers introduced sulfite treatment of wood pulp, but "chemical wood"—a pulp that produced a strong, durable, and inexpensive printing sheet—was not widely available for another twenty years.[18]

A century's worth of ardent searching might have been expected to produce a speedy, accurate, and dependable typesetting machine, a machine to supplant printing's slow and expensive hand compositors. It did not. Hordes of skilled workmen, their numbers steadily increasing, formed a logjam in print production, slowing work, and driving up costs. Despite innovations everywhere, typesetting became the last printing task to be mechanized.

Printing's Longest Revolution

Typesetting was simplicity itself. Nineteenth-century compositors came equipped with their typesticks and their skills, employing printers supplied the type, and that was pretty much that. Setting type was routine, repetitive work that almost everyone, especially youngsters, found intrinsically dull. At some point during a long and boring day at the case, the idea surely occurred to every apprentice that if ever a machine was called for, it was in composition. In Hannibal, Sam Clemens had been such an apprentice. "I worked," Mark Twain famously remembered, "not diligently, not willingly, but fretfully, lazily, repiningly, complainingly, disgustedly, and always shirking the work when I was not watched." In time Twain became a ceaseless investor in equipment that might ease this occupational pestilence. Boredom was the issue for Sam Clemens, not creeping production rates, and one hundred years worth of journeymen printers easily agreed.[19]

Costs of production did, however, concern John F. Trow. In typesetting machinery as in so many other shopfloor contrivances, the New Yorker Trow led the way. Beginning in 1855, he became the first to incorporate "automatic" typesetting equipment into commercial operation. Trow used a machine called a Mitchel Composer, introduced two years earlier by the American inventor and machinist William H. Mitchel. Mitchel's invention was rudimentary. Responding to an operator's keystrokes, the machine dropped standard metal types into an accumulating and undifferentiated line of letters.[20] The operator subsequently punctuated the letter string by hand and divided it into words. Trow installed and used a dozen Mitchel machines to set his city directories. His firm became "the first printing-house in the world in which type was regularly set by machinery."[21]

By 1855 printers and inventors had already been trying to mechanize the process for a while. As far back as 1822, William

Church, a native Vermonter living in London, patented a mechanized system for setting type. Church found no manufacturer for
his prototype; it failed and vanished. Then, some twenty years
after Church's effort, the United States government issued a
patent for an imported British machine. The Pianotyp, devised by
the Englishman James Young and a French colleague, Adrien
Delcambre, resembled a musical instrument fit for a parlor. Its
name derived from its aspiring bank of type channels that rose behind a letter keyboard, an arrangement that made the Pianotyp
look less like a piano than a pipe organ.

Still, mechanical typesetting lagged badly compared to the rest
of printing's equipment. The remarkable thing about John Trow's
entrepreneurial innovation was how singular it was and how late.
Printing press technology had flourished since the introduction of
the Stanhope iron press in the first decade of the nineteenth century. Columbian and Albion presses and dozens of other printing
devices ensued, all complex in innumerable ways. Developments
in mechanical typesetting, however, lagged far behind. It seemed
impossible to replace human compositors, men and women whose
task required them to make hundreds of small judgments each
hour, each decision unique, however tiny.

But during the decade of the 1850s, inventors introduced a
handful of new efforts. In 1857 both W. H. Houston and Timothy Alden patented automatic typesetters, and the search for viable machinery accelerated with the conclusion of the Civil War.
By the end of the century, the United States Patent Office had
registered more than 1,500 patents for composing machines.
Some thirty years after John Trow experimented with his Mitchel
typesetters, Ottmar Mergenthaler's "revolutionary" Linotype
would be but the latest in a lengthening line of variously useful
composing machines.[22]

Labor Organization

By that time, the end of the century, any typesetting equipment
that would displace handsetting journeymen printers faced the
potential opposition of strong and well-organized trade unions.

Throughout the nineteenth century, printing's craft union movement was as vigorous as any in the land. Like many skilled nineteenth-century workers, a printer often worked autonomously at discrete tasks that eventually dovetailed with the work of others. Those tasks—a section of newspaper copy, a book chapter, part of an annual report—eventually required pooled energy and shared labor. Deadline pressures demanded certain shopfloor harmonies that at any time might strain the communal good will. Stresses on individual compositors within this structure were centrifugal. Because compositors were pieceworkers, they received pay in direct proportion to the amount of type they set. Each compositor's worth was a function of his speed, which, in turn, dictated his wage. The system constantly required a reconciliation of contentious individual claims with those of a group. Shopfloor journeymen, as they had done for centuries—in New World or Old—organized themselves into "chapels" and elected a "father," or chairman, to lead them in equitable rules of work distribution and social conduct.[23]

Nineteenth-century printers thought that the skills and effort a worker brought to a job constituted a "labor property right." Working hours were a journeyman's own property, which he sold to an employer. Innovative equipment altered the straightforward nature of such a transaction. Typically, according to the historian David Montgomery, "machinery belonged to a company, which sold the workers' output for its own profit in intensely competitive markets." To survive and grow within that market, "a company was obliged not only to hold its labor costs as low as possible but also to introduce new machinery to raise output and eliminate workers."[24] To maintain autonomy and standing within this power relationship, printers had each other and a courage of confrontation, part of a printer's repertoire of insistence. In an unfolding nineteenth century, harnessing the one to the other increasingly demanded an extension of chapel organization into strong labor unions.

Throughout the nineteenth century, American printers were among the earliest and best organized working people in the nation. Dating to 1852, the National Typographical Union was the first national trade union.[25] Through local "societies" of Revolutionary-era printers, the Typographical Union could trace itself to a tradition of ancient European labor guilds, organizations devoted to common responses to persistent printing problems, significant among which was the ongoing difficulty with partially trained printers who willingly worked below standard wage. Access to the trade—printing's gatekeeping function—was an ancient problem, fundamentally important to the definition of gainful wage. In nineteenth-century America, as always everywhere, this access preoccupied working printers and precipitated their union movement.

Duff Green forced the issue. Green published the *United States Telegraph* out of Washington, D.C., and in 1834 opened what he called a training school for apprentice-aged compositors. Offering a single year's worth of on-the-job instruction, Green promised to teach the trade to two hundred boys between the ages of eleven and fourteen. Naturally, the arrangement was far cheaper than paying journeyman scale to competent printers. Three decades later, women's rights advocates would use an identical tactic to gain access to printing's labor market. In the meantime, Green's plan implicitly recognized an approaching fact of industrial life in the United States. Large shopfloors teeming with typesetters were replacing the local job shop, and lightly trained, runaway apprentices surfaced on many of those shopfloors. Green, by contrast, insisted his program was sensibly responsible.

Duff Green had devised a factory scheme for training typesetters, an alternative to the existing apprenticeship apparatus. Printers thought Green demeaned their profession and impoverished its artisanry, and they needed a way to contend with his threat. In 1850 Horace Greeley, founder of the *New York Tribune*, helped establish the New York Printers' Union. According to Greeley, "the first if not the most important movement to be made in advance of our present social position is the organization of Labor." Dismayed by challenges to a decent printing wage, Greeley presumed that the "basis of all moral and social reform lay in a practical recognition of the right of every human being to demand of the community an opportunity to labor and to receive decent subsistence." Two years later at a printing convention in Cincinnati, New York's union became Local No. 6 of a brand-new national organization, one of fourteen original members.[26]

The International Typographical Union (ITU) built on years of local print union organizing, movements themselves heir to a craft guild tradition. Their problems nonetheless remained chronic. The Duff Green episode had forced the issue of gatekeeping—the definition of membership and what it meant to be a "practical printer." From the start, the ITU sponsored the traditional apprentice system as a means both of training printers and of certifying union membership. The fusion of purpose seemed crucial. Delegates to printing conventions endlessly discussed apprenticeship programs.

Gatekeeping control provided the ITU a way of offering professional cohesion to its membership. It also raised the issue of sovereignty. From the start, the ITU was a federated organization that divided authority among union locals and an overarching national office. Rural locals representing far-flung and disparate printshops occupied a different world from that of city delegations representing composing room staffs that numbered in the hundreds. Printers of Keokuk, their concerns easily buried by the agendas of city delegations, quickly claimed a unity offered by a national organization and favored a strongly centralized, overarching ITU sovereignty. New York printers, however, required the strength of a national union far less. The New York printing union's designation as Local No. 6 of the ITU quickly provided its nickname, and the powerhouse "Big Six" subsequently dominated labor affairs well beyond its own jurisdictions. By the last quarter of the nineteenth century, contested sovereignty permeated all substantive issues, from wages and hours to women on the shopfloor.[27]

Greeley and Reid

Horace Greeley had been, in the language of printing, a "practical printer," a complete printer. Himself a product of the apprentice system, he exemplified it as well. Greeley rose from a hired journeyman to become a master, an employing printer, and subsequently he founded the *New York Tribune.* Greeley initially would not hire a college graduate who did not show he could overcome the "handicap" of a college education. Once, when a college-educated fledgling reporter applied for work, Greeley grumbled "I'd a damned sight rather you had graduated at a printer's case!" and passed him to his managing editor, Whitelaw Reid.[28] Reid, a college man with no printing experience whatever, gave the young man the job. When eventually he succeeded Greeley at the *Tribune,* the skills, attitudes, and expectations Reid brought to his tasks were those of a corporate executive, not a master printer.

Whitelaw Reid also became the dark star of a journeyman's world. After the business panic of 1877, Reid offered his compositors reduced wages, hired nonunion replacements, and combated union printers at every opportunity. Reid's *Tribune* composing room was entirely nonunion. Under Greeley, the newspaper had been home to fast typesetters such as Ben Glasby and Hugh Morton. Veteran *Tribune* compositor Amos J. Cummings thought Glasby and Morton had been "the fastest good typesetters in New York for years."[29] Unwelcomed by Reid, all the celebrated fast typesetters abandoned the *Tribune.*

Employers such as Whitelaw Reid forced a paradox on journeymen printers. By midcentury, the best compositors in the world no longer damped paper, ran a press, or performed the range of printing tasks. Many of those accomplished printers worked at book printing plants or large job-printing shops, but most of them toiled at metropolitan newspapers, where, despite Whitelaw Reid, the wages were highest. Big city dailies paid them the most, but required only their quick and nimble typesetting. A skilled artisanry stood hours on end at its typecases. For journeymen compositors, it meant that the pathway to printing excellence—to pride of workmanship, accomplishment—had narrowed to speed alone.

2 The Arensberg Wager and the Swifts

AT FIRST THEY CALLED HIM "THE BOY." IN 1869 A fresh-faced twenty-year-old printing compositor named George Arensberg arrived in New York. Within a year he would be famous, shopmates at the *New York Times* would call him "The Velocipede," and the nickname would last the rest of his life.

Arensberg had E. A. Donaldson, a composing room foreman at the *Times,* to thank for his nickname and much else, as well. That winter, Donaldson, a "sporting man," offered young Arensberg an opportunity to prove that he was fast enough to set four stickfuls of type in an hour. Then Donaldson, a noted "boat puller, billiard player, and base ballist," spread the word. Printers from throughout New York's newspapers and printing shops converged on the composing room of the *New York Sun,* neutral territory, to "invest" in Arensberg. On the afternoon of February 19, 1870,

Arensberg set 2,064 ems of solid minion type in a single hour, becoming in the process "the world's fastest typesetter" and an authentic journeyman hero.[1]

Swifts

Almost everyone has forgotten typesetting races. In fact, there was celebrity to the nineteenth-century printing life, and racing played a large role in it. At newspapers and job shops throughout the country, printers called compositors "typos" or "comps" and referred to particularly fast ones as "Swifts." After midcentury, Swifts began to compete with increasing energy, in widening circles. Printshop composing rooms held contests, kept records, published challenges, and generally encouraged interest in what had been the industry's intramural sport. By the 1880s, names such as "Bangs" Levy and "Kid" DeJarnatt dominated what was becoming a circuit of touring professionals, auguring a later era's golfers and bowlers.

It is well to remember that compositors had raced from the day there were two of them, usually for beer. Betting accompanied drinking and was part of the life. Sometimes, around youths or printers with morals, the wager became a purse. In 1846, when a very young Robert Bonner won a contest, the hands at the *New York American Republican* left ten dollars for him.[2]

Printers measured their races in "ems." In the long years of metal type, an "em space" had become the standard of typographic measurement. The name came from the letter *m,* the widest of the alphabet. Usually, no matter how large or small the type, something between two and a half and three characters constituted an em. Printers were pieceworkers, which meant that their employers paid them by the amount of work they did, not by an hourly wage. The result of a compositor's work, the text he had set in type, contained a measurable quantity of "em spacing," a measure of area, that printers used for wage calculation. They arrived at a total by multiplying the length of a line by the number of those lines, rather than attempting an actual count of letters. Ordinarily, in fact, printers simply wound a piece of string around the block of type they had set, measured it, and were paid accordingly. A fast printer set a "long string."

Different sizes of type once had names. Printers since the late nineteenth century have used a point system to measure the size of type. Large text type, such as might appear in a book, is 12- or 14-point. A big black newspaper headline may run a full inch in height, in which case it measures some 72 points. Before measuring type sizes by points, printers gave them names. Until the very late nineteenth century, printers referred to 12-point letters as "pica" type. The phrase "agate type," which is still used to describe the tiny text of baseball box scores or classified ads, is a vestige of this older system. Nineteenth-century competitors used various sizes, sometimes a type called "bourgeois," similar in size to today's 9-point. It was, in fact, large for newspaper work, which was usually 6-point type called "nonpareil" or the slightly larger "minion." Large type is easier to read, but more to the point, bourgeois (which everyone pronounced "burjoyce") was easier to handle.

On average, a compositor could set and correct 7,000 ems of type in a day of ten hours. This amounted to 700 ems an hour at a normal workaday pace. Most shops assumed 10,000 ems (1,000 an hour) was too much to expect from their workers in a day. In setting 1,500 ems an hour (as one might do in spurts), the compositor's hand reached into the typecase some 4,000 times. Two thousand ems an hour, the fastest racing pace, required 5,400 reaches, which was 85 to 100 letters picked up each minute. An extremely fast typesetter, his arm pumping like a piston, went back and forth from case to stick seven or eight times every five seconds.[3]

George Arensberg simply did this faster, with acceptable accuracy, than anyone else. In the process, he culminated a long shopfloor tradition, most of it anonymous. Renown required special circumstances. In 1852, at a time when 1,500 ems an hour seemed very fast, Thomas T. Sutcliffe had set 2,487 ems during a period of an hour and a half. A logotype manufacturing firm had tried to convince the *New York Courier and Inquirer* that by using logotypes (shortcut letter combinations), the paper could set 1,500 ems in an hour. The *Courier and Inquirer* said they had compositors who already could do that, and trotted one out—Sutcliffe. The logotype company trimmed the lead editorial from that day's paper and challenged him to set it faster than they could. He did.[4]

Typesetting racing enjoyed particularly widespread popularity during the twenty years from the end of the Civil War until the mid-1880s. George Arensberg's racing career was exemplary. When Arensberg began racing, prizes of fifty dollars were significant amounts. Sums such as this turned heads when printers working at the top of their profession earned thirty dollars a week. Quickly, racing enthusiasts upped the ante. In 1877 foreman John Bell, on behalf of the *Cincinnati Enquirer*'s composing room staff—its "Big Ten"—challenged any and all other composing rooms for $1,000. In 1881 Thomas C. Levy won $1,000 competing at Winnipeg.[5] Harry Cole's New Year's Day 1881 face-off with Myles Johnson in the rooms of the *New York Herald* was lucrative and immediately made Cole famous.[6]

While the world awaited mechanized typesetting, and as long as editors did not demand a college background or art school training, compositional skill and speed commanded respect. In the middle of the nineteenth century, the Swift was an elite workman, a member of the International Typographical Union (ITU), the oldest and best-established labor union in the land. Artisans at some big-city dailies achieved a sort of gentility. The *New York Tribune*'s ace compositor, Thomas Rooker, wore diamond-studded shirt fronts.[7]

In fact, however, typesetting remained the tedious labor it had always been. This was particularly true of columnar tasks, the "straight" typesetting of long text passages that characterized much newspaper work and most of what was done at book printing firms. Among themselves, printers easily admitted that composition had become a specialized occupation by the second half of the nineteenth century. William C. Barnes, a blazingly fast Swift, acknowledged that his own broad range of skills had shrunk in favor of speed. Formerly, a printer "needs be able to perform all the different duties appertaining to the trade," Barnes said, "now, he has but to be proficient in one."[8] Changes in the levels of ordinary literacy also encroached on a printer's domain and on his codebreaking skills. Formerly arcane rules of grammar and punctuation in time became the equipment of every high schooler. An informed, bureaucratic society was fast intruding into an elite worker's special realm of literacy.

The Shopfloors of Swifts

Typesetters worked in composing rooms. By midcentury large printing firms had outgrown the village printshop, and various aspects of such establishments, from editing and business offices to the pressroom, became segregated by their functions. Up to three dozen compositors, each by now expected to set type and little else, stood before banks of typecases, five or six abreast. Within the trade, when a journeyman compositor found regular work, he was said to "hold" cases. In fact, with the exception of smaller shops and newspaper advertising tasks, one compositor's typecases were identical to all the others. Holding cases was a territorial claim; journeymen worked at the same location each day. When the journeyman Edgar Yates found work at the *Providence Journal,* Rhode Island's largest newspaper, his space was his property, not his type. "I got cases after a while," Yates reported, "and was slug 9, in the centre alley to the left of the head of the old stairway."[9]

A typical composing room at any large plant was inevitably large and even cavernous if blessed with ventilated, high ceilings. In addition to many compositors and their cases, the room contained space sufficient for the proofing, proofreading, and pagination that preceded presswork itself. Large cabinets contained extra, or auxiliary, types. Compositors "pulled" proofs of completed work on one of several small proofing presses. Proofreaders sat nearby. Other printers gathered and arranged the work of compositors into pages, or "forms," and secured them for the pressmen to handle.[10]

A composing room at a large printing plant was normally a busy scene, and its hectic pace under a looming deadline could approach chaos. In newspaper composing rooms, filled with

The composing room of the *New York World* at the end of the nineteenth century.
(Courtesy, New-York Historical Society, New York City; neg. 58714

journeymen who might easily put in sixteen-hour days, it was necessarily a convivial place, as well. Most large newspapers, certainly those publishing an afternoon edition, employed a small day force. The bulk of composition, however, took place from seven o'clock in the evening until four o'clock the following morning. If there was room for him to work, a compositor might arrive for work at ten o'clock in the morning. Usually, however, one o'clock in the afternoon was a typical time to begin. Compositors began setting type immediately if there was late copy, stories needed for the afternoon edition. Afternoon work was ordinarily distribution time, the time when a compositor broke down standing text blocks and replaced the used types in their cases—a chatty time of otherwise mindless tedium. Dinner hour arrived at six o'clock, and at seven o'clock composition began in earnest for the next day's morning edition. Compositors took a half-hour lunch break at about eleven o'clock at night. Work necessarily ended at four in the morning, a deadline required by the pressroom schedule.[11]

"Exhausted after the tiresome night's work," the Swift Joseph McCann once explained, journeymen compositors "sought the convivial cup to restore their shattered nerves."[12] A printing life was this sort of daily round of long hours of tedious labor. Moreover, a journeyman awaiting copy combated languid boredom interspersed with sudden and frenetic spurts of activity, when, for instance, the shipping news came in. The erratic pace easily led to the absenteeism and drunkenness that had long been typical of the trade. "In order to keep the irregularity within bounds," says the cultural historian Robert Darnton, printing employers "sought out men with two supreme traits: assiduousness and sobriety."[13]

Journeymen, in other words, were not hired simply because they were fast, but also because they were dependable. Among printing employers, speed mattered less than sober reliability. "If he also happened to be skilled," says Darnton, "so much the better." Composition required many hands; the marginal utility of a single individual's typesetting speed was slight and fully negated in the instance of an unreliable Swift. On the shopfloor, then, an inherent tension existed between compositors, for whom speed meant skill, and employers, who depended on steady docility. Although their purposes seemed to mesh with those of the firm, fast typesetting Swifts were rarely employees of highest value. An independent spirit might easily burden a shopfloor.[14]

Composing rooms naturally encouraged a shared esprit. Busy compositors stood elbow to elbow, an arrangement that offered easy interaction. "On my right was Leavitt," recalled the *Providence Journal* journeyman Edgar Yates, "and on my left was Jim Williams," each of whom was something of a local celebrity. Other notable alley regulars included Withee—"slightly lame in one foot"—and Press Willard, who "chewed tobacco, set type and swore with remarkable ease, skill and fluency." In Yates's view, the *Journal* composing room "was certainly made up of the greatest gang of 'characters' that ever gathered under one low and stifling roof." Many composing rooms might have said as much.[15]

Emphatically what Yates did not describe was the shopfloor of a printing establishment specializing in book manufacture. By the second half of the nineteenth century, bookmaking, like newspaper printing, had hived away from the traditional local printing shop. Book manufacture occupied printing's middle ground between newspapers and job work, and many journeymen viewed book compositors' tasks with thinly disguised contempt. "There is no class of men connected with the printing business," declared *Inland Printer*, "whose interests are so frequently overlooked by their fellow craftsmen as the book compositors." News and job compositors considered them "hybrids," typesetters who were held to high standards on uncomplicated work. According to *Inland Printer*, "most typos" considered book work "a mechanical operation that needs little skill and less thought."[16]

Book printers, of course, usually favored their own composing room workers over newspaper compositors. The famous New York printer Theodore L. DeVinne thought that the demands of newspaper typesetting required the "least skill." As the trade journal *Inland Printer* pointed out, "bookroom obligations are imposed to which the news compositor is a stranger." Book proofreaders, for example, returned for correction instances of uneven linespacing that newspaper typesetters routinely considered acceptable. Book compositors were often required to set technical texts that demanded levels of literacy approaching those of proofreaders, standards rarely demanded of newspaper Swifts.[17]

DeVinne, however, also claimed that newspapers paid their journeymen "the lowest price," which industrywide was demonstrably untrue. Among book printing proprietors, such claims justified exacting standards. According to most journeymen, however, employers rarely paid book compositors up to those expectations.

Pages of book text type often required extensive revision, perhaps a complete resetting, noted a writer in the *Inland Printer,* but "in nine cases out of ten the painstaking compositor receives from five to ten cents less per thousand ems than the rusher on a morning or afternoon paper." The way union printers saw it, book houses expected a great deal from their typesetters, and those employees expected far too little in return. "Is it any wonder then that under these circumstances a majority of the most skilled compositors forsake the book for the news room," wondered *Inland Printer,* "preferring recompense to honor."[18]

Working conditions were always better at book offices. The steady workflow of book production recommended it to stable and sober compositors, family men, and quite often to nonunion printers. According to rank-and-file print journeymen, any of this explained the routine welcome that book plants offered women employees. For their part, women in the book industry found steady work that remained otherwise unavailable to them. From the late 1850s Harper and Brothers in New York employed dozens of women compositors. Henry Houghton's Riverside Press in Cambridge, Massachusetts, used women compositors from November 1849, when Houghton first experienced a printers' strike.

By the late nineteenth century, Riverside Press ran a clean and tidy shop filled with hundreds of specialized workers. Book employees worked daytime hours. Deadline demands and consequent job pressures were far less severe. Riverside, like many other large firms, provided a range of benefits for its printers and generally prided itself on their lengths of service.[19]

Compositors composed. Their activity—setting, justifying, distributing type—was universal. Their institutions, however, varied greatly, and so did their behavior. Book people, especially their employers, considered newspaper journeymen drunken sots. Newspaper people thought book printers nothing more than dupes at work for small change. Book compositors might incidentally be fast, but well-run shopfloors of book houses discouraged racing. Swifts, without exception, worked elsewhere.

A Saloon Society

Swifts inhabited three primary institutions: the printing shop-floor, the union hall, and the bars and taverns of their social life. They gravitated to large city shopfloors, where crowded newspaper composing rooms formed the core of a distinct printing cohort. Most big races and heavily bet challenges took place in the workrooms of metropolitan dailies such as those at the *New York Sun*. This was where the hard-eyed professionals hung out, men who liked to bet and drink and who were renowned in their own working circles, sometimes beyond.

Swifts composed a portion of what modern observers have described as an emerging nineteenth century "sporting-male culture." According to historian Howard Chudacoff, the years following the Civil War became nothing short of an "age of the bachelor," a relatively rootless period of urban migration, declining family ties, eroded artisanal standards, and the bewildering challenges offered by socially emergent young women. A variety of urban institutions, particularly saloons, attracted young working-class men. From billiard rooms and barber shops to dance halls and amusement parlors, city life offered footloose men complementary outlets for the peer sociability that came with drinking, gambling, and similarly masculine behavior.[20]

Swifts, like all compositors, spent most of their waking hours at work, on their shopfloor. After work—perhaps four o'clock in the morning—and at leisure, independent young men gathered at favorite saloons. Finally, while few Swifts were leaders in the labor movement, all were staunch members of their local chapter of the International Typographical Union. Swifts stood out, easily recognizable on their shopfloors and in their saloons and union halls. They were young, unmarried men, mobile and adventuresome and convivial within their peer groupings. Swifts were capable and smart and proud of being both, and they were autonomous to the brink of irresponsibility. Above all, Swifts were what they did. They set type faster than most of their brethren. Most important, they raced.

Other fast typesetters did not race. Book compositors, for example, might be highly skilled as well as speedy, but they worked outside the institutions of the trade. Book workers, family and wage-earning men and women who went home in the evening to responsible lives and regularity, often remained unaffiliated with printing unions and avoided both the saloons and the union halls that defined the life of a Swift. Book compositors often accepted a lower wage than that of their newspaper counterparts in exchange for cleaner working conditions and, with it, a finer civility. Newspaper compositors viewed with disdain the endless pages of routine "straight matter" that typified book work. Of course, it was an issue of style; much newspaper composition was as straightforward as the typesetting of books. In manner as much as task, such people seemed dull sorts to newspaper journeymen.

Over the years, printers had earned a reputation for drinking, and many cultivated it. Drink had long been part of shopfloor life. A village journeyman easily might have worked as he drank his beer, sending shop boys periodically to top off the jug. As the community of the workplace—apprentices, journeymen, and master—hardened into working and managing classes, spirits of various kinds became the drink of ownership, of the bourgeoisie. The rest of the shop drank beer, as it always had. Drink paced the day of a printing society, and in that sense accompanied the chatter and the philosophizing and the badinage that was required to get a compositor through his wearying task.

Swifts widely epitomized the drinking reputation. The Swift Joseph McCann expressly made the link, noting that piece work fostered both racing and drinking. According the McCann, "the piece system was the parent of the swift." Productivity alone dictated wage. The system rewarded speed, but at a cost of intense effort under deadline and hot gaslight. Fast typesetting, said McCann, led to "excessive drinking," and eventually it "developed an undesirable class that brought discredit on the profession." Others agreed. New Yorker Amos J. Cummings, a longtime compositor at Horace Greeley's *Tribune*, remembered the *Times*'s "instinctive" Mort Rainey. "Like the majority of instinctive type-

setters," said Cummings, "he was given to joviality and good fel-
lowship." But once he took stick in hand, Rainey, "no matter how
shattered his nerves or how obfuscated his brain," was lightning.[21]

Some printers, hoping to modify a particular onus on Swifts,
minimized drinking problems by explaining them away. One such
writer, Alton B. Canty, allowed that printers, especially night compositors, indeed drank to excess. Still, Canty thought, a man who
worked all night and subsequently unwound by drinking would
necessarily display that drunkenness in public. Others, working by
day, might imbibe as much, but they could sleep it off and "present a sober appearance the following day."[22] Canty would exoner-
ate the particular drunkenness of Swifts through the universality
of drink within the trade.

In union hall or saloon, journeyman compositors rarely drifted
far from the manners of the printing shopfloor, their working habi-
tat. The trade journal *Inland Printer* routinely criticized what it
called an excessive "contempt for the conventionalities of society"
among journeymen printers. Swifts spoke in a "code of slang," the
magazine noted, and indulged in "unwarranted familiarity." Compositors commonly "jerried" each other. The word referred to
shopfloor noise raised when someone "rendered himself ridicu-
lous," or in other words, farted. Men rapped their knuckles on
their type cases or drew a reglet sharply down the boxes of their
upper cases. It made the sound of a stick dragged along a picket
fence, and turned a composing room of several dozen typesetters,
never a tranquil atmosphere, into a raucous din. *Inland Printer*
thought boorish behavior represented a blight on the profession.
Common courtesy, the magazine complained, need not be "evidence of effeminacy."[23]

Standard shopfloor masculinity became noisome by hygienic
standards as well. Many a journeyman, claimed the *Inland Printer,*
was "the hog in human shape." The man "makes a trough of his
alley." He "smears the passage ways with streams of tobaccoed
saliva," reported the magazine. "He should be weeded out as un-
ceremoniously as an obnoxious plant is plucked from a flower
patch."[24]

Some commentators, such as Robert S. Menamin, editor of the authoritative *Printers' Circular,* thought they saw improvement. Dissolution among journalists, Menamin thought, had declined, "and to some degree in the composing room." Typeracing Swifts seemed particularly sober to Menamin. "There are few large composing rooms in which a considerable number of such men may not be found."[25] Editor Menamin's double negative seemed a hedged bet, even by the prolix standards of nineteenth-century prose.

Labor Unions

Most typeracing Swifts were firm trade unionists. The printing historian Alexander Lawson called the journeyman Swift an autonomous "free spirit," and paradoxically the structure of the union allowed such attitudes.[26] Of the guiding institutions of a Swift's life, his labor union importantly provided freedom, independence, and autonomy. Few nineteenth-century compositors felt themselves the unfettered captains of their own ship. They worked too hard, earned too little, and died too soon to make such claims. Rather, nineteenth-century compositors felt the most free when they felt autonomous and uncoerced. Their union, the local assembly of the venerable International Typographical Union, wrested wages from ownership on their behalf. As important, thanks to their union, journeymen compositors worked remarkably free of an employer's intervention, to say nothing of his coercive tyranny. Days might pass without a boss on the shopfloor; printers answered to shop foremen, not employers. In contrast, proofreaders were constant problems. A proofreader, also a union member, read a compositor's proofs, and the faults he might find cost a typesetter money. Journeymen typesetters hated proofreaders.

Compositors made hundreds of tiny decisions every day, choices that embodied a printer's autonomy. The first commandment of the typesetting trade was to set texts "as written." The second was a supervisor's admonition to correct obvious errors, "slips of the pen." The distinction was never sharp, but compositors were expected to know it. Confronting a garbled manuscript in an age of handwritten copy, a compositor's literacy, his unparalleled skill, informed his guesses. Beyond this, a compositor's autonomy governed his wordspace choices, his line drops, the propriety of his end-of-line word breaks. These choices combined to produce the look of his printed page. In time, new men on the shopfloor would command even these typesetting skills. Art directors and graphic designers added their directions to those of foremen and proofreaders. Unlike the others, however, these new voices did not merely correct the errant compositor, they also eroded the range and efficacy of his choices and diminished him.

Among Swifts, union membership legitimized racing, an inherently unstable activity. Nineteenth-century typesetting racing, like all shopfloor athletics, was timeless and intramural. After the Civil War, as racing events expanded in scope, union locals easily offered racing rules and respected referees. Soon, however, the larger unions understood that racing offered employers a kind of shopfloor production standard—a Swift's phenomenal speed raised the bar for all compositors—and discouraged competition.

Swifts themselves, however, required the sanctioning organization of their unions. By the mid-1880s New York Swifts had devised a codified set of racing rules on behalf of the city's Local No. 6 of the ITU. Without these regulations, local events lacked standing. Certainly contestants were expected to be printing unionists in good standing and freelancers fell outside the pale. The midwesterner George A. "Cleve" Barber, widely considered the first to issue broad public typesetting challenges, was such an outlaw. As early as October 1866, the brash Barber, then in Detroit, had challenged the world to a week-long race, ten hours a day of "solid, straight matter." Barber was offering enormous wagers, bets ranging from $2,000 to $5,000, outrageous sums guaranteed to attract a young man's attention, and sure enough, according to Barber, George Arensberg had already deposited $100 as a first installment of a $1,000 stake. Plans thereupon stalled. According to William Barnes, Arensberg "refused to notice" Barber's challenge because Barber was not in the union.[27]

In their union affiliation, as on their shopfloors and in their saloons, journeymen compositors lived in an artisanal world of "reciprocity and mutuality." They used their unions to race, and gambling, of course, fueled those races. When it did, it cemented their fraternity. To many working-class Americans, money was more than a personal reward for honesty, industry, frugality, and piety. It was a lubricant of group behavior, a "means of conviviality." All of it was premodern, rarely political, and certainly not "class conscious" in any adversarial way. It was an alternative, not oppositional, pattern of life. As long as typeracing remained in newspaper offices, printing adhered to artisanal modes long after society moved toward regimentation.[28]

Membership in the local chapter of the International Typographical Union was the glue that bound journeymen printers. Union membership of course offered benefits, such as increases in wage or the potential reduction of hours, but it also meant mobility, and mobility meant opportunity, the freedom that came with options. Many journeymen printers—almost all Swifts—routinely traveled.

By age thirty, for instance, George Arensberg had worked in most major cities in the eastern United States. Printing unions everywhere sponsored this kind of mobility as a means of regulating workforce and wages. Printing journeymen called jobs "situations"—"sits," in the argot—and they called migrations from one to another "tramping." Theoretically, this mobility was an important union labor tactic, and the International Typographical Union sponsored a system of identification cards that required employment or at least hospitality upon presentation. Journeymen compositors, often highly mobile bachelors working at day-wage piece rates, were willing to travel in search of work. Tramp printers followed high wages and fled low. A union card opened doors to cardholders and closed them to those without cards.[29]

Insofar as the system worked, tramping produced a modified free labor market, the labor union regulating an "authorized" workforce tied to straightforward supply and demand. Many printers simply enjoyed moving around, and by their widespread tourism, journeymen compositors, especially Swifts, gave printing a certain adventure. Certainly tramping was an honorable, even mythic, aspect of the life. "A characteristic tramp," an essayist commented in the printing journal *Printers' Circular*, "is he of the festive nature, who walks into a town tired, hungry, solemn, sober, and penniless; poor but respectable; shabby, but very skillful; shoeless, but with a good understanding; all but hatless, with a remarkable idea-box."[30]

The description conformed to a printing ideal, but tramping carried some unamplified negative connotations, as well. Tramp printers were fabled drinkers, which employing printers viewed at best with mixed feelings. Some printers became tourists, using their trade to see the world. At worst, such printers were undependable. But others tramped when their lives required it, when work proved unavailable locally, and occasionally these printers crossed picket lines and broke strikes.

Fast typesetters were almost invariably tramping typesetters. Once typeracing left the job shop, once a particular Swift felt he had bigger fish to fry, travel was the essence of it all. Between 1873, when he was working for the *Bridgeport Standard*, and 1884, George Graham, soon to be New England's champion Swift, worked in nine different states—"much," according to William Barnes, "as the average printer's life is passed, roaming about the country."[31]

The speed of a compositor, given reasonable sobriety, made him inherently valuable to shop foremen. Fast compositors easily found employment, claimed one observer, something that inclined them to travel, and so "in former years many of the best men were found in the floating contingent of the type-setting fraternity." Current composing room staffs seemed more settled than this, "and it is said that the itinerant disposition is on the wane."[32] In fact, rates of travel among compositors rose during the years following the Civil War. The printing historian William Pretzer describes a peak in tramping as late as a period from 1888 to 1892, as the Linotype "sent men scurrying for work."[33]

George Arensberg began his career on the move. Born in 1849,

he grew up in Pittsburgh peddling the local *Dispatch.* Newsboy
tasks introduced him to other edges of newspaper life. Arensberg
hung around printers, and soon he was learning the trade. In
1864, when he was fifteen, Arensberg applied for membership in
Pittsburgh's Local No. 7 of the International Typographical Union.
Local No. 7 considered him young and rejected him. Arensberg
spent a year persisting, and the union acquiesced. In 1865 a
teenaged Arensberg commenced his printing life.

That meant traveling. He first went to New Orleans, wending
his way by the Ohio and Mississippi riverways. The union local in
New Orleans looked askance at the boyish Arensberg and decided
Pittsburgh had broken the rules by admitting him. Cast out of
New Orleans, young Arensberg began working his way home. He
signed on as a cabin boy, worked his passage upriver to Memphis,
and got a job at the local *Bulletin.* From there, in short order, it
was Louisville, where he stayed a year and a half, learning typesetting from some compositors of renown. In Louisville he met
Victor O. Loomis, Charles B. Church, and Bill Mason, big names
in the field and transient men who would surface and resurface
throughout Arensberg's career. By the late 1860s Arensberg had
returned to Pittsburgh.

By now Arensberg was in every sense a journeyman—a "jour,"
in the lingo. While journeymen printers in America wandered
much less than romance would have it, Arensberg took to it readily. He worked for a time at the *Pittsburgh Commercial* and then
for an ill-fated sheet called, simply, *The Paper.* When it collapsed,
Arensberg was off to Washington, D.C., where he set type at the
Patriot until it, too, perished. By 1869 Arensberg was in New York
applying for work at the *New York Times.* He was twenty years old
when his historic race made him famous.[34]

The Wager

By the early 1870s Luther Ringwalt's *Encyclopedia of Printing*
could report a growing list of people rumored to be capable of setting 2,000 ems of type in an hour. It was no longer certainly

impossible, and it was becoming something of a standard—printing's four-minute mile. Reports varied widely. As early as 1845, John J. Hand, deputy foreman of the *New York American Republican,* famously tried to set 32,000 ems of solid minion in twenty-four hours, a pace short of 1,500 ems an hour. In Rochester, New York, printers claimed their man, George Dawson, averaged 2,700 ems of brevier an hour when he set a reported 27,000 ems of brevier in ten hours. Henry Keeling, of Utica, New York, set, distributed, and corrected 100,950 ems of solid 8-point brevier in six ten-hour days. In 1858 William Mink, at the *Pittsfield Eagle,* set 10,046 ems in four hours and forty-five minutes.[35]

These tests involved stamina as well as speed. Pure sprinters had special reputations. Carlos Comens, a printer in Rochester, "frequently set up notices of sheriff's sales containing but little short of 1,000 ems of nonpareil" in twenty minutes. In 1853 Charles McDonnell, foreman at the *Portsmouth Tribune,* set 8,240 ems in four hours, an average of better than 2,000 per hour. In a Toledo, Ohio, match race, the hometown's C. C. Wall beat George A. Barber of Cincinnati, 4,288 to 4,054, in a little over two and a half hours. Chicago's Andrew W. McCartney was a legend at the *Evening Post.*[36] On the West Coast the *Sacramento Union*'s "rushers," a nickname favored there, averaged some 1,333 ems per hour, very speedy for an entire room, "even," one commentator remarked, "in this fast age."[37]

Gambling fueled the era of speed. William Barnes thought professionalism *meant* betting. For every local hotshot at the case, there was a composing room full of cohorts willing to bet money on him. Printing firms sometimes staged competitions to speed production on individual projects. Charles K. Neisser, for instance, won such a prize working on a Philadelphia city directory.[38] Most contests, however, were plain races during a gilded age particularly receptive to them. Colleagues thought the Swift Harry Cole was something out of Mark Twain: "If he saw two birds sitting on a fence he would bet on which would fly first." An era of wagering introduced "hippodroming," a descriptive new phrase. A hippodrome was a rigged result, a thrown game, a fixed race. Journeymen throughout the trade understood an 1886 typesetting race in Providence, Rhode Island, to have been a hippodrome and ignored the results.[39]

Harry Cole was on hand the afternoon of February 19, 1870, when George Arensberg picked up his stick and rule in the composing rooms of the *New York Sun*. *Times* foreman E. A. Donaldson knew his man, as did large numbers of New York journeymen. The affair also drew doubting outlanders, most of whom, according the *Sun*, "backed time." Donaldson had seen to that. The race drew a colorful lot. The "handsome Hanlon of the *Sun*" showed up. So did Briscoe of the Washington, D.C., government printing office, "himself a very fast 'crab.'" Watkins, "the 'fat' compositor from Boston," was there and Thompson, "the exquisite night foreman" for the *Times*. It was a gathering of aces, of sharks, and sobriquets such as handsome and exquisite took on full double meanings. Such compliments referred professionally to the look of their cases and to their workmanship—their composed pages—but also and especially in these circumstances it suggested lace-cuffed stars of the gaming table.

All the local color was out. Howe of Vermont bet heavily on Arensberg. Becker "had put in three straight weeks and put it all on the 'Velocipede.'" And then there was Jeptha Jones, "the Walker," who as a captain in the 14th Brooklyn during the Civil War, had always walked toward the enemy. And Bowen, "the tallest and loveliest man in the business, but whose friends fear that he will kill himself with hard work." Reed was there, the *Times*'s popular proofreader, "if such a thing," reported the *Sun*, "can be possible." Stanley, "the shortest and best compositor in the business" was on hand to referee. The Arensberg Wager drew baseball stars, as well, notably Jimmy Woods, "the celebrated second baseman of the [Brooklyn] Ekford base ball club" and a sporting confederate of Foreman Donaldson.

And so, at 3 P.M., they were ready, Stanley judging for the house with a stopwatch "of celebrated foreign make" and the *Dominion*'s Payne judging Arensberg with an American timepiece. Arensberg started fast—too fast, some said. "Backers of 'time' felt quite

jubilant, showing," reported the *Sun,* "greenbacks." The Velocipede completed his first stickful in thirteen minutes, fifty-five seconds. But then he finished his second even faster, by five seconds,
and his doubters began to hedge their bets. When Arensberg
came in with a time of fourteen minutes flat for his third stick, the
issue was settled. Barring collapse, Arensberg could walk home in
eighteen minutes and three quarters. Losing bettors frantically
sought takers for a side bet against his setting 2,000 ems in the
hour. But Arensberg carried the day. Not only did he finish his
fourth stick in fourteen minutes and ten seconds, but he also
worked on the fifth stick handed him for the balance of the hour.
He had rung up a total of four stickfuls in fifty-five minutes and
fifty seconds, winning the bet, and he covered all sides by hitting
2,064 ems within the hour. Shopmates mobbed him at the finish.
Backers challenged the entire world. This was the fastest typesetter in Creation.[40]

The Legend

Arensberg's successful *New York Sun* wager of 1870 became
typesetting's Everest. Moreover, dispelling all fears of a fluke performance, the Velocipede repeated his victory the following
month. Once again at the *New York Sun,* he won another bet, setting 1,800 ems of "lean, solid minion" to 24 ems in fifty-nine and
a half minutes.[41] Word of the Velocipede's success reverberated
throughout the printing world, striking sparks wherever working
typos felt themselves as fast as they came. Rumors had long flown
of astonishing speed in far-flung places. In a shrinking nation,
speedy printers—shopfloor athletes—wanted those tales sub-
stantiated; they wanted to know how they stood.

Arensberg's performance seemed convincing in ways others
had not. In the first place, it happened in New York City, a widely
acknowledged media hub. Further, New York was the home of
Local No. 6 of the International Typographical Union. Among
member chapters of the nation's oldest labor union, Local No. 6
was unquestionably most mighty. When "Big Six" crowned a
champion, what challenge could journeymen in Dubuque offer?

Printing literature quickly examined Arensberg's achievement. The *Typographical Messenger* called it "the greatest feat in typesetting on record." Philadelphia, never presuming itself a printing backwater, was home to the *Printers' Circular,* since 1866 the official trade magazine of the ITU. Immediately upon learning of Arenberg's match, magazine editor Robert S. Menamin invited Arensberg to Philadelphia. He wanted to see the phenom for himself and offered a purse for convincing proof of his speed. It was something of an audition, a command performance. At Philadelphia, Arensberg's 1,764 ems in an hour fulfilled conditions of his visit, but fell slightly short of previous records. Menamin accepted excuses, noting that Arensberg had not distributed his own type and so found it difficult to pick up, the type having "settled down in the case."[42]

George "The Velocipede" Arensberg, for years the fastest Swift of them all and always the most famous.
(From *A Collation of Facts Relative to Fast Typesetting,* New York: Concord Cooperative Printing Company, 1887)

Still unsatisfied, Menamin decided that legitimacy demanded a match that was as widespread as its claims and organized a postal contest open to printers far and wide. All variables, from type and line measures to copy text and race supervision, were identical. Union officials monitored local contestants. A special committee of the ITU read final submitted proofs. On May 10, 1871, Arensberg beat an "international" field and accepted the winner's solid silver composing stick, "richly chased and furnished with an elegant rosewood case lined with satin." There remained, it seemed, few mountains to climb.[43]

Arensberg therefore stayed put for a while in Philadelphia. By June, when Editor Menamin delivered Arensberg's freshly engraved typestick prize, the Velocipede was working at the *Philadelphia Sunday Mercury*. The lure of the road, however, persisted. In time, he left Philadelphia for Pittsburgh and a hometown visit. By some point in the early and mid-1870s, Arensberg "drifted to Boston and floated out again," shaking up conservative Boston, according to locals, "injecting a vim into some of the staid residents which made their veins tingle."[44]

By this time, Arensberg was simply legendary. He could work when and where he wanted. In 1877, on his way to Cincinnati, he visited Cleveland and Toledo. Late that year, Arensberg arrived at the *Cincinnati Enquirer*. They were expecting him. In December John Bell, foreman of the *Enquirer*'s composing room, had offered what *Printers' Circular* called "a bold challenge from the West."[45] For a price beginning at $500, the *Enquirer* was prepared to back its fastest Swift against any other shop's challenger, its fastest pair against any other shopmate pair, and thus through any comparable ten-man typesetting staff. The *Enquirer* backed its entire composing room "Big Ten" to the tune of $1,000. Well it might. Foreman Bell had accumulated a lineup of all-stars. Joe Hudson was there, as were Charlie Church and Al Ulrich. All were Swifts with widespread reputations. Still, *Printers' Circular* found it "improbable" that the nation's ten fastest compositors worked "in one composing room in Cincinnati."[46] Perhaps Editor Menamin thought the Velocipede was still in Philadelphia. George Arensberg, however, was in Cincinnati, working, if only once a week, at the *Enquirer*. He was there to race. He was the swiftest Swift in a room full of them.[47]

Arensberg and the rest of the Cincinnati Swifts had no interest in prolonged employment, at the *Enquirer* or anywhere else. They were mercenaries, heroes of the trade with "breezy ways," cocky and full of "aggressive, sometimes vehement, unionism." Dashing they might be but perhaps "reckless of consequences." In shopfloor slang, men such as Arensberg "'tossed up' one 'sit' and 'caught' another 'on the sheet across the way.'" They "made the staid 'homesteaders' stare in amazement."[48] The Velocipede was anathema to sober men with production schedules. The Swifts embodied a printer's notion of manly independence. They stood astride a working world.

3 The Gendered Machine of Timothy Alden

GEORGE ARENSBERG WAS SPLENDIDLY FAST AT A TASK that collectively mired an industry. Swifts aside, the inability to speed composing rooms bedeviled both labor and management. This was true throughout the printing industry, but especially true in newspaper composing rooms. All printing was frenetic and deadline driven. Printers naturally examined ways to increase the output of their presses. Newspaper printing epitomized this competitive breathlessness.

At the end of the Civil War, printing employers who would increase productivity and reduce cost confronted some fairly simple equations. Typesetting machinery remained technically unproven and prone to breakdown. Equipment innovation might boost output, but overhead costs soared. Conversely, overhead costs in a composing room filled with handsetters remained minimal. The tools of typesetting, after all, were absurdly simple. A compositor required typestick and rule, the emblems of his task, but he needed little else. Once a company bought its type, further outlays—lighting, ancillary equipment such as rule miters and saws, cabinetry—were relatively small. A composing room would incur most such expense in any event. When an employer wished to set more type, he simply hired more typesetters, as long as there were places to put them. Armies of compositors resulted. In this system, most of the cost of setting type became wages. It followed that in order to minimize this cost, many printing employers hired workers willing to work cheaply, beneath scale.

By midcentury, large printing employers, especially newspapermen, tended toward two basic business approaches. One sought market expansion and increased readership and naturally led to content refinement and a product that more and more people would eagerly read. A second tactic emphasized cost cutting and workforce productivity. The two strategies focused differently on their workers. Within a decade, Joseph Pulitzer's *New York World* and Whitelaw Reid's *New York Tribune* expressed these strategies best. Pulitzer increased readership at the *World* by lowering the price of his paper to a penny and by manufacturing news. Reid, instead of chasing readers, committed his *Tribune* to innovative production technology and a reduction in shopfloor wages. By the early 1880s, he was combining mechanical composing equipment with nonunion handsetting employees.

Throughout the Civil War period, however, most printing firms, and especially newspapers, followed tried-and-true tactics: they relied on increasing their sales. Among newspapers, the model was James Gordon Bennett's *New York Herald*, an established daily with a history of cheap editions and sensational journalism that dated to the 1830s and the rise of the original "penny press."

Timothy Alden's Typesetter

In this context, the inventor Timothy Alden offered the nation's printers his brand-new and innovative Alden Typesetter. Boredom, however, had originally inspired Timothy Alden, not sluggish production schedules. Like George Arensberg, young Alden apprenticed at the typecase. The similarity ended there. Young Alden was six generations removed from the Plymouth colony's John, a hallowed inheritance, and the wealth and honor that might come Timothy's way would only cap an ancient lineage. In contrast, George Arensberg had grown up on the Pittsburgh streets. Arensberg and Alden shared long hours of boyhood drudgery at the case, but from there their paths diverged. A printshop offered life to young Arensberg as well as a meal ticket and a travel voucher. Printing stifled Alden and made him feel robotic.

Contemporaries claimed that a weary Timothy Alden conceived of his typesetting machine while setting type. According to one journalist's report, Alden announced that, "if his life should be spared to him, he would invent a machine that would relieve compositors of that offensive profession they were led to follow." Since time out of mind, compositors had used shopfloor conviviality to combat the intrinsic boredom of long and text-heavy typesetting chores. The routine grind especially burdened active apprentices. Few journeymen remembered zesty youthful hours at their typecases. Alden, for instance, prefigured Hannibal's Sam Clemens, whose talents were not inventive, but whose youth at the case convinced him that a machine to do the cursed work was worth his investment. In time, Clemens famously would plow the proceeds of *Huckleberry Finn* into a machine called the Paige Typesetter. Solving the typesetting bottleneck promised fabulous riches. The Swift William Barnes, for instance, reckoned that "the wealth of a Croesus, and a place in the temple of fame" awaited the successful inventor. Hate, however, seemed importantly part of the equation. Scions of wealth or status, such as Timothy Alden, doubtless found typesetting apprenticeships a particular drudgery. By 1857 Timothy had hatched a machine.[1]

Timothy Alden also died in 1857, not yet forty years old. In twenty years of constant, driven effort, the inventor of the Alden Typesetting Machine had worn himself out. In the overwrought prose of the era, he literally perished with a dream. "Night after night he tossed feverishly upon his bed," declared the *New York*

Times. "Day after day he studied and planned without result, until one night, waking suddenly from a deep sleep, he saw full and clear before him the long-sought vision, and rushing to the table, seized his ever ready paper and pencil, and as if by inspiration, sketched upon the sheet the very plan from which the machines are made today." Quickly young Alden moved from plan to product and cobbled together his contraption. Reporters made much of the fact that Timothy had lived to see his typesetting machine work. He called in his friends and, "with glistening and flushed cheek," he explained his idea "and then, exhausted by the greatness of the deed, fell fainting in his seat. . . . Six months afterward he died."[2]

If Timothy Alden lived to see the fruits of his labor, he only barely did so. Surely he died unsatisfied, bequeathing to Henry W. Alden, his cousin and business partner, a long list of imperfections in his machine design. Timothy Alden was an inventor, a fanatic in the pursuit of a miraculous machine, a man who had long since lost contact with the merely viable. Other men, notably his cousin Henry, would take over the task of marketing the machine to a skeptical workplace. Silent and in the background until his cousin's death, Henry Alden had already spent $40,000 on the project. In his inventive idealism, Alden was similar to other innovative geniuses. The inventor Ottmar Mergenthaler, whose Linotype would later find the success that eluded Alden, would have to be shouldered aside before a cadre of businessmen found ways to market his imperfect machine. Left to Mergenthaler, the Linotype machine would never have been completed, and neither, it seemed, would have the Alden.[3]

Like the Mitchel Composer and indeed all typesetting machines, the Alden employed a keyboard. The operator sat at the side of a circular table and pressed one key for each of 154 characters, symbols, and logotypes. A wheel approximately two feet in diameter sat in the center of the table. Around the wheel were thirty-six fingerlike conveyors, "setting antennae," and beyond these arms was a series of grooves where the types were stored. The wheel revolved, impelled by a printer's available motive power—foot treadle, horse, or steam—and the conveyors picked type as the operator poked. When the wheel revolved, it brought the types around from whichever groove was indicated by the keyboard operator. As the wheel passed a drop point, it deposited the types one by one into a tray corresponding to a typesetter's stick. "Could anything be more like brain turned into brass?" asked Alden's brochure.[4]

The contraption even contained a rudimentary memory. Because an individual type spent a certain amount of time between original retrieval and subsequent deposit in conveyor transit, the machine could "store" up to sixty keystrokes, "thereby leaving a certain amount of work to be done by the automatic intelligence of the machine." Printers might anticipate happy moments of shopfloor larking. While waiting on the machine, the operator "may rest, read copy, eat, drink or do any of the thousand things which suggest themselves at the moment." All of this was marvelously intricate. Journeymen had scoffed at "a mechanism

Twenty years before Ottmar Mergenthaler's Linotype, the Alden Typesetter showed great promise, especially when operated by Augusta Lewis.

(From *American Dictionary of Printing and Bookmaking,* New York: Howard Lockwood & Co., 1894)

that can think," but here was a machine doing something much like it.[5]

However thoughtful, Alden's typesetter could neither space words effectively nor, originally at least, replenish its own type supply, a pair of problems well past the fast fetching of letters. Word spacing was a first order of business. Journeymen compositors, men such as George Arensberg, routinely began a project by taking a sheet of manuscript copy "off the hook," where hung all incoming work, and propping this copy on his type cases. These were paired, one sitting above the other, the upper case filled with capital letters and the lower with small. Beginning work, his single letters formed words and soon lines of composed type. The words of each of these lines required uniform spacing within that line, and it was a compositor's job to see to this. This seemingly simple task became difficult when all lines of type were to end at an identical length, as in most book and newspaper composition—never ragged. Word spacing (accomplished by the insertion of tiny pieces of metal) in any given line might vary from that of the preceding line, but printers expected internally consistent spacing within each line. In achieving all of this, some words surely required division on their appropriate syllables, and that line would end with a hyphen. Word break hyphenation, of course, followed rules of its own, rules that were second nature to capable typesetters. A compositor's workday was a ceaseless series of all of these tiny judgments.

Printers called the process "justification," and justification was a problem for those who would devise machines to replace hand compositors. Indeed, figuring out a quick way to get single types into a line—the presumptive problem—was never difficult. Almost anyone could envision a gravity-drop mechanism triggered by a keystroke. Until, however, someone figured out a way to tell a machine how to get the spacing right, justification required a second printer working in tandem with the machine operator, a worker whose sole function was to justify lines of type. By midcentury, no one had made a machine that could do this, while a competent hand compositor did it routinely as he set the type—in the instance of a racing Swift, with lightning precision.[6]

"Distribution" was a second major headache for inventors. Among printers, distribution actually meant redistribution, the recycling of used letters back into their appropriate typecase boxes. The task was generally the first order of workday business, and most compositors spent a couple of hours each day "tossing type" before commencing fresh work. Devising a keyboard that could both fetch type and subsequently replace it vexed everyone. Some twenty years later, Ottmar Mergenthaler's genius would lie, not in devising a machine that could set and distribute type, but in devising one that avoided distribution altogether by melting down and reusing the metal.

When in 1857, after "years of study and years of toil," Timothy Alden finally devised his typesetter, he did so "only to wake up to the conviction that no labor was saved by it unless its companion—the distributor—was also brought to light." An employee might distribute machine-set type by hand, of course, but little advantage was gained that way. In time, the Alden machine, like others, solved the problem by using type specially cast for its equipment. Each character carried a distinctive "nick," which instructed the conveyor arms in their return trip to the proper grooves. The Alden company went so far as to turn its distribution requirements into strength. "The type," read their brochure, "may be cast at one-half cent less per pound than that made in the usual way, which is readily accounted for by the saving of metal." Moreover, Alden breezily suggested that shop machinists could always nick existing type "of any description" and could do it "by the thousand with a simple plane."[7]

In August 1862 the *New York Times* became a believer. "The only point to be determined," according to the *Times*, "is whether the enormous pressure which the demands of a great daily will bring upon so nice a piece of mechanism will not overtax its powers." It might well have wondered. Beyond design features, the simple durability of complex printing machinery was a constant source of complaint. Machines broke down too easily and often at inopportune moments. The Alden company, in response, pointed to ease of maintenance. Alden machines used no springs. The machine itself was entirely iron and steel and brass. It used "a thimbleful" of oil a month. If a printing shop could not accommodate harnessed horses, human pedal power would do. "We will defy any one to find the least fault with any portion of this novel affair," crowed the company, "there being a provision made for any and every emergency throughout the entire machine." Above all, fingers never touched type. "The machine can make no mistake; for its task is reduced to perfect law."[8]

Journeymen and Machines

By the end of the century, Ottmar Mergenthaler's Linotype would steamroll the composing machine market, a conquest so complete as to make his Linotype seem unprecedented. Mergenthaler's machine appeared to fall from the sky.

Mergenthaler's "revolution," however, culminated a slow evolution in composing machines. Twenty years before the earliest Linotypes, Timothy Alden's new typesetter became the latest in what was already a lengthy parade of similar efforts. As described earlier, John F. Trow became the first successfully to incorporate typesetting machines onto a working shopfloor. In 1855 Trow used the Mitchel Composer to set the New York *City Directory*. As Trow installed his Mitchel equipment, W. H. Houston of Belfast, Maine, began experimenting with yet another machine, a variation on the Mitchel.

All these devices were flawed. Each was a marvelously complex mechanism for accomplishing something so rudimentary as stacking individual characters next to each other in an undifferentiated row. Inabilities to space, break, and generally manipulate words remained problems that limited their use to the simplest, most straightforward, typesetting tasks. Limited as they were, early typesetting equipment nonetheless easily malfunctioned, prey to an array of technical and mechanical glitches.

Most important, each was fatally vulnerable in a business sense. Most midcentury printers continued to set type by hand. Printers who were looking for ways to reduce the production cost of that handwork required the same things in a machine they wanted in their people: cheap and ceaseless reliability at acceptable speed. Almost all nineteenth-century typesetting machines were devices by which an operator selected single types by touching a keyboard. Even if that operator outpaced an ordinary journeymen, his speed only slightly exceeded that of, say, George Arensberg. Machines, in other words, remained relatively slow.

Problems of type distribution and justification were even worse. Distributing used type by hand, the old-fashioned way, compromised any gain in machine productivity. Similarly, all early-nineteenth-century typesetting equipment required a second journeyman to justify lines. Because of these manpower requirements, most printing establishments adhered to the old ways. An entire printing industry—everything from printing press, paper, and ink technologies to literacy rates and advertising—would have struck Johannes Gutenberg as strange, but he would have been perfectly at home in any mid-nineteenth-century composing room.[9]

Machines fit best where typesetting work was straightforwardly repetitive and there was a lot of it. The work of routinely stacking lines of type in book texts was such work, especially when coupled with the sheer length of such tasks. Large urban book printing firms quickly understood the factory nature of the work, innovated earliest with machines, and invited women to operate them, as well as set type in the traditional manner.

After the Civil War, most printing employers, including newspaper editors, anticipated the day when a handful of typesetting machines would empty their composing rooms of accumulated journeymen. Efficient equipment would reduce costs and might even increase productivity. Not surprisingly, working printers noticed a potential problem. Whatever the model, any typesetting machine promised to diminish a compositor's prosperity. Standards of productivity, wage and hour rules, technological innovation—all were classic workplace labor issues. A journeyman printer belonged to his local chapter of the International Typographical Union in order to protect himself from threats such as typesetting equipment.

In fact, throughout its nineteenth-century history, three recurrent issues dominated the agendas of the International Typographical Union: wages, production quotas, and the nature of the union's federal structure. Of these, the most important concerned the maintenance of high wages, which printing unionists understood to be a gatekeeping function. Like all unions, the ITU sought adequate recompense for its members. Cheaper labor—"rat" labor, in printing parlance—performed by nonunion workers or incompletely apprenticed boys eroded a journeyman's prosperity. Union printers therefore spent most of their time discussing incompetent youths, the apprentice system, and workers who accepted wages below industry standard.[10]

Printing unions had long governed the terms of printing employment, insisting that only "practical printers," journeymen sculpted by a prolonged printing apprenticeship, might work throughout their jurisdiction. They therefore routinely discussed the jurisdictional issues raised by "two-thirder" boys, escapees from partially completed apprenticeships. Print unionists endlessly analyzed the shape of their apprentice system, a system that they reckoned was dismal and getting worse. Especially in cities, shopfloors were filling up with youngsters, workers who set "straight type" and performed beneath the printing union's authorized wage scale.

Accepting such work was a grave violation of a journeyman's code. But "two-thirders" were mere boys, after all. When mature journeymen worked at substandard rates of pay, union printers labeled them rats and ostracized them. Women, however, also went where the work was. With the onset of the American Civil War, women filled shopfloors vacated by journeymen at war. When women entered composing rooms during and after the Civil War, they acquired some customary derogatory labels. Women were not boys and never would be men. Neither were they apprentices nor likely to be, and women walked straight into an old and ongoing problem.

Union printers expected to manage their own labor force. Employers who independently hired printing workers from outside the ranks of union journeymen incurred their wrath. However ubiquitous in printing shops around the country, women faced a classic double bind. They needed apprentice training to earn the union imprimatur, and unable to join unions, they lacked access to apprenticeships. Thus, women who traditionally had worked more cheaply than men continued to work outside the union system. That system of access to a printing livelihood was a gatekeeping function that union printers discussed endlessly. Necessarily, after midcentury, these discussions routinely included the role of women on shopfloors, as well.[11]

What union printers did not discuss was typesetting equipment. If journeymen printers foresaw in machinery a threat to their livelihood, no records of that fear remain. New York City's Local No. 6 of the International Typographical Union first took up the subject as late as the 1880s, after paying "very little attention" up to then. Even when the Alden firm placed its typesetters in the composing room of the *New York World,* the introduction elicited scant horror. According to union minutes, machines such as the Alden were "never seriously regarded by employers," and therefore "neither was there any apprehension among journeymen as to the possibility of their general introduction." The new machines, however, had yet to be linked with women, and journeymen who were skeptical, even ignorant, of innovative printing equipment knew all about the threat women posed to their printing unions.[12]

Employing printers introduced shopfloor machinery in order to reduce their costs of production. Working printers, however, never saw it that way. Immediately after the Civil War, typesetting machines and women entered shopfloors together. Paired in that manner, machines that might have sparked a market-driven workplace dispute, one that classically pitted labor against capital, seemed something else to journeymen. Working printers quickly reckoned typesetting equipment not as an expression of management perfidy, but as an episode of gender rivalry. After all, both print managers and equipment manufacturers presented the issue in these terms. The promising Alden typesetter came coupled with nonunion women operators.

Gendering the Alden

On his deathbed Timothy Alden had bequeathed his invention to his cousin Henry, along with various recommended modifications. Henry did what he was told and in 1862 produced a working model intriguing enough to attract a contract with the *New York Times*. According to its own report, the *Times* tested the Alden, "and being thoroughly convinced of its vast superiority to all other methods of composition, we have deemed it a necessity to order twelve of the machines for the use of the *Times* establishment." The newspaper called it "*the* invention of the Nineteenth Century," and predicted a "new era in newspaper publishing will date from the day of introduction."[13]

That day proved not as imminent as they wished. Delivering a dozen Aldens was more than Henry Alden could handle. Having exhausted his bankroll on his cousin's behalf, Henry ran out of money and ceased production. He had constructed three working models, only one of which was actually running when he gave it all up.[14]

Short months later, Charles C. Yeaton resurrected Alden's idea. Yeaton, a New York businessman, bought the Alden company, infused it with his "indomitable perseverance and energy," and formed a $100,000 joint stock company. He also hired the composing room foreman at New York's *Irish-American,* a man named Welch, to set a promotional brochure using the Alden typesetter itself. With the energy of renewed commitment, the Alden company threw its doors open to the public. Those doors were in Manhattan at the corner of St. Mark's and A Avenue. Their machine consisted of 14,600 separate parts and weighed 1,560 pounds. It cost $2,000. Every hour, claimed the firm, brought "some celebrity" in to look it over.[15]

The Alden typesetter, wondrous as it might be, got nowhere until the company stopped trying to persuade people how fast it was—how "smart" it was—and started convincing employers that women could run it. When the *New York Times* was first attracted to Timothy Alden's early version, it claimed "the public was ready to believe that a revolution in the art of printing had been inaugurated by his invention, and only waited to see the machine in general use among publishers of all printed matter." But the machine performed erratically. According to the *Times,* "unforeseen difficulties were in the way, and those of such a nature as to be overcome only by the nicest mechanism, and that the result of much thought and the patient labor of years."[16]

The *New York Herald* was next in line. On May 19, 1864, Charles Yeaton placed an improved Alden "in a printing office for the first time in its history." The road-testing chores this time fell to William Leaning. Assistant foreman of the *Herald* composing room, Leaning was also a respected Swift, "one of the most rapid compositors in New York."[17] The new Alden would earn highest merit if it could impress the best. Leaning would wrestle with the machine, learning its operation and working out the bugs in the distribution system, for over a month. Finally, on June 29, 1864, he produced "the first paragraph ever set by machinery in a newspaper office." The Alden company rejoiced. The *Herald* called the little piece "Skyrockets" and ran it the next day. The single inch of column text ran to three sentences. After forty-one days of tinkering, it had taken Leaning three minutes and thirty-two seconds to set.[18]

Problems persisted. Printing ink, necessarily viscous, was a sticky and smelly fact of life to workmen long used to grime. In a typesetting machine, however, ink-smeared type might easily clog its channels, especially in the smallest sizes. The Alden, as constituted, could set brevier (8-point) type, but it would never handle agate, and newspapers used large quantities of this smaller type.

Further, despite Alden's claims, its mechanism seemed too complicated. Maintenance threatened to require someone's full-time efforts, and the job seemed beyond the scope of the newly targeted operators: women employees. Yeaton, ready in 1865 to introduce yet another Alden, admitted as much. "No one could learn how to take care of it," he said of the older model, and furthermore, "if this were possible, it would take a man to do it." Still, "women could be successfully introduced as operators of the new machine."[19] That was promising. Indeed, it was becoming the goal.

When in 1865 Yeaton introduced a new and improved Alden machine, the third such advance, he also fully embraced the sales potential of women. Nine months after failing to impress William Leaning and the *New York Herald,* a new Alden associate, J. T. Slingerland, helped Yeaton produce a typesetting machine capable of handling the smallest type. At the same time and more important, Yeaton altered his sales pitch. The company's 1863 promotional brochure, *The Wonderful Type-Setting and Distributing Machine,* had been a small wire-stitched pamphlet. Now the firm hired Theodore L. DeVinne, executive officer of the New York printing firm of Francis Hart and Company and soon to become renowned in the field, to produce a prospectus of grand dimensions. Yeaton's volume, titled simply *Manual of the Alden Type-Setting and Distributing Machine,* contained exquisite typography, splendid woodcuts, and embossed leather binding. It was a marvelous book to herald a wonderful new machine. Yeaton wrote the descriptive text himself.

The message of the *Manual* pointed straightforwardly to composing room personnel changes. At the same time, the company hired a woman to demonstrate it. Selling the Alden no longer required men such as Welch, Leaning, or anyone else of shopfloor standing. "Miss Willard, formerly of the *World,*" explained the prospectus, was "engaged to work the machine, and after a few days' study became quite an expert operator." Willard arrived fresh from the *New York World*'s recently established women's typesetting staff. On September 12, 1865, without error, she set and distributed 1,000 ems of solid agate in ten minutes using the new Alden. Newspapers such as the *New York World* were obviously feminizing their work forces, and Alden positioned itself accordingly.[20]

Willard was the first woman to try the Alden. Assuredly, said Yeaton, she was the first of many. "I have never seen any man

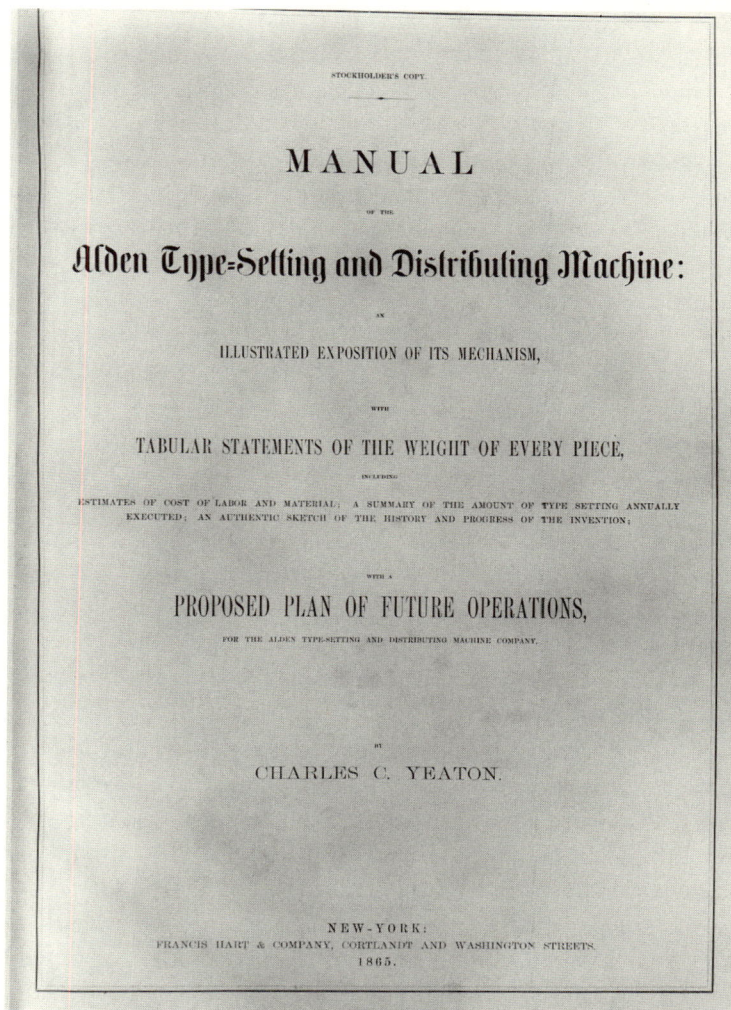

STOCKHOLDER'S COPY.

MANUAL

OF THE

Alden Type=Setting and Distributing Machine:

AN

ILLUSTRATED EXPOSITION OF ITS MECHANISM,

WITH

TABULAR STATEMENTS OF THE WEIGHT OF EVERY PIECE,

INCLUDING

ESTIMATES OF COST OF LABOR AND MATERIAL; A SUMMARY OF THE AMOUNT OF TYPE SETTING ANNUALLY
EXECUTED; AN AUTHENTIC SKETCH OF THE HISTORY AND PROGRESS OF THE INVENTION;

WITH A

PROPOSED PLAN OF FUTURE OPERATIONS,

FOR THE ALDEN TYPE-SETTING AND DISTRIBUTING MACHINE COMPANY.

BY

CHARLES C. YEATON.

NEW-YORK:
FRANCIS HART & COMPANY, CORTLANDT AND WASHINGTON STREETS.
1865.

The title page of the *Manual of the Alden Type-Setting and Distributing Machine,* perhaps the most exquisite equipment sales prospectus ever printed. The book, an elephant folio, is filled with woodcut illustrations, the printing of which established the reputation of Theodore Low DeVinne, who produced the volume for New York's Francis Hart and Company, printers.

(Courtesy, American Antiquarian Society, Worcester, Massachusetts) manipulate the keys as rapidly, or set so clean a proof," he claimed. "I am convinced, that if girls can endure the fatigue of night work, they will make by far the best operators upon the machine; and henceforth the proprietors of newspapers and book establishments will no longer be entirely dependent upon men to compose the matter they use." Yeaton continued to pound his moral. "The machine has never been known, so far, to strike for higher wages or stop work," he said. Neither, of course, had women compositors. "It will tend to elevate their position, and that of the working class generally," declared a pious Yeaton.[21]

Most printing employers understood Alden's sales pitch, and a line of them was forming. Alas, tested once more by the *World's* Willard, Alden's machine again failed. Newspapers, deadline driven, demanded smooth, maintenance-free action. If a typesetting machine was to succeed, its mechanisms must meet the sternest demands. Most New York dailies—the *Tribune,* the *Times,* the *Herald*—printed from stereotype plates, cast-metal reproductions of rows of hand-set letters. The *World,* however, printed from the actual types as they were assembled by compositors. The Alden machine clogged on inky type.[22]

In 1865 the *New York World* had begun a program of hiring women compositors "for the sake," the trade paper *Printers' Circular* would later say, "of giving practical aid to the movement for enlarging the sphere of women's work." Between 1865 and 1868 the *World* hired one hundred women typesetters at beneath union wage rates, segregated them from the men, and brought them slowly up to speed. Indeed, after the Civil War many employers began attempting to identify typesetting as women's work. Union printers called it a "petticoat invasion" and objected.[23]

Alden in 1868

In the fall of 1868, the typesetting staff of the *New York World* walked out of a rancorous dispute with the management of the paper. Wages and hours underlay any labor conflict, but the men at the *World* complained loudest about women printers. For at least three years the newspaper had hoped to cut costs by hiring women, installing machines, or combining the two. By using women to set straight matter, the newspaper repeatedly and by now routinely crossed Local No. 6 of the National Typographical Union.

The *World* ran a women's shop that was segregated from the men. The women's tasks were book- and job-related straight matter that the *World* conducted on the side, as it were, in a manner traditional to newspaper printers. The newspaper, however, also called upon the women to set for its columns, and when that happened, the women seemed to the men to be nothing less than "rat" printers, nonunion personnel who worked at less than scale. Local No. 6 and the *World* spent the summer of 1868 hacking out an agreement.[24]

Coincident with the *World* strike, Alden announced the readiness of its latest model. Speaking for all newspapers, the *New York Times* was ecstatic. For some eleven years since 1857 and Timothy Alden's first typesetter, "the public was ready to believe that a revolution in the art of printing had been inaugurated by his invention," and printers everywhere awaited his miracle. Now, thanks to the patented work of J. T. Slingerland, all the bugs were ironed out, and "we are at last upon the threshold of this revolution."[25]

When the *New York World* and Local No. 6 resolved their differences, the men returned and the *World* fired all of the women—all, that is, except for a woman named Augusta Lewis. As it had done repeatedly, the *World* sent Lewis to test Alden's latest model, and Lewis set more type faster than ever. As important, Lewis was both smart and articulate. According to the *American Artisan,* she "explain[ed] the scientific and complicated operations to visitors with great clearness."[26]

Still, this Alden would fail, as had all the others. Weary of work stoppage and now disappointed by Alden, the *World* could but wave its arms and demand a renewed effort to develop a competent mechanical typesetter. It was high time, said an exasperated editorialist, and "discreditable to the inventive genius of this country that the one great mechanical want of the time is still unsupplied." The newspaper offered a half-million-dollar prize for a successful composing machine.[27]

Augusta Lewis's work on the Alden in 1868 had been better than Willard's best effort. Unlike her predecessor, however, Lewis was merely beginning her tricky cruise among the men of the printing industry. Her performance established a reputation. Women who showcased machines did badly in the labor market and often disappeared. Such women were doubly threatening, as working females and operators of job-threatening machinery. Lewis, however, used her Alden experience to advance.

4 | Augusta Lewis and Women's Typographical Union No. 1

FIRST AMONG ITS VIRTUES, THE ALDEN TYPESETTER was fast, faster even than George Arensberg. Therefore, any woman who operated the machine would be fast as well—faster, naturally, than the vaunted Velocipede. Augusta Lewis might, it seemed, outdistance any Swift and by extension all their journeymen brethren. In other words, Lewis's Alden disturbed the likes of Arensberg and threatened their workplace prowess in the process. In the case of the Alden, the machine failed, but the operator succeeded famously. As it turned out, the Alden's great gift to printing was Augusta Lewis herself. Quite apart from technology, Lewis spearheaded a challenge from women that printing would not soon forget.

In four remarkable years, from 1868 until 1872, many people in printing discovered a use for Augusta Lewis. Along with many others, she began at the *New York World* as cheap, replacement labor. Then the Alden Typesetting Machine Company hired her to demonstrate its equipment. The International Typographical Union (ITU) next used her as a lever for enlightened, gender-inclusive unionism. New York printers' Local No. 6 of the ITU, initially at odds with the national organization, first considered her a working-class enemy, but later it found her to be an effective tool for beating back a dual-union threat. Susan B. Anthony used her to recruit women to her alternative feminism, before writing her off as a classic union dupe. Pulled by conflicting claims, Lewis transcended all of them. She was a competent compositor, a famous typesetting-machine operator, and a pioneering labor organizer. In time, having left the shopfloor far behind, she became a gender hero and a valuable memory among the men of the oldest labor union in the land.[1]

Augusta Lewis forced a pair of responses to the gender issue. When she and the women she represented became impossible to ignore any longer, print union officials for the first time in any trade authorized a separate, segregated women's affiliate within the ITU. Swifts and other rank-and-file journeymen members of the union, however, were not so accommodating. Rarely an obliging bunch among themselves, shopfloor typesetters now defended their masculine turf by equating it with printing prowess. George Arensberg and Augusta Lewis bloomed concurrently, if in vastly different venues. When Arensberg became a famous Swift, he launched a quickly accelerating series of typesetting races that reinforced the connections among speed, skill, and masculinity.

The Apprenticeship of Augusta Lewis

Augusta Lewis faced a fundamental conundrum in that she literally had never paid her dues. No women had, because in 1868 they could not join a printing union. In Lewis, organized journeymen had a seriously contentious printer on their hands. She and her colleagues were challenging an entire masculine world, the gender solidarity of shopfloor and printing union. Lewis and many other women could be competent typesetters, and most men knew it. As it stood, partially trained boys filled city shopfloors, and the bumbling did not stop there. In truth, many journeymen were terrible typesetters. Thoughtful union printers, however, wanted to retain a system that offered people—men— job security without regard to external standards of minimum skills or the production quotas of the marketplace. They could do this as long as they guarded the ancient mysteries of their craft. Those mysteries were evaporating, as the ease with which gate-crashing printers found work attested. For years, printing's typical response urged more attention to its apprentice programs.

In 1869 Augusta Lewis founded and led Women's Typographical Union No. 1, the first all-women's labor union in the land.
(From *American Dictionary of Printing and Bookmaking*, New York: Howard Lockwood & Co., 1894)

Moreover, unlike almost everyone else in printing, Lewis was never an ordinary shopgirl. Born in 1848 and subsequently orphaned, she was raised in affluent Brooklyn Heights. Lewis's childhood playmate there was Seth Low, a next-door neighbor who eventually became mayor of New York and president of Columbia University. Lewis began her working life as a writer, spending several months as a newspaper reporter. She later claimed that she learned to compose type as a means of enhancing her career as journalist and writer. "I contributed articles to the New York newspapers," she later told the printing historian George A. Stevens, "and learned printing as an educating factor to help me in writing." Young Lewis also learned French, certainly another "educating factor," first at the Brooklyn Heights Seminary and later at the convent school of the Sacred Heart in Manhattanville, where she also took courses in the classics, literature, and philosophy. She graduated with honors. While a teenager, she wrote for *Courier des États-Unis,* a French-language paper in New York. Even among compositors, labor's "intellectuals," her schooling was exceptional.[2]

In 1867 Lewis left a reporting job at the *New York Sun* in order to learn typesetting at another New York daily, the *Era.* Soon she joined the *New York World,* where the compositors had walked out. Everything Lewis knew of printing she learned during that first year on the job. Little wonder that old-timers griped. In the first place, she was eighteen, and in the middle of the nineteenth century that was far too old to begin printing. And of course an apprenticeship of a few months' duration was simply a joke.[3]

Lewis's tenure at the *World,* however, quickly became a novitiate in labor relations. When Local No. 6, Big Six, of the International Typographical Union struck the *World,* Lewis and her women colleagues, generally perceived as "rats" willing to set type cheaply, immediately became a corps of female strikebreakers, replacement "scabs." After the union and the newspaper resolved their differences, the men returned and the *World* fired all of the women.

The *New York World* had fired all its composing room women by the time the men returned to work—all, that is, except Augusta Lewis. We are told that Lewis thereupon walked out of her job in sympathy. Certainly she left the premises. It is likely, however, that the *World* "retained" her because she was already working out of house. The *World,* like all newspapers, consistently explored ways to reduce its composing bill. This, of course, was why it hired nonunion women workers. Denied a battery of women typesetters, the newspaper sent Lewis to test the cost alternative of the Alden typesetting machine. Lewis proceeded to master the machine and displayed it in the Alden showrooms to visitors from throughout the world.[4]

It is unclear who filled her pay envelope. The Alden company put Lewis to work not on *New York World* copy but on an assortment of showy exhibition projects. Lewis and her Alden typesetting machine made quick work of Appleton publishing company's *Cameos of English History.* She set portions of Charles Dickens's *David Copperfield,* which the appreciative author used for public readings. Most spectacularly, Alden gave her the text of a new G. P. Putnam and Sons edition of *The Legend of Sleepy Hollow.* Lewis set 24,993 ems of solid agate in six hours and thirty-nine minutes, a rate of 3,800 ems an hour. This was exceptional speed. The Alden turned heads in corporate boardrooms and newspaper composing rooms alike. Lewis had made the new machine dance.[5]

The year 1868 was a pivotal one for Augusta Lewis. At the *New York World,* she and the rest of the women got a wage from five to ten cents per thousand ems less than that paid to the men. Eager women were naturally satisfied with their pay envelopes, however ambivalent they might have been with their status as rat printers. Lewis, however, hated the situation and began looking for solutions. Before the year was out, she had met with Elizabeth Cady Stanton and Susan B. Anthony to help form New York's Working Women's Association. Anthony used her to organize the production staff of *Revolution.* In October Lewis successfully established Women's Typographical Union No. 1, the nation's first all-female labor union. Yet by year's end, everyone—Big Six, Anthony, *Revolution,* the *New York World*—had at some point been unhappy with the twenty-year-old Lewis.

Since its charter in 1852, the International Typographical Union had refused to admit women to membership. Although women found work setting type throughout the nineteenth century, a newspaper constituency remained the power behind Local No. 6 and all the other ITU affiliates. By the 1860s, however, the attitudes of organized labor toward gender roles began to change. The numbers of women setting type were growing, driving down wages. Seeing this, some in the labor movement thought women might be a greater threat outside the union than within. New York's Local No. 6 encouraged the 1867 Memphis convention of the ITU to "throw around their sisters the protecting power of their organization." The convention took no action.[6]

By year's end, further challenges had appeared. Augusta Lewis's role in the *New York World* strike of 1868 was part of a complicated web of tactical maneuvers. Local No. 6, representing the striking journeymen at the *World,* originally accused the newspaper of work-rule violations, specifically union guidelines on acceptable kinds of copy. The compositors at the *Brooklyn Eagle* were already striking over a wage dispute, and *World* journeymen complained when their employer put them to work setting type for the *Eagle,* forcing one set of union members to scab another. Local No. 6 struck all the interested parties. The *World* thereupon hired and, when necessary, trained women replacements. Some typographical union members, such as Robert McKechnie and Alexander Troup, had the foresight to realize that if women were already in the ITU they would be unavailable as strikebreakers.[7]

While working printers chewed on their problems, Susan B. Anthony provided two new paths out of the mess. She first of all offered work to the freshly unemployed women printers, hiring several and teaching others at *Revolution.* In addition to this assistance, she proposed a support organization, a Working Women's Association.[8]

The *New York World* strike marked a moment when working-class women printers and middle-class suffragists found common cause and clear-cut male oppressors. According to *Revolution,* the sin of the *World* was not in replacing unionized men with women substitutes but in paying those women less. Cogently and persistently throughout the strike, *Revolution* attacked the journeymen of Local No. 6 of the ITU, saying that women printers should under no circumstances knuckle under to charges of scabbing, that the union was getting what it deserved, that Local No. 6 prohibited women from its membership, and that it would eagerly fill their places at the end of the strike. By the end of the job action, the point of view of the *World* quickly evolved to fit the opinions of returning union printers. In firing their women, the paper cited a catalog of incompetence with which most members of Local No. 6 agreed—women could neither spell nor justify, and, worst of all, could not read sloppy manuscripts. Women were careless and neglected ancillary duties. The *World* and Local No. 6 agreed that these shortcomings were virtually genetic.[9]

Anthony offered Lewis a forum in which to protest the *World*'s action if Lewis would bring her printing colleagues to support Anthony's causes. As Elizabeth Cady Stanton described it, Anthony had ambitions for Lewis and the rest of the typesetters. "One of Miss Anthony's most cherished plans is to have a magnificent printing establishment, and a daily paper, owned and controlled and all the work done by women, thus giving employment to hundreds and making the world ring with the new evangel for women." On the evening of September 18, 1868, a group of those women launched the Working Women's Association as Augusta Lewis delivered her typesetting troops, "several still in girlhood, and of unusual comeliness and intelligence."[10]

Lewis promptly entered a dispute with Stanton and Anthony. Fresh from a day's labor on behalf of Alden, "Gussie," as her friends called her, wondered why Anthony and Stanton considered the vote their highest priority. Lewis rejected making the working women's group a suffrage organization, insisting that "women's wrongs should be redressed before her rights were proclaimed." To use the word "suffrage" in the name "would couple the association in the minds of many with short hair and bloomers and other vagaries." Lewis thought that working women should combine to improve their economic conditions. That improvement having been achieved, women might then be indoctrinated to suffrage and other reforms. The coalition between working-class and middle-class women, so quickly formed, was just as rapidly crumbling. In Philip Foner's phrase, the "young ladies who were present who were workers" sided with Lewis. The organization would become the Working Women's Association, leaving "suffrage" out of the title altogether.[11]

Women's Typographical Union No. 1

Augusta Lewis wanted a labor union. She rejected a general reformist group out of hand, but would examine the shape of an alternative printing alliance. Women's Typographical Union No. 1 accordingly emerged from a classic debate over labor tactics, specifically dual unionism. Originally, all the women at the founding of the Working Women's Association wanted something resembling a "cooperative female printing office." Women printers in San Francisco had organized such a group under circumstances similar to those of New York. San Francisco's union printers, however, had rejected the cooperative. The Anthony-Stanton faction of the Working Women's Association welcomed such a separation, but New York's women typographers did not want it to happen to them. From the start, Lewis wanted to use her union to force open the doors of the men's ITU.[12]

On October 12, 1868, Susan B. Anthony offered to the first meeting of the Women's Typographical Union one of the most patronizing chats in labor history. "Girls," she intoned, "you must take this matter to heart seriously now, for you have established a union." Lewis listened, probably impatiently, beginning to understand that Anthony too often talked like this. At the *New York World* Lewis had set type at journeyman speed. What did Anthony know about printing, the shopfloor, or working women at all? Anthony and Stanton wanted a suffrage organization with a newspaper that women would print. Lewis appreciated the work but nonetheless demanded a women's printing union. She thought she was a good printer and wanted pay at union rates. Local No. 6 of the International Typographical Union would not let her in, but Anthony's middle-class gang did not seem to be helping. "For the first time in woman's history in the United States," Anthony went on, "you are placed, and by your own efforts, on a level with men, as far as possible, to obtain wages for your labor. I need not say that you have taken a great momentous step forward in the path of success." That was so. Woman's Typographical No. 1 soon boasted forty members. Augusta Lewis was its first president, and she could not wait for Anthony to leave and for work to begin.[13]

The women printers did not wish forever to remain rats. Lewis, along with Emily Peers, Eva Howard, and others, had long petitioned Local No. 6 for membership, and if the union demanded better apprenticeship training of them, they urged that reform as well. By October 1868 and the end of a long strike, the women found some support at Big Six. The union sent a pair of its members, Robert McKechnie, composing-room foreman at the *New York World*, and Alexander Troup, secretary-treasurer of the national union, to reach an accord.[14]

Emily Peers rose to this occasion, speaking the plain words of the shopfloor working class. At times Lewis needed this kind of help. Lewis had been raised and educated to middle-class standards, and many people deferred to that background and manner. Few considered her a garden-variety shopgirl. Lewis told the meeting that the *World* had always treated her right. "I have heard that there is a decided prejudice in the Union against women setting type among men," she said. Was this so? To the working women assembled, Lewis's question must have seemed needlessly disingenuous, and Peers chose to be more direct. "Will the Union allow ladies to join their ranks as members?" she asked Troup.[15]

Troup could play the innocent, too. "I never knew of any woman applying for admission," he replied. "I can speak for Mr. McKechnie . . . as being in favor of women working at case with equal rights and privileges as the men. But he is not in favor, nor am I, of women coming in to undermine the prices paid to men."[16]

Accounts of the meeting began to read like operetta lyrics or an invitation to the dance. Peers offered Troup a dollar, the entry cost to the ITU. "Will you take my initiation fee now, if you please?" she asked. "Yes, of course I shall; and will propose you as a member," he said.[17]

Troup, however, was serious, and well aware of the dangers of dual unions. On behalf of Local No. 6 he would "hire a hall for your meetings, furnish you with books, stationery, etc., and assume all other expenses which it may be necessary for you to incur in getting your association into working order, and to continue to do so until your Union shall be in a condition to support itself." He explained how Women's Typographical No. 1 should apply for an ITU charter. The women accepted the union's support and eagerly formed their union.[18]

Skill and the "Manly Competence"

Men printers liked to think what they did was a truly "manly art" that combined intellectual and manual labor. Augusta Lewis and many other members of Women's Typographical No. 1 admired these manly men and many would marry them, but the intelligence and dexterity of competent composition seemed to have little to do with masculinity. In Lewis's case, composing equipment had augmented her typesetting skills. From there, her strong leadership urged women to shoulder more of the broad-ranging tasks a culture required. She found few intrinsically masculine problems standing in her way, save, of course, the men themselves.[19]

Printing journeymen considered her an occupational gate-crasher. Men often claimed that women such as Lewis diminished the overall skills required of their work, but the requirements of hand composition remained the same no matter who was setting type, and most compositors acknowledged the minimal demands of straight typesetting. It remained difficult to insist that women "deskilled" the craft. Machinery, however, might actually reduce what a compositor needed to know, and when women ran that machinery, it was a different story. Mainly, however, journeymen typesetters simply accused Lewis and the rest of the women of being women, which translated into a general charge of incompetence. Others, of course, were inadequate as well—two-thirder boys, for instance. After the Civil War, women merely added gender to a preexisting labor problem. In any event, often enough men were incompetent, some of them slower and less deft than most. Their shopmates called them, among many other things, "shoemakers."

The saga of Olive Miner doubtless sobered many male

judgments. The booming business of California's gold rush pressed young Olive into a regular situation at the *Lodi Democrat,* where she set a routine daily 6,000 ems. She earned as much as $1.86 a day, a "fine little sum" by modest journeyman standards. Olive, as it happened, was "about twelve years old" with three months' experience. Olive Miner lacked the speed of a Swift, but was nonetheless unarguably competent. Miner was a preadolescent girl doing the work of full-grown journeymen, a child rolling the bowling ball from between her legs and watching all the pins fall down—repeatedly. More Olive Miners and the mysteries of print composition might unravel entirely.[20]

Printers disdainful of these implications lamented the limited range of their youngsters. Theoretically, apprentice training supplied them with broad printing skills—paper preparation, the inking of forms, press techniques—but these proved to be skills men never employed. Therefore, the calumny men heaped on women had little to do with a diminishing range of skills and much to do with a kind of occupational degradation, a process social scientists came to call "demasculinization." Partially trained boys, for all of their inadequacies, nonetheless remained boys, apprentice men. At their worst, they presented the craft with an abridgement of manly competence, a hedged resume. Although in this they might resemble women and girls, in the fact of their sex they resembled men more, and there was no question among printers whence came a complete, good standing in the trade. True men fulfilled an apprenticeship and carried a union card. As skills alone could not, the judgment of one's betters and subsequently of one's peers defined a man. In other words, skill or prowess did not confer competence, but rather became a component of it, a part of a totality to be judged by a community of printers. As long as this equation obtained, printing simply defined women out of its workplace. By 1868, however, what heretofore was a problem of shopfloor pubescence, nagging and recurrent, had escalated into a predicament of gender—and a calamity.[21]

Book and Job Strike of 1869

Women's Typographical No. 1, the nation's first all-women's labor union, hit the ground running. In January 1869 Local No. 6 led a strike against the book and job printers of New York City, whose numerous women employees typified nonunion typesetters willing to work for substandard wages. These were workers appropriate for an appeal from Women's Typographical, and the women looked for a response from the new union. Perhaps more important, so did Big Six.

Led by Lewis, the women's union joined Local No. 6 in supporting the striking printers. Lewis invited women involved in the job action to apply at Women's Typographical No. 1. Lewis and her union could place competent women typesetters. Emily Peers and others fired by the *New York World* had landed at the *Anti-Slavery Standard* and made good money, union scale. Lewis herself remained on the staff of *Revolution,* where she had been since leaving the *New York World*.[22]

This presented a problem. The labor policy at *Revolution* remained that of its founders. *Revolution* was itself produced by Gray and Green Printers, a Manhattan job firm. Several months earlier, S. W. Green and J. A. Gray, sympathetic to the feminist goals of Anthony and Stanton, had agreed to an ongoing on-the-job training plan for working women, a program designed to provide women with the skills they were denied because of the exclusionist union policies. In response to the strike, Gray and Green offered a crash two-week training program that would furnish replacement typesetters to affected companies. Gray and Green trained scab labor.

As had been the case at the *New York World,* a gendered technology compounded the labor problem. In 1857, coincident with Timothy Alden's first typesetter, W. H. Houston patented his Houston Typesetter and Distributor. The machine languished for a decade until, in 1867, Gray and Green Printers bought the patent. The firm renamed the machine the Green Typesetter, built a dozen of them, and Messrs. Gray and Green installed them all on their own shopfloor. By 1869 Gray and Green had filled its composing room with nonunion women machine operators. Local No. 6 howled. *Revolution*'s editorial response was immediate and hostile to the union printers.[23]

Susan B. Anthony had sided with the owners of the city's book and job shops. Union printers, including Augusta Lewis, quickly found the *Revolution* guilty of the worst sort of rat printing. Lewis protested to Anthony and subsequently to her employers, Gray and Green. They fired her. Lewis thereupon confronted Anthony, who protested that her hands were clean; she did not employ any typesetters and had no control over the policies of the firm that did her printing. Anthony claimed merely to have appealed to employing printers "to open the way for a thorough drill to the hundreds of poor girls, to enable these women to earn wages with men everywhere," and could not understand why Big Six or Augusta Lewis were upset.[24]

The strike ran eleven weeks into the summer of 1869 and concluded on terms favorable to New York's union printers. Anthony and the Working Women's Association took a particular beating from the city's journeymen. Anthony lost and would never regain her reputation as friend and representative of women workers everywhere. The Women's Typographical Union had much to do with this outcome, and Augusta Lewis's stock soared among union brethren.[25]

The implications of it all were hashed out in August 1869, when Anthony appeared at the annual meeting of the National Labor Union representing the Working Women's Association. The convention offered another arena for tactical maneuvering. Anthony voiced her standard position; she wanted to establish an independent women's voice within the ranks of labor, and she favored alternative, and separate, organizations. Lewis and the working women had demanded decent wages and had, throughout the spring, gained a good deal of respect from their peers. For union printers, the equation was simple. Local No. 6 of the ITU had struck the job printers, Lewis's Women's Typographical Union supported Big Six, and Gray and Green had fired Lewis. From a union point of view, Anthony's printing project at *Revolution* was a simple scab-training program.

What followed was a classic episode of nineteenth-century gender politics. Delegate John Walsh, on behalf of the typographers, accused Anthony of running a rat shop and challenged her right to participate in the convention. Anthony responded from the floor. Yes, she said, she had used the *World* strike as an opportunity to train women as compositors; it was the only way women could get experience in the trade. Austin Puett, not himself a printer, defended Anthony from what he hoped was some theoretical high ground. Puett believed in equal rights for all and hoped that everybody would "enter upon the grand platform of competition, and I do not care whether he is a 'rat' or a mouse."[26]

John Walsh could not believe his ears and counterattacked. Plainly disgusted, he observed that Puett and his ilk knew nothing of real working men and would not know a rat if they saw one. Insofar as Augusta Lewis was concerned, he might have stopped there. But Walsh was on a roll. "The lady," Walsh said, referring to Anthony, "goes in for taking women away from the wash tub, and in the name of heaven, who is going there if they don't? I believe in a woman's doing her work, men marrying them, and supporting them." This reasoning, of course, was why there were no women in labor unions to begin with. Lewis wanted badly to change this attitude. For the moment, she was stuck with it.[27]

Susan B. Anthony considered the young woman a union dupe. Anthony knew women were second-class citizens. They would be first-class only with change, and change could come only with the power of the vote, not with labor solidarity narrowly focused against management on the one hand and existing rank and file on the other. According to Anthony, women would be given equal treatment in the trades, would be taken seriously, only when fully enfranchised. "We ask for a change, we ask for a chance."[28]

Anthony lost her case before the Philadelphia convention. She had contended for power within the ranks of labor and had lost. Insofar as working men and women were concerned, Anthony had

had her chance and had blown it, showing herself to be a class enemy, incapable of improving the lives of real people.

Cultural Segregation and the ITU

Augusta Lewis was making the most of her new reputation. In short order, the International Typographical Union welcomed her women's union into the fold. Scant weeks before the 1869 National Labor Union (NLU) convention, the typographers had convened their own national gathering in Albany. On behalf of Women's Typographical No. 1, Lewis and Eva B. Howard petitioned the organization for a charter of membership. The ITU, acknowledging the support from New York City's Local No. 6, quickly accepted the petition.[29]

Lewis and the members of Women's Typographical No. 1 had chosen a kind of segregation. Still, Women's Typographical never became a separate entity, a rival union. The International Typographical Union was a federation, and the women became members of the parent ITU, equal in standing to rank-and-file men journeymen. Because the men of New York City's Local No. 6 would never admit them, Women's No. 1 accepted a compromise and became an anomaly, officially a part of a national organization but separate from the muscular Big Six, that union's main source of strength. This distinctive status may have seemed a bad bargain to some. In 1869, however, convention delegates Lewis and Howard had all they could handle in avoiding the same treatment as the complete apartheid facing printers of color.

In 1869 Albany's ITU convention opened a door to Augusta Lewis and her women printers as it slammed it on racial minorities, and in the process offered women printers a dose of hard realities. At Albany, a Government Printing Office employee named L. H. Douglass forced the racial issue on American printers. Douglass, the son of the famous abolitionist Frederick Douglass, had applied for membership in his local Washington, D.C., printing union, Columbia Local No. 101, and the union had rejected him. On Douglass's behalf, Daniel Flynn of the District thereupon urged a resolution "that it will be flagrantly unjust for any subor-

Eva Howard and Augusta Lewis, the first delegates from Women's Typographical Union No. 1, are front and center in this group photograph of the 1869 Albany, New York, convention of the International Typographical Union.

(Courtesy, Albany Typographical Union No. 4 Archive, McKinney Library, Albany Institute of History & Art)

dinate union to deny admission to any printer merely on the ground of race or color." After "prolonged discussion," convention delegates tabled the resolution, 57 to 28.[30]

J. T. Halleck then tried to head off the issue by a vigorous statement of local autonomy. Halleck, also of the District of Columbia, offered a resolution alternative to that of Flynn that decried the imposition of "religious or political" tests for union work. The office of the *Congressional Record* had insisted on hiring Douglass and needed union authorization. Halleck castigated this "wanton attempt of the congressional printer" to force Douglass on Local No. 101. According to Halleck, the issue had nothing to do with race. Douglass was "an avowed rat" and thus met "our unqualified condemnation."[31]

A ruckus having been raised, convention delegates decided to devote an evening session to "the negro question." John McVicar, a delegate from Detroit, tried to clarify the issue. Clearly, McVicar insisted, the sentiment against Douglass was racially motivated and had nothing to do with Douglass's "rat record." The transgression had happened in Denver, where Douglass had worked in an "unfair office," because, McVicar claimed, nobody would let him into a union. Douglass had "positively insisted" on being paid the union scale, to no avail. Among Douglasses, according to McVicar, union vigor practically ran in the family. In 1863 the upstate New York *Rochester Democrat* offered nonunion composition work to Frederick Douglass, Jr., L. H. Douglass's brother, and Frederick refused the offer. He wanted union journeymen to know "that although they would not admit him to the union on account of his black skin, he . . . would do nothing to jeopardize their interests in the strike."[32]

After "a very full discussion," the Albany convention delegates defeated a straightforwardly exclusionary resolution barring admission "of any negro into a subordinate union." Having thus sidestepped a racist regulation, the delegates addressed Douglass's rat status, not his race, and in a 48 to 37 tally, felt free to reject his claim.[33]

In the meantime, membership in Susan B. Anthony's Working Women's Association sagged. Recruitment among working women declined precipitously, and personal antipathies lingered. From the start, the imperious Anthony seems to have annoyed the never-deferential Lewis. Anthony had organized the association in order to earn her credentials as a delegate to Philadelphia's National Labor Union convention. Then she simply leaned on the women for their endorsement. Lewis had squirmed, then protested. "What good," she asked a stunned Anthony, "will that do?" Not much, reckoned many working women. Soon all that remained of the Working Women's Association were wealthy middle-class women seeking new ways to speak on behalf of inarticulate seamstresses.[34]

Subsequent meetings of the International Typographical Union mirrored this shift in power. Those attending the 1870 ITU convention in Cincinnati heard accounts of the NLU ruckus the preceding year and declared Anthony to be "an enemy, not only to the working men, but to the working women of New York." They then turned to Augusta Lewis for confirmation. Lewis agreed. Anthony's organizational efforts, Lewis consistently claimed, were "inefficient" in a "working-women's association" and Anthony was undermining Lewis's hard work on behalf of Women's Typographical Union No. 1 and those of working women everywhere. Anthony was becoming a punching bag for union printers, with Lewis leading the attack.[35]

The 1870 convention thereupon named Augusta Lewis its corresponding secretary—presumably to reward this valuable recruit in the gender wars, or maybe the membership was persuaded by its leaders that a gesture was in order. No woman had ever before held office in the ITU. Indeed, only recently had any been allowed to join. No woman would ever again be thus distinguished. Possibly, therefore, in anointing Lewis, Cincinnati's delegates wished to reassure themselves of some noble purpose. In 1870 the race issue, personified again by L. H. Douglass, reemerged, and as the ITU added its brightest woman, it buried an entire African-American constituency. When the printers discussed their gender issue, castigating the viper Anthony and rewarding the stalwart Lewis, their special committee on interracial membership expressed "regret" that the "negro question" had ever been introduced in the first place. It was "contrary to the progress of civilization," the committee claimed, "to legislate on the color of printers seeking membership." The issue, therefore, should be left to the discretion of subordinate unions. John McVicar, vocal as always, considered this "a lame conclusion" that surely invited trouble.[36]

Union Official

Lewis turned her secretaryship into anything but a sinecure. During her one-year term, she energetically sought a better deal for nonunion women typesetters. Certainly she worked within the union, encouraging it to accept women members. Women, Lewis felt, deserved equal pay for equal work. To get it, they needed equal training. Such training could come only from an ITU-sponsored apprenticeship program. The union, Lewis insisted, must make room. Such persuasion and cajolery were hard work for Lewis.[37]

Problems outside the union were just as intractable. Lewis attempted to persuade employing printers to hire women at the established union rate. She argued that print shops should employ union printers but that women must never be made to scab. In making this case Lewis encountered the perfidy of Susan B. Anthony.[38]

Anthony fostered and exploited rat printers. In addressing the delegates at the 1871 ITU convention, Lewis, alluding to the printers Gray and Green, described a shop in New York "that . . . boasts a branch known as the 'Women's Printing Office.' I believe well-known authoresses patronize this office, intending to help female compositors; yet every injustice possible is suffered on account of that office." Lewis told the delegates how in three weeks fifteen female learners had been "taken in" to learn the rudiments of typesetting. During the year that Lewis herself worked there, one hundred such novices passed through. Lewis and other experienced women had done all the work, Lewis complained, and the novices got "all the fat, all the reprint." Anthony's system asked accomplished women to work more for a cause than a paycheck.[39]

This was an argument the men could understand, presented in a way they could follow. In the battle for the heart and soul of New York's women printers, Lewis accused Anthony's printing and publishing empire of sweating its workforce. "The *Fireside Companion*," Lewis told the delegates, "is the only office in [New York] which will employ none but union girls"—unlike Anthony's *Revolution*. Lewis wryly informed the convention that she was still waiting for satisfaction from those proprietors "who have solemnly promised, when their present contract expires, to have the *Revolution,* a union office, paying the full scale alike to men and women."[40]

Having warmed hearts within the ITU, Lewis lit into them. Women still did not trust printing unions but could be able compositors, Lewis insisted. The union should recruit them, train them, and see to it that they are paid to scale. Only in this way could organized labor combat rat printers and class enemies such as Anthony. "It is the general opinion of female compositors," Lewis scolded, "that they are more justly treated by what is technically known as 'rat' foremen, printers, and employers than they are by union men." Susan B. Anthony had been saying as much for years.[41]

Lewis may have seemed credulous and perhaps naïve to feminist rivals, but she expected a great deal from changes within her union. She wanted journeymen printers to accept a woman colleague as a woman, not as "one of the boys." Lewis was on hand on December 17, 1871, when the International Working Men's Association sponsored its famous parade in New York to commemorate the Paris Commune. The glory of the American left turned out—African-American Civil War regiments, Irish nationalists, Cuban patriots, and Victoria Woodhull and Tennie C. Claflin, "walking in one of the front ranks and carrying a red flag." As grand as it all was, for Lewis the event heralded a coming era in gender equality. "Women marched arm-in-arm with their husbands, and many were accompanied by their children," she marveled. Moreover, Local No. 6 was on hand, "presenting a fine appearance." Many members had joined the International, Lewis happily reported, and organized themselves as Typographical Section No. 1. "It was the most genuine Democratic affair that was ever witnessed," Lewis declared.[42]

Lewis admired libertarian politics but loved being a part of the printing trade. She never merely picked up a pay envelope. She wanted to be among "real" printers as badly as she wanted to reform them. By 1871 she supplied a monthly column to the *Printers' Circular*. Late in December, Lewis wrote admiringly of publisher Robert S. Menamin's brand-new *Encyclopedia of Printing* and the "reverent spirit" it inspired.[43]

Augusta Lewis thought that women could be both printers and

parents; after all, men were. Lewis persistently believed that men's institutions would open to women when men saw that women were as capable as men. Lewis, however, was discovering that women, no less than men, considered gender expectations as problematic as job skills. She refused to allow unions to degender women before admitting them. She urged three tasks on the men. First, unions must reach out in good faith to women, offering the full advantages of membership. Second, the unions must quiet fears that full union recognition would not cost women their traditional homemaking roles. And third, men on the shop floor must refrain from sexist ridicule.[44]

She might as well have tried to halt the planets in their orbits. Journeymen had always pointed out that women, however skilled or conscientious, found their true occupation in the home and all too readily abandoned their careers for a chance at marriage. The charge hit home at Women's Typographical No. 1: four of its roster, including charter members Eva B. Howard and Kate Cusack, soon married. On June 12, 1872, Augusta Lewis did as well, thereupon moving to New Haven, Connecticut. Members of Local No. 6 wished them all well with punning condescension. Never mind that one of the women was fast enough to be called a "velocipede," nor that another had quit a book-composing job in union solidarity, nor that a third, Cusack, was a past president of the women's union. Cusack married a man named Storey, a journeyman printer, as it happened. "If *Mrs.* Kate will discharge the new duties . . . as well as did *Miss* Kate," glowed the *Printers' Circular,* "she need no fears of *her* Storey having anything but a happy ending." Even Lewis could not resist these coy tributes. Colleagues Howard and Cusack, she announced, had organized "a *new union* in places where Unions already exist." She hoped the union would not mind such a transgression, but feared it would take the opportunity to "tell us to 'Go and do likewise.'" Which, of course, is exactly what Lewis did.[45]

Without Augusta Lewis, the post–Civil War generation of women printers survived only into the 1880s. Women's Typographical No. 1 collapsed in 1878, but that collapse said as much about the parent International Typographical Union as it did about the numbers of women throughout printing locals. Printing, as all working culture, revived during the mid-1880s, and the typesetting races of that time became emblematic of that resurgence. Building on what Lewis had bequeathed, women would race, and they would beat the Swifts at their game. But first, printing had to enter the new sphere of public amusement.

5 Joseph McCann Takes the Swifts to the Show

AMID ACCUMULATING SHOPFLOOR STRAIN—WOMEN to the left of them, machines to the right—Swifts did the only thing they knew how to do. They went even faster. By the mid-1880s, journeymen Swifts resembled mythic Irish elks and modern athletes. They had become the best ever on earth at what was becoming irrelevant. One Swift in particular, an Irishman named Joseph McCann, led the way. McCann aimed for the renown that came with the eclipse of the great George Arensberg. In tackling the legend of the Velocipede, McCann and a group of racing Swifts created cultural theater.

Joseph William McCann was born in 1856 in Williamstown, Ireland, a village south of Dublin that was rapidly becoming suburban. In 1869, when he was twelve, he began a printing apprenticeship in Alexander Thom's government printing office. He served five years of a standard seven-year printing apprenticeship there and completed his printing education at the Dublin *Evening Mail.* Once a journeyman, McCann quickly joined his union, the Dublin Typographical Provident Society, and landed jobs at the *Dublin Express* and later, *Saunder's Newsletter.* Later he moved on to the *Freeman's Journal.* In 1881, restless, barely solvent, and weary at his third profitless local newspaper, McCann opted out. On May 14, 1881, he applied to the union for his traveling card and for the foreign emigration allowance the union paid to members of good standing who intended to leave Ireland.[1]

Printing unions throughout Britain sponsored migration as a means of regulating workforce and wages. Indeed, when American printers called this mobility "tramping," they borrowed an earlier coinage. In Ireland, tramping usually meant emigration to England, but also, of course, to America. In the spring of 1881, the twenty-five-year-old McCann put a deposit of two pounds on a steamship ticket to New York City. Philip Little, Joseph Fennamore, and Michael Wall, three friends, vouched for him. The union gave him money—eight pounds, fifteen—and launched his new career. "JoeMac" had worn well on people. For his going away present, mates gave him a silver-plated composing stick engraved with their good wishes. McCann would gather more of these, as mementos and prizes. He sailed May 28 from Queenstown (now Cobh), near Cork.[2]

Joseph McCann arrived in New York in June 1881. With countless other late-nineteenth-century migrants, at first he worked where he could. McCann bounced from book offices and job shops to newspaper departments, finally finding a spot in the composing room of the *New York Herald.* An ambitious McCann thought there might be more. Briefly, in the fall and winter 1882–83, he tried his fortune in Boston, where he held cases at the *Globe.* But by May 1883 he was back in New York at the *Herald,* where he began astonishing shopmates with his speed.[3]

Evolution of an Event

When, in 1886, the *New York Tribune* inaugurated its brand-new Linotype composing machines, it capped a printing revolution. The implications of that revolution arrived first among hand-setting compositors. In time, the Linotype forced an industrywide displacement of these printers. The particular skill the industry jettisoned first was speed. Speed, of course, defined Swifts.

In 1886, however, throughout the eastern United States and coincident with the installation of the *Tribune*'s Linotypes, the fastest Swifts launched a series of highly publicized typesetting races. Chicago and Philadelphia staged the largest tournaments, and from Boston to Memphis printers throughout the eastern United States raced at setting type. The races happened not on shopfloors, but in public arenas, pleasure bazaars known as dime museums, before thousands of fascinated citizens. In other words, confronting equipment far faster than they, machines that might easily spell their occupational doom, Swifts decided to celebrate their speed. Instead of raising angry hell, compositors put on a show. English workers, similarly challenged, boycotted. Frenchmen marched. In the United States, compositors raced.[4]

It actually began late in the year 1885 at Tousey's Printing Office in New York City. There, Joseph McCann accepted a challenge by William C. Barnes. The city's journeymen, as usual, gathered and placed their bets. Unlike typical shopfloor contests, however, this match race turned its contestants into public people and introduced a workplace sport to the world at large. What that world watched were displays of astonishing competence in the face of advancing technology. Not in five hundred years had technology been a compositor's equal. Swifts reaffirmed that autonomy for all of an industry. Sovereign workmen might yet conquer an insistent technology. These were dances of defiance.

By 1885 typeracing was breaking out of the print shop. Bigger races attracted barroom attention usually reserved for billiards, bicycle racing, or boxing. Throughout the eastern states, citywide contests extended an essentially intramural activity to include meetings of the best of several printing establishments. George Graham beat a gathering of Boston's best printers. In the South, W. H. Van Bibber triumphed at Memphis. William C. Clarke won at Pittsburgh, Joseph Farquhar at Rochester. Journeymen printers were becoming municipal assets. Cincinnati's Alexander Duguid returned home a conquering hero after winning a national meet in Philadelphia. On April 15, 1886, he basked before testimonials at a Grand Hotel merchants' banquet. "Our guest," proclaimed one toast, "Cincinnati is proud of him."[5]

Joseph W. McCann, whose goal was always to surpass the Velocipede. (From *A Collation of Facts Relative to Fast Typesetting,* New York: Concord Cooperative Printing Company, 1887)

Challenges circulated widely, increasingly farther from the confines of individual shopfloors. One such challenge, appearing in the *New York Sun,* caught the eye of Mannis J. Geary, the assistant composing room foreman at the *New York Herald.* Geary answered with a public challenge of his own—the *Herald*'s composing room dark horse, a mysterious "unknown." Joseph McCann had been at the *Herald* for two years, and, as he later liked to recall, "I was the unknown."[6]

Ira Somers answered the *New York Herald*'s challenge. Somers, then at the *New York World,* suggested a three-hour contest, winner to fetch $500. "The challenge was accepted on my behalf," said McCann, "by my friends, Myles Johnson, Harry Cole, two of the fastest compositors in the country, and Al Mohr, all of the *Herald.*" Somers, younger than McCann, was a prodigy. The *New York World,* newly purchased by Joseph Pulitzer, had made peace with New York's Local No. 6 of the International Typographical Union (ITU) and by the 1880s had hired some notable Swifts. Somers had been but a teenager when, in the summer of 1882, he astounded Philadelphia by setting 2,019 ems of solid minion in one hour. Few had set type faster. Then for a couple of years he hit the road, showing up in 1885 at the New York City convention of the ITU.[7]

Labor historians like to dwell on plenary sessions of union conventions. There is where issues of apprentice training and wage solidarity were discussed and labor bigwigs sat with politicians. The International Typographical Union held its 1885 meeting at New York City's Irving Hall, and as the session got under way, Henry George, the famous author of *Progress and Poverty,* addressed the delegates from the left hand of Mayor W. R. Grace.[8]

Meanwhile, faster action and journeymen of a different stripe arrived at the composing rooms of the *New York Sunday Star.* Joseph McCann and Ira Somers raced that day, and three hundred noisy shopmates got their money down. McCann won the match, building an early lead and holding on. Somers had been nervous, committed several early errors, and spent valuable time revising his stick. He was unable to rally. Nonetheless, colleagues found much to admire in Somers's performance, a deceptively easy motion. "He does not appear," commented the journeyman William C. Barnes, "to be setting type as fast as he really does."[9]

Bill Barnes miscalculated. As he watched McCann dispose of Somers, Barnes saw McCann's jerky style, compared it with Somers's smooth yet seemingly slow manner, and concluded that McCann could be beaten. Intent on forging his own reputation, Barnes nonetheless should have known better. A native of Toronto, Canada, he had won matches at Montreal and Hartford before joining the staff of the *New York World.* Twice on wager in 1885 he had surpassed the 2,000-ems-per-hour standard. That

September, having sprinted to an hour's total of 2,160 ems, Barnes challenged McCann to a mid-December match race: four hours for $500 a side, winner take all.[10]

As a shopfloor celebration of working-class culture, few events equaled the typesetting match that pitted Joseph McCann against William Barnes. Like all such competitions, the race brought journeymen together to renew acquaintances and reexamine pecking orders. Printing royalty came out for the big matches, such as the Arensberg Wager fifteen years earlier or the McCann-Somers race. "Of course," a reporter said, "no competition among printers would be complete without the presence of 'Arry Cole." Himself very fast, Harry Cole was "a true friend and a sincere enemy" within the fraternity and its union, a man whose "sporting operations spread over half a continent," stopping only at Chicago, "because the roads to San Francisco were bad." He liked McCann, indeed sponsored him, and the "coolness and precision of Barnes played havoc with his usual cheerfulness." Local legend "Poohbah" Gill was there with his celebrated "stocking" full of cash. He backed Barnes, as did many others, who for several days had placed up to fifty dollars in early-line wagering. E. A. Donaldson, the man who had arranged the famous Arensberg match, arrived "with a cigar and an air of nonchalance."[11]

The race, however, proved difficult to bet. While McCann filled his composing stick to its twenty-line capacity, Barnes was emptying his after only nineteen lines. To onlookers, Barnes therefore seemed faster. McCann's friends, however, remained confident. Myles Johnson smiled the famous luminous smile that made him such a popular Swift and "threw a halo around McCann and lit up his space box." The Irishman even pleased Grove Thompson, who "brought up the rear in his usual phlegmatic way." He didn't look "nearly as glum as is his wont."[12]

Victory profited people differently. When the McCann-Barnes match ended, proofreaders pulled galleys, scanned them a last time, and declared Joseph McCann the winner. McCann won by setting more type than William Barnes and by providing a cleaner proof, as well. It was the last that undid Barnes, who hoped to win in proofs. Thus, he resigned without revisions, "shook hands with McCann, acknowledged his superiority, and the referee gave the match to McCann." Naturally, money changed hands. Pooh-bah Gill got "downed mercilessly." Jack-of-Clubs Kearney "looked as if his heavy high hat had telescoped." Jubilant supporters gave McCann a gold badge, and McCann, in turn, "made even" in a short speech. Honor remained a significant issue here. McCann, Barnes, and most of the rest sought a kind of ratification. "Honor," according to the historian Elliott J. Gorn, "had no existence outside group life, for only reputation and the esteem of others conferred it." That sort of honor came when men bought drinks, spent money, shook hands, and "made even."[13]

Joseph McCann was not, however, racing for the simple prestige of the thing. Cash prizes could be enormous. Occasionally, purses totaled $1,000. The purse for this race, $500, was a lot of money when New York journeymen compositors, earning at the top of their trade, made $30 a week. Still, most matches offered much less, anywhere from $10 to $50. Money around such contests circulated and recycled among their betting shopmates. Often, in fact, medals or trophies sufficed.

Typeracing awards, especially trophies, were as outrageously rococo as was printing's beloved circus-poster typography. In 1877 Montreal offered its winner $1,000, but the runner-up made do with an inkstand and $4, and third place bagged no more than a composing stick and $3. Composing sticks were the most popular prize, after cash, and the best ones were sterling silver. Items made of gold tended to be watches or, more often, medallions that ordinarily featured—little wonder—Franklin, in relief. When, in 1874, J. R. McBride won his division of a Washington, D.C., meet, he took a gold breastpin. Second prize was a print encyclopedia and, in third, H. C. Tarleton nosed out George Parklin for a thermometer.[14]

Something was changing, though. Within a week of the McCann-Barnes duel, a promoter and former talent scout for P. T. Barnum contacted both men. J. R. Davis was recently responsible for the celebrated arrival of Jumbo the elephant, and by

1884 he had helped Barnum gather "a good collection of Nubians, 'hairy people,' Nautch dancing girls, sanctified cattle, and a 'sacred' white monkey." Now Davis worked for Kohl and Middleton, operators of a chain of dime museums, and offered the Swifts an opportunity to race on tour.[15]

Knights of Labor

Ten years had passed between George Arensberg's famous wager and the day Joseph McCann stepped off the boat from Cork. The 1870s had been economically depressed, hard days among the American working rank and file, and printing journeymen felt the pinch along with everyone else. Among printers, one disturbing result was the withering of their organizations. From 1876 to 1879, the International Typographical Union, the institutional capstone of printing workers, lost two-thirds of its member locals. In 1876 Philadelphia's annual midsummer convention of the ITU had attracted ninety-eight delegates representing eighty constituencies. Three years later, in 1879, delegates from only twenty-seven locals attended the Washington, D.C., event.[16]

Nor were things better locally. New York City's Local No. 6 of the ITU served the journeymen of the nation's printing and publishing center. Until the late 1870s, Big Six was easily a stronger voice on behalf of its membership than was its "parent" organization, and the same could be said of most big city locals. From 1876 until 1879, membership in No. 6 "declined rapidly," according to its historian George A. Stevens, "showing a drop of nearly 160 per cent in that period." When the panic of 1873 ended in late 1879, "a trifle more than 1,000 members" remained from the 2,644 on the roll in 1876.[17]

Other union locals languished, as well. In Providence, Rhode Island, for example, few printers attended local meetings, and by 1878 nobody attended the national convention at all. Providence's typographical union dated to 1857, and the newly formed local had immediately acquired a charter of national affiliation as Local No. 33 of the ITU. Union membership in Providence, national and local, remained stable until the mid-1870s. From 1874 to

1878, however, Local No. 33 lost virtually all of its members, and showing "a decided lack of interest," remaining members ceased keeping even rudimentary minutes of their meetings. Attendance at those meetings repeatedly failed of quorum, until, in 1878, a dozen stalwarts voted to dissolve the local's association with the ITU. By 1880 Providence Local No. 33 itself was moribund.[18]

Unions routinely used two tactics to combat defection. They either tried to do a better job of what they normally did—extract better wages, hours, and working conditions from ownership—or they mounted vigorous membership drives. Typically, New York's Local No. 6 chose the first option, as did most other unions. Higher wages attracted members, and printing locals consistently tried to stimulate interest in their unions by improving their bargaining techniques. In 1880, however, the tactic was not working.[19]

Conditions were ripe for a different way, perhaps an alternative labor movement entirely. The Noble and Holy Order of the Knights of Labor offered such an alternative. Formed late in 1869 and since 1879 led by Terence V. Powderly, the Knights of Labor offered American workers significantly fresh representation in the marketplace. Unlike printing organizations, the Knights of Labor was not narrowly a craft union. Knights were members of an authentically national labor movement, the first workers' organization that was from its origin more than regional in membership or influence. Knights believed in the essential unity of all working people and tried to enlist the entire range of skilled and semi-skilled workers, indeed anyone who could be considered a producer. The organization tried to do this without regard to sex, race, or trade. By the mid-1880s, thousands of local "assemblies" were championing a variety of causes and reforms, from eight-hour workdays to women's rights and child labor legislation. Much of this agenda broadened the mission of the Knights to include cultural and educational goals. The Knights would redistribute land, stifle religious hypocrisy, advocate temperance, reform the currency, and denounce swearing. The organizational push of the Knights was tremendously successful during the mid-1880s, a standing challenge to existing craft organizations. Sparked by the successful sponsorship of an 1885 strike against Jay Gould's South-western Railroad Conglomerate, the appeal of the all-inclusive re-definition of labor expounded by the Knights of Labor swept the country. In 1886 Knights membership numbered more than a million American workers. Not the least of the organization's popularity was its encompassing social component.[20]

The rapid growth of the Knights of Labor offered ideas and tonic to the sagging International Typographical Union. By 1883 whatever authority inhered in printing's national office was merely titular. The typographical union, for instance, lacked something so fundamental as a salaried staff. Not surprisingly, the organization existed mainly to stage the annual convention. In the summer of 1882, Mark L. Crawford, secretary-treasurer of the national office, began a reinvigorated solicitation program, one that emphasized languishing locals such as that in Providence. Noting their five-year hiatus in affiliation, Crawford told a group of Providence printers that "typographical matters were booming all over the country" and that Rhode Island ought to get on board. "I will torture you with communications till you take some action in the matter," Crawford said. Thirty-two members signed up, and in April 1883 Providence's Local No. 33 was rechartered. Following this kind of success, the national office of the ITU named a chief organizer and began organizing brand new unions, sometimes superceding local organizations in the process.[21]

Innovative outreach seemed the order of the day. Anyone could see that the Knights of Labor was particularly good at beating bushes, of exciting people to its cause. Typeracing, it seemed, might be a highly visible way of attracting attention to the union. On March 1, 1886, Printer's Assembly No. 1735 of the Knights of Labor sponsored Rochester's citywide typesetting championship.[22]

Large crowds gathered that day at Rochester's Odd Fellows' Hall on Clinton Street to watch the *Rochester Morning Herald*'s Joseph Farquhar prevail over four other local journeymen. Composing rooms at each of the city's daily newspapers entered their fastest. The men were literally on a stage for the first time in their lives and were nervous, but "at the call of time each man dropped to his work, and for an hour nothing was heard but the 'click, click,' as the five contestants hustled for local honors." It was, reporters observed, the "first public appearance" for any of them "and it is very probable any of them could have done better if not subject to the gaze of a crowd."[23]

In the end, Joe Farquhar and the typeracing Swifts entertained that crowd splendidly. At the conclusion of racing, both printers and public highstepped straight from the typecases to an adjoining Odd Fellows' ballroom. There the sponsoring Knights of Labor presented a "dance programme of some length" to assist worthy sick and disabled printers on behalf of their cause. "As can easily be imagined this fund has occasional drafts made upon it, while the means of repletion are not so numerous."[24]

Public Amusement, Dime Museums, and a National Championship

Rochester's race pointed toward a mingling of several late-nineteenth-century energies. Enthusiastic new labor tactics intersected with an accelerating public inclination to amusement. The result was a convergence—of the culture of the Swifts, the hegemonic culture of bourgeois society, and an emerging mass culture of consumption.[25]

This is the context in which Promoter J. R. Davis proposed a public typeracing tour. Judging from their recent efforts, Joseph McCann, William Barnes, and typeracing generally seemed immensely popular. On behalf of Kohl and Middleton, "the Chicago Museum Managers," Davis sought the two Swifts as headliners of a series of races that would pit the reigning champion and his chief competitor against the best local talent, first in Chicago and then Philadelphia. Arrangements that Christmas season were still incomplete, but Davis presumed engagements in Boston and New York City and possibly others would follow. On December 23, 1885, a week after the McCann-Barnes match, Davis requested a picture of McCann for publicity purposes. Here was giddy prospect. It fairly turned the head of Joseph McCann.[26]

Kohl and Middleton's South Side Dime Museum billed its race the "championship of the world." The printing trade paper *Inland Printer* announced it "a novel attraction for Chicago sightseers." The event revived a calling among dime museums. Originally, museums supplied an important dimension of nineteenth-century American democratic culture. As the name implied, they were inexpensive places for clerks, mechanics, and other ordinary people to examine improving books, artifacts, and performances. Henry Tappan, president of the University of Michigan, had hoped such oases—he had the British Museum in mind—could be sanctuaries of scholars, a place of Muses. As the nineteenth century progressed, this liberal dream intersected with the marketplace show business of men such as Barnum and evolved into something altogether less exalted. After the Civil War, the dime museum became "a place of amusement," according to its historian, where Americans would find "a theatre, some wax figures, a giant and dwarf or two, a jumble of pictures, and a few live snakes."[27]

Dime museums proliferated throughout the 1880s and 1890s. As pillars of working-class culture, they ranked with concert saloons, vaudeville stages, and the ballpark in appealing especially to young men. "Women and married men also could be found at most of these entertainment centers," says the cultural historian Howard Chudacoff, "but commercial recreation played a special role in the lives of bachelors, helping to create as well as to reinforce both the alternative and, on occasion, the countercultural aspects of their lives." Dime museums, according to Chudacoff, offered young, unattached men a middle ground between the circus and the playhouse.[28]

The firm of Kohl and Middleton Museum Managers stood ready to exploit this segment of the population. Chicago's South Side museum, host to printing's first public race, was one of several such franchises that the Kohl and Middleton company opened in cities such as Milwaukee, Cincinnati, Louisville, Cleveland, and Minneapolis. As a measure of prosperity returned to the United States by the mid-1880s, the dime museums of an American entertainment industry went into high gear, peddling all manner of

KOHL & MIDDLETON'S

SOUTH SIDE DIME MUSEUM.

COMMENCING MONDAY, JAN. 11.

TYPE-SETTING TOURNAMENT!

Racing for Seven Days

FOR THE

Diamond Medal and Championship of the World,

Under the Management of the Typographical
Union of Chicago.

JOS. McCANN.

Of the New York Herald, the present Champion of the World.

W. C. BARNES.

Of the New York World, ex-Champion.

W. J. CREEVY, of the Chicago Inter-Ocean.
"KID" DE JARNATT, of the Chicago Tribune.
JOS. M. HUDSON, of the Chicago Mail.
THOS. C. LEVY, of the Chicago Evening Journal.
LOU MONHEIMER, of the Chicago Daily News.
UNKNOWN, from Chicago Daily Herald.

A GRAND MONSTER STAGE SHOW

FOR THIS,

OUR BANNER WEEK!

The type used in this contest has been furnished by the Chicago Mail.

Kohl and Middleton's South Side Dime Museum hosted Chicago's 1886
national typesetting championship.
(From *Chicago Tribune*)

zesty experience, from model renditions of gynecological offices to the chambers of the Inquisition. Entertainment entrepreneurs wanted above all to sell tickets, to profit. They booked typesetting Swifts because they knew they could draw crowds.[29]

But the veneer of sophistication or the gratification of learning also sold tickets. The better museums consistently tried to appeal beyond wandering young men to a broader population—a growing middle class that wanted to be associated with refined amusements or immigrant families tasting a novel American culture. As later generations would say of television, there was a good deal of objectionable junk in dime museum fare, but one might always find a good thing to watch. Swifts who winced at sharing a billing with a checker-playing automaton recovered when they found themselves slotted among moral dramas, religious tableaux, or patriotic displays. Printers who considered themselves a working-class elite might easily confuse the onset of a culture of popular amusement for a pathway toward mainstream bourgeois respectability.[30]

Dime museums took typeracing off shop floors and out of beer halls, and thereby turned honest, mundane toil into a public entertainment. Some printers found it scant improvement. Like all the others, Chicago's museum occasionally enlightened the public, but it always entertained it. Typesetting week, shouted the Sunday ads for the South Side Museum, would be "our banner week!" The tournament would not only produce a champion of the entire world, it would crown that champion in diamonds. The museum knew not everyone longed to watch typesetting racing, and so it provided the standard fare of vaudeville acts. Throughout the week and accompanying it all would be "a grand monster stage show."[31]

On January 11, 1886, Kohl and Middleton's Museum was ready and so were the stars, McCann and Barnes. Alongside the New Yorkers, both of whom would participate in the afternoon's opening heat, stood two of the local talent, William J. Creevy of the *Chicago Inter-Ocean* and Joseph M. Hudson of the *Evening Mail*.[32]

Shortly after 2 P.M. on Monday's first day of racing, a "short, thick-set man with a good-natured, red face trotted down the main floor" of Kohl and Middleton's, paused among compositors poised in front of their typecases, and then cried "Time!" It galvanized the contestants—galvanized all, that is, except McCann, the reigning champion. According to a reporter from the *Chicago Tribune,* "the look of determination that had irradiated his features a few minutes before had faded away into an expression of dreamy cogitation, and he stood, his 'stick' in his listless left hand, gazing vacantly into space." A man nudged his elbow. "Time's called, McCann," he whispered. McCann awoke. "Is that so?" Then, "after an eagle glance at his active fellow-competitors," Joseph McCann "went to work with a will." He had spotted the field a minute and a half.[33]

When McCann froze at the start, William Barnes took an early lead, held it throughout, and won the event in something of an upset. McCann had been favored, coming off his victory over Barnes in New York City. To be sure, McCann would break Arensberg's famous single-hour record at Chicago, but it resembled a consolation prize. To the dismay of his backers, McCann never could catch his New York rival.

Thanks to Joseph McCann's laggard start, Barnes jumped in front and led after the first day's competition. Each of the seven competitors participated in an afternoon heat lasting an hour and a half and repeated the effort at night. Race format called for two afternoon and two evening stints, with the cast of characters dividing and recombining among them. In this way the museum converted the marathon of sustained effort typical of typesetting into a series of sprints. It kept the action fresh and fun to watch.

For the most part, opening-day form held throughout the entire week. McCann set more type than did Barnes or anyone else, but he also made many errors, which allowed Barnes to pull back ahead in proofing. First-day errors also ruined the chances of the *Tribune*'s heralded Clinton "The Kid" DeJarnatt. A miserable evening heat left the Kid's proof "so badly marked up" that the early Chicago favorite slid into last place, far behind his mates.

McCann finished the day in second place, DeJarnatt brought up
the rear, and nothing in six more days of racing altered the standing of either.[34]

At Chicago the Swifts raced with "solid minion," by which
printers understood roughly 7-point type set with no line spacing.
Solidly stacked letters meant less time spent emptying typesticks.
The *Chicago Evening Mail* supplied Kohl and Middleton's minion type. Small type could be difficult to handle and typographical errors were common. Typos were easily corrected, but an improper line-ending word break could be calamitous. Its correction
might force entire syllables onto a subsequent line. An "out," more
disastrous still, was an inadvertent omission of a word or phrase.
Such errors involved extensive rejustification of entire lines, the
single mistake ramifying throughout the set piece. On these occasions the museum's proofreader, Fred Rae, became particularly
important, because a well-composed line was a nicely spaced line,
without gaps, and Rae could insist on it.[35]

DeJarnatt's showing disappointed many Chicagoans. Hometown Swifts had itched to strut their stuff. Chicago's printers "must
have a match," observed the trade paper *Printers' Circular.* "Several of her compositors had great records and plenty of friends to
back them." DeJarnatt's collapse, however, typified an overall failure by the hometowners to challenge the New Yorkers. Later,
Barnes could be magnanimous in victory. DeJarnatt, he said, "was
in ill health during the Chicago match, as his appearance indicated, and in consequence he was extremely nervous."[36]

In fact, the entire Chicago contingent seemed nervous. Some
local printers thought the *Daily News*'s Leo Monheimer was faster
even than DeJarnatt, but "the call of 'Time' appeared to 'rattle'
him badly," noted the *Tribune*'s reporter, "nearly a minute elaps-
ing before he had fumbled through his first line." The *Inter-
Ocean*'s Will Creevy, a New Orleans native who had worked in
Chicago for five years, "did not appear to be in any hurry." Joseph
Hudson, of the *Evening Mail,* also carried a stately pace. The veteran Hudson at least had a plan. He hoped to win by avoiding mistakes, and his style owed more to careful method than nerves.

Finally, the *Tribune*'s reporter discovered "a look of languid sadness, whether habitual or accidental . . . had overspread the countenance of Thomas C. Levy, the *Journal*'s representative, as he slowly picked up his 'stick' and went to work."[37]

A Showcase of Stars

McCann, the reigning champion, got most of the early attention. Even though he performed badly from the start, "JoeMac" attracted crowds. "By far the greatest number of curious visitors grouped themselves in the vicinity of McCann," said the *Tribune*. But by midweek, McCann's backers, "many of whom are alleged to have bet considerable money on him," seemed to the *Tribune* "very lugubrious . . . and the admonitions he received to 'go slow' were as numerous as they were emphatic."[38]

The participants at Chicago's 1886 national typesetting championship. Standing, from left: DeJarnatt, Hudson, Creevy, Barnes, Levy, McCann, and Monheimer. Seated: Rae and McLaughlin.
(From *A Collation of Facts Relative to Fast Typesetting*, New York: Concord Cooperative Printing Company, 1887)

Soon enough William Barnes unseated the Irishman as the event's main attraction. Barnes combined speed with an exceedingly smooth manner. Paradoxically, Barnes insisted his speed derived from slowing down. Barnes set type by evenly repetitive, uninterrupted movements. If his fingers missed a type, Barnes pretended otherwise, bringing his empty hand routinely to his typestick. Similarly, if by accident he fetched two characters, he carried both to the stick, dropping one of them or neither. His goal was metronomic regularity. "Barnes's record for fine workmanship continues and he is the favorite by heavy odds," reported the *New York Times*. "His action was not nearly so rapid to the eye as that of McCann but a great deal more regular," observed the *Tribune*. "An old printer, whose mouth was distended in a grin of professional delight as he watched him at work, said he would back Barnes against McCann in a day's work from start to 'jig-up' at long odds."[39]

Barnes offered tricks as well as style. Between the two evening heats of Tuesday's racing, he entertained the crowd in a half-hour exhibition with his typecases reversed. Hand compositors worked facing two trays of type and placed the tray containing capital letters above the lowercase tray. The ancient arrangement bequeathed us our contemporary "uppercase" and "lowercase" terminology, and, if reversed, presented most typesetters with difficulties akin to asking them to set in Cyrillic. Museum goers could not get enough. The contestants usually spent mornings "throwing in their cases," replenishing their own supplies of type, each in the manner they most preferred. Before racing began the next morning, Barnes reversed his cases again for "his customary group of admirers." By Wednesday, the Swifts were becoming a big hit. "To judge by the number of spectators on hand interest in the contest for the typesetting championship had not waned."[40]

Barnes quickly became a financial as well as an artistic success. By the end of his second Wednesday heat, Barnes had twice exceeded a pace of 2,000 ems an hour, a feat that "gained him a prolonged round of applause and caused substantial fluctuations in his favor in the betting." Barnes then shifted to high gear during

Thursday's afternoon intermission. He first set type from reversed cases, and then awed the crowd by setting blindfolded, copy being read to him. Finally, getting all the balls into the air, he set blindfolded from reversed cases. Barnes made only two mistakes during his blindfolded effort at Chicago, a spacing error and a typo. This was "work never before attempted by any other compositor." It was also bettable work, and it kept the cash flow alive.[41]

William C. Barnes, Chicago's national typesetting champion.
(From *A Collation of Facts Relative to Fast Typesetting,* New York: Concord Co-operative Printing Company, 1887)

Barnes swept the field at Chicago. By the second day of competition, Chicago's contingent had shaken off its opening round lethargy and "appeared to have got rid of the nervousness which characterized their work of Monday." Will Creevy in particular improved, "and the anxious glances he had cast from time to time at his competitors Monday were altogether wanting." Leo Monheimer, who learned his trade in Bloomfield, Iowa, had come into the race confident of winning. Quickly, however, the city's printing fraternity recognized what their colleagues were up against. Two days into the tournament, news reporters were now locating something more rustic than charming in their adopted Iowan, noting that Monheimer "appeared on the platform in the same shirt that he wore when he left there."[42]

At twenty-one years of age, Monheimer and DeJarnatt were the youngsters of the tournament. DeJarnatt's youth had earned him his nickname, but printing ages were deceptive. "In his day," according to the *Inland Printer*, Joseph Hudson had been "the lightning compositor of Chicago." At race time the over-the-hill Hudson was all of thirty-six years old. (In 1886 an average printer's lifespan was scarcely longer, a short thirty-seven years.) Hudson, a native of Baltimore, also had many miles on his resume. Nine years earlier, he had been a member of the *Cincinnati Enquirer's* "Big Ten." Hudson certainly acted the graybeard, beginning with his idiosyncrasies. He stooped at the case and "offset the action of his right hand by an incessant oscillating motion of his left shoulder-blade." Then, presumably weary, he simply sat down.[43]

In his dotage, Hudson's steady style nonetheless easily moved him ahead of his fellow Chicagoans and into third place. Hudson, who arrived in Chicago in 1880, quickly became a betting shoo-in for third place and the bragging rights of his adopted hometown. Bettors who once liked Hudson because he was fast, backed him now because he was clean. In an early hour-and-a-half heat, he set 2,500 ems with but two errors, a record no others approached. Smart money also knew that Hudson's *Evening Mail* had supplied the tournament types, thus providing him with his house type. Languid of pace, each day when the others fell back in proofs, Hudson reemerged just behind the New York leaders.[44]

In the end, Chicago proved to be Joseph McCann's worst showing. At Kohl and Middleton's he averaged 1,921 ems an hour, the only time in his racing career that he failed to average 2,000 ems. McCann was not above griping about the results, often mentioning the museum's "noise and bustle." The shopfloor atmosphere of fast-lane typeracing was rarely serene. Neither, however, was it public in the manner of Kohl and Middleton's, with hundreds of patrons more or less randomly milling around. On opening day, McCann attracted most of those customers. Still, the "galaxy of gazers didn't appear to disconcert him in the least, and save for an occasional glance in the direction of his most formidable rival over the way, Barnes, his eyes never left his copy." By the end of the week, McCann had changed his tune. "McCann," reported the *Tribune,* "attributes his failure to repeat his performance of beating Editor Pulitzer's fast printer to the noise made by the crowds of spectators round his case, which disconcerted him badly for the first three days."[45]

Joseph Hudson thought he had more to complain of than McCann. Hudson performed well from the start and occupied third place throughout the week. His Tuesday afternoon heat seemed particularly well raced; the "performance elicited considerable applause." By Thursday Barnes and McCann were certain winners, and therefore the battle for third place took the spotlight. Necessarily, the third place finisher would become champion of all Chicago, and thus the competition was of "keen popular zest." Monheimer and Creevy stayed consistently close, and repeatedly passed Hudson in quantity of type set, but Hudson swung back ahead in proofs.[46]

Form held until the final day, when the *Evening Journal*'s Thomas C. Levy, the event's forgotten man, staged a rally. "Bangs" Levy was twenty-seven years old, a veteran compositor from Oshkosh, Wisconsin. Like Hudson, Levy carried some impressive public typeracing credentials. Five years earlier, while working in Winnipeg, Manitoba, he defeated James McCaw of the *Toronto Globe* for $1,000 and the 1881 Canadian championship. He once set 2,220 ems in an hour's test at the *St. Paul Pioneer,* and fully a year before the Chicago match an *Inland Printer* correspondent thought Levy "may be reckoned as the quickest known." The magazine agreed: Levy "can make a stick and rule hot in about ten minutes." Still, Levy's early "apathy" landed him back in the field at fifth, and by midweek he struggled to stay ahead of the fevered Kid DeJarnatt.[47]

Until the very end, many onlookers thought the match was over, with Joe Hudson secure in third place. Barnes, the leader, was getting odds of 5 to 2, "with few takers." McCann "virtually concede[d] the battle to his grim-visaged rival, who has given utterance to a determination to wipe out the disgrace of his last defeat by the Irishman."[48]

Levy, however, was gathering momentum. Perhaps to reward a faithful following, Levy had saved his best speed for last, picked up his pace on Friday's fifth day of racing, and when he completed work on Saturday, his gross score had moved him ahead of Hudson. Still, proofreading and corrections on Saturday's work remained for Sunday morning, and routinely throughout the week Hudson regained ground in proofs. Not, however, this time. "The exceeding closeness of the result, which gives Levy third place and Hudson fourth, is unparalleled," the *Tribune* reported.[49]

Levy's big Saturday had held up in corrections. Still, there was high drama before the issue was settled. Sunday night's finals paired Levy and Hudson in a showdown match race. Levy drew away from Hudson during that last hour and a half, working hard, "plunging." Reporters observed "his ears were stuffed with cotton batting" to stifle the noise of a packed crowd, and "his black eyes bulged out as he rapidly but nervously snatched the type from the case." Pandemonium reigned. "Soon the shrill voice of a female sounded above the din." She was drunk and insulted, and she attacked an offending cop. "Poor Levy was frantic," recalled onlookers. He stamped his foot. "For God's sake, gag her," he cried.[50]

Levy's rally almost upstaged the centerpiece of the tournament. On Sunday, by arrangement, the New Yorkers Barnes and McCann each attempted to break George Arensberg's famous single-hour record. According to McCann, "during this tournament Mr. Barnes and I determined to dispose of the much-talked-of record of Arensberg's of 2,064 ems made about sixteen years previously and which had never been beaten." Barnes had outdistanced the field, and Kohl and Middleton's welcomed a further way to keep the turnstiles moving to the end. "Both Barnes and McCann are anxious to eclipse Arensberg's great New York record," announced the *Tribune*, "but neither of them intends to attempt it until the last day, and possibly the last heat of the tournament."[51]

That they did. Both Barnes and McCann surpassed the great Velocipede in a special hour-long Sunday night heat. It was redemption for Joseph McCann. He had lost the "national championship" to Barnes, but Arensberg remained a legend, and his single-hour mark was a shopfloor standard. McCann's 2,150 ems at Chicago easily outdistanced the Velocipede and edged Barnes by fifty.[52]

Sunday night was awards night, a convivial gathering of Chicago's printing fraternity. Andy McLaughlin, president of

---

NATIONAL RULES.

———— ❈ ————

FORMALLY ADOPTED BY THE CONTESTANTS IN THE PHILADELPHIA TOURNAMENT AS A STANDARD TO GOVERN TYPESETTING MATCHES.

1. Membership in the Typographical Union is necessary to qualify printers for the National Typesetting Contest.

2. The type used to be solid minion or nonpareil, without paragraphs, and the column width to be 25 ems of the minion, or 28 ems, if nonpareil.

3. The hours of contest for each contestant to be fixed by the referee.

4. The copy, cases, stands, gas-jets, type, etc., to be identical in character for each contestant, and the selection of the stands to be decided by lottery previous to the contest.

5. The proofreader to be appointed by the referee, and a revise taken to insure correction of all errors marked in first proof. Twenty-five ems shall be deducted from the total amount of work performed for every minute occupied in correcting proof, and corresponding fractions of a line for fractional parts of a minute.

6. The contestants are required to empty their sticks, and they shall receive no aid whatever from others. Contestants are at liberty to select sticks and composing-rules to suit themselves, but the sticks must be set and examined at the discretion of the referee.

7. All types, letters, spaces and quadrats must be kept in their recognized boxes, and the following stipulations strictly observed : Three-em spaces shall be used in composition, and in spacing out the lines nothing thicker than two three-em spaces shall occur, unless necessary to use thicker spaces to fill the line tight. No word or syllable of a word shall be turned over that can be got into a line without the use of thin spaces. · A line may be thin-spaced to get in a word if the contestants so choose. Not more than one and a half ems shall be allowed in correcting.

8. Justification is expected to be performed in a workmanlike manner, and the referee shall carefully examine all work in this particular, and be required to deduct such amount from the total of a contestant as in his judgment may appear proper in case he finds this portion of the work slighted. If a line shall be a five-em space short, it shall be an error, and marked by the proofreader.

9. Either Webster or Worcester shall be authority on dividing words, but no word of four letters only shall be divided, nor shall a syllable of a single letter be permitted at either end of a line.

10. Each contestant shall distribute his own type.

11. Any contestant failing to respond to the referee when "time" is called, either to begin or end composition or correction, will be considered out of the race.

12. In case of questions arising not covered in the preceding, the decision of the referee or his representative shall be final, and from which there can be no appeal.

By the mid-1880s codified rules sanctioned typesetting races. (From *A Collation of Facts Relative to Fast Typesetting*, New York: Concord Co-operative Printing Company, 1887)

Chicago's Local No. 16 of the ITU awarded the prizes "in a neat speech." First prize was "a handsome championship emblem in the shape of a gold star pendant from a scroll. In the centre of the star was a large diamond, and on the scroll the words: 'Championship for Fast Type Setting.'" McCann's runner-up prize was a sterling silver water service. Levy got a silver hunting cup for third. According to the *Tribune,* "All of the contestants received a fair compensation for the week's labor." And then they all retired to a late banquet at the National Hotel. "A large number of the members of the Typographical Union were present, and the conviviality was continual until a very late hour."[53]

From the Shopfloor to the Show

Chicagoans came out to see Joseph McCann and William Barnes, and the New Yorkers fulfilled their missions. McCann, at Chicago, chafed under the burden of George Arensberg's reputation. He always would. In 1884 McCann had actually gone looking for Arensberg. That February McCann's composing room foreman, Mannis Geary, had challenged the entire city of New York, "Arensberg preferred," on behalf of McCann. To McCann's annoyance, Arensberg declined. Much later, recounting his career in 1906, McCann twice pointedly omitted Arensberg from any personal listing of outstanding Swifts. Arensberg, in the Wager of 1870, took "liberties," or so McCann claimed. Referees allowed a "quad line," a mostly blank line containing metal but few letters, in each stickful. Arensberg, McCann thought, ordinarily got away with "any old spacing."[54]

McCann called the Kohl and Middleton tournaments "exhibitions." He meant that they were paid regardless of tournament outcome, irrespective of who won. McCann and Barnes, then, received "appearance money" on top of whatever merchandise they might capture as prizes. It offended purists, notably Geary of the *New York Herald.* Geary had originally gotten McCann into all this, sponsoring his unknown speedster many months before. It proved difficult to contain a rising star. When J. R. Davis made the Kohl and Middleton offer, McCann immediately agreed. "Some of my friends opposed it," he said, "but I was determined to accept." Geary felt betrayed and never, claimed McCann, forgave him.[55]

Nonetheless, McCann said, "money, novelty, and experience were the factors that enticed me." By the end of spring 1886, he had earned enough for a triumphal return to Dublin, and while he was there, he outfitted himself. In August 1886 McCann ran up a bill of £55 on suit jackets alone at the Dublin clothing establishment of C. Martin, Practical Tailor. It was a couple weeks' worth of wages for most journeymen.[56]

Mannis Geary and shopmates back at the *Herald* doubtless thought Joseph McCann had forgotten them. Others objected to the typeracing tour because they hated the hype. Barnum's Jumbo the elephant may have died, but museum people seemed to supply the Fastest Typesetter on Earth alongside JoJo the Monkey Boy. Robert S. Menamin, the Philadelphia printer and publisher, found the testimonials and hero worship pernicious. All the speed was shaming the solid and steady 1,200-ems-an-hour fellows. "Worshippers of favorite typesetting heroes," Menamin noted, overpraise their "rushers, rattlers, slingers, and dabsters."[57]

Kohl and Middleton's Dime Museum made stars of them all. Chicago's Swifts had found a path that led not merely to fame and celebrity, but also to testimonials—to *endorsements!* Shortly after the match, Barnes, McCann, and the other competitors emerged in the pages of trade papers boosting Barnhart Bros. and Spindler, typefounders and suppliers of the tournament types. Those types, they said, seemed "as near perfection as any we have ever set." Overnight, the men became industry models, ethical paragons. "Persevere till you do succeed," the *Inland Printer* advised apprentice compositors, "and it is quite possible your record may some day outrival that of Barnes, McCann or Arensberg."[58]

Chicago's national championship typerace had grown out of a dispersed kind of intramural sport. Half a continent away, the *New York Times* reported "a large crowd of newspaper men and printers" at the start of the Chicago match, "and this interest manifested was very deep." Interest was all the deeper because for the

first time the public was invited. Ordinarily, compositors competed within their subculture, behind the scenes. Until 1886 the
Swifts raced and bragged among other journeymen on shopfloors,
at union meeting halls, and in saloons. At Kohl and Middleton's
Museum, racing became for the first time a public amusement,
attended by hundreds, occasionally thousands, of an amusement-
consuming middle class. At Chicago, productive labor became
cultural theater, but among Swifts an ideal was being imparted:
autonomous and indomitable workmen triumphant in the face of
technology.[59]

In Chicago in 1886 ordinary people discovered a shopfloor
sport. Entertainment provided a path by which printers could
enter a wider world, leaving behind unions and workplaces, the
traditional sponsoring agencies of a life of production.

J. R. Davis, Kohl and Middleton's race organizer and talent
scout, was already planning the next event. On February 16, he
alerted Joseph McCann to the Philadelphia tournament scheduled for the middle of March. Bradenburg's Ninth and Arch Street
Museum would host the next "national championship." Train tickets were on their way. Trade papers understood that the Chicago
event augured a series of races featuring Barnes and McCann. A
tournament was scheduled for Boston as well as Philadelphia. At
Boston, however, everything began to change.[60]

6 Fast Women: The Boston Typesetting Races of 1886

ON FEBRUARY 21, 1886, THREE WEEKS AFTER WILLIAM Barnes won the Chicago championship, Boston crowned the champion typesetter of all New England. In a spirited week-long competition that was similar in many ways to that of Chicago, George Graham triumphed over three others. He won an engraved watch, cash, and the cheers of a crowd gathered at Austin and Stone's Dime Museum. Barnes, with many other Swifts, quickly acknowledged Graham among a dozen of America's fastest typesetting racers.

In 1887 Barnes, McCann, and Alexander Duguid, another famous Swift, collaborated in compiling a book called *Fast Typesetting*. The book was a manual of technique, a record of match results, and a general overview of printing's state of the art. The editors applauded Graham and also tucked a brief sidebar alongside their account of the New Englander's rise to prominence. In

addition to George Graham's championship, *Fast Typesetting* noted
that a women's race had also been held in Boston and that a "Miss
Kenney" had won it. The women's performances seemed speedy
indeed. According to reports, the women had outscored the men,
but "as much latitude was allowed the ladies in the matter of time
and proofs, their scores cannot take rank as genuine records."[1]

That, the dismissal indicated, was enough of that. In fact, no
"latitude" seems to have been given the women at all. Austin and
Stone's Dime Museum staged the women's contest to be identical
in every way to that of the men, and L. J. Kenney, as Barnes noted,
defeated three rivals. Race results, however, merely opened this
tale. Not only did she win, but Kenney also set more type faster
than had Graham, the men's winner, the freshly crowned champion of all New England. More interesting still, two of Kenney's
female challengers also posted results superior to those of Graham. Three of the four women racing that February in Boston
outperformed the entire lineup of male counterparts.

Women Printers

The Boston races marked a crest for the women's movement, at
least within the printing industry. Without Augusta Lewis, Women's
Typographical Union No. 1 had foundered. Sustained by Lewis
for two years following its establishment in 1869, by the summer
of 1872 it was no longer sending a representative to International
Typographical Union (ITU) conventions. In that year the parent
union opened its membership and prohibited further charter of
women's locals. Instead of welcoming women, the tactic now en-
veloped the occasional extraordinary woman, absorbing her but
offering diminishing opportunities for most women to enter the
trade. In 1874 female union membership, once fifty, had dwindled
to twenty-eight. Remnants of the women's union lasted until its official demise in 1878. Six years later the ITU's annual report listed
only 106 women members throughout its entire national ranks.[2]

Still, the late 1870s had been the low point for the ITU generally, suffering as did all of organized labor from a depressed economy. And thousands of women, after all, almost all of them

unorganized, remained at work throughout the printing industry. Useless to women to begin with, by 1886 a weakened International Typographical Union confronted a threatening rival in the Knights of Labor. Knights recruited vigorously among Boston's women printers, and incidentally provided those women the union affiliation Boston's championship required. The women took it from there, flaunting their talent and gaining admission into the Boston Typographical Union. The 1886 typerace showed what the recognition of a middle-class public might do for the cause, and it forced the hand of Boston's Local No. 13. But it was a last gasp, not a renaissance. Women were fading fast from shopfloors and union halls to say nothing of saloons, the major institutions of a masculine trade.

In the mid-1880s, public entertainments, not printing institutions, offered Boston's women their opportunity. As in Chicago, popular amusement halls in Boston and other Eastern cities discovered and promoted typeracing. Also as in Chicago, this bit of entrepreneurial innovation removed an age-old printing pastime from shopfloors for the first time. In Boston, Austin and Stone's Museum staged its women's race as a simple and innocent adjunct to that of the men. As a result, Austin and Stone's provided sponsorship previously unavailable to women and to their printing skills. For a brief—and entirely unintended—moment, Austin and Stone's Dime Museum replaced standard printing enclaves as a source of occupational legitimacy. To the interest of some and the consternation of others, L. J. Kenney outperformed the men.

Austin and Stone's Dime Museum

Austin and Stone's Museum, located on the west side of Tremont Row, hosted the Boston races of 1886. The museum held its championship in February, slotting it between Chicago's national championship and a big Philadelphia tournament scheduled for March. Boston billed the race "The Typesetting Championship of New England."

Austin and Stone's Museum differed little from its Chicago or Philadelphia counterparts. Like all the others, Boston's dime museum occasionally edified folks, but it always entertained them. "Vastness, originality, and abundance," shouted the museum, "our motto!" To make room for the printers, but only reluctantly, Austin and Stone's moved the monkeys out of the Great Hall. In case the typesetters bombed, the museum laid in a bill of vaudeville acts to keep the turnstiles moving. The compositors at Austin and Stone's competed with each other, and with a pair of singing sisters, an Irish comic, a blackface act, and The Great Annie Hindle, the Apollo Belvedere.[3]

Still, the museum accommodated the printers with some style. During the weekend before the races, a gang of forty carpenters, gasfitters, and upholsterers turned the museum's lecture hall into a replica of the composing room of a large daily newspaper. Austin and Stone's enlisted the assistance of the Dickinson Type Foundry Company in providing such necessary items as type and cabinetry as well as in providing expertise in ensuring an authentic feel to the place. "As very few of our patrons . . . have access to the composing room of newspaper offices," said the museum, "this

Austin and Stone's Dime Museum hosted Boston's typesetting races of 1886.

(Courtesy, Billy Rose Theatre Collection, New York Public Library for the Performing Arts, Astor, Lenox and Tilden Foundations)

The trappings of Boston's typesetting race were typical throughout the Eastern United States.
(From *Boston Globe*)

contest will afford thousands an opportunity to see how type is set, and by a group of acknowledged expert compositors!" The museum's mission was instructional: "Go and see how your favorite morning newspaper is made up!" Then, to keep things hopping, the museum hired a band. For two weeks, Swifts at Austin and Stone's worked to "the inspiring strains of a military band." Indeed, they enjoyed it and talked of "demanding music hereafter in their respective composing rooms."[4]

By the Monday morning of February 15, Austin and Stone's "composing room" was ready, and at ten o'clock, Melvin R. Crosby of the *Boston Record* walked to his typecase, followed by three others of Boston's fastest: George Graham of the *Globe,* Richard Cross of the *Herald,* and John A. Grant of the *Post.*

The Men's Race

Crosby of the *Record* took an early lead, breaking away smartly on Monday's first day of competition. The *Herald*'s Cross was hot on his heels, closely followed by Graham, with Grant trailing. The rules called for three racing sessions a day, forty minutes in the morning and the afternoon and sixty minutes each night. Each period was further divided into twenty-minute heats. The daily format, then, consisted of seven sprints beginning at ten o'clock in the morning and lasting until ten at night. Judging from the early turnouts, it was a popular plan. While it cost a thin dime to watch the races at Austin and Stone's, ready cash flowed steadily among the patrons. Type slingers were racehorses, and short heats kept interest alive. "Crowds stood around the perspiring compositors and enthusiastically cheered their favorites on."[5]

Melvin Crosby seemed a crowd favorite. Barely twenty-one years old, he was the youngest of the contestants. Born at Albion, Maine, Crosby apprenticed at the *Manchester Union* and in 1884 he moved to Boston in time to help the *Record* get out its inaugural issue. He had since been a stalwart in the *Record*'s composing room. For the first four days, Crosby and George Graham would trade leads, one or the other faltering, depending on the slightest mishandling of the very small types.[6]

Much of Boston's New England championship followed the recent Chicago model. As at Chicago, Boston's Swifts raced with minion type, set solid. Boston contestants contended with the same escalating calamities of typographical error and improper word breaks. Austin and Stone's proofreader was J. R. Burns, as stonily adamant as proofreaders anywhere. Job mobility—tramping—characterized Boston's competitors as it did those elsewhere. The *Herald*'s Dick Cross, twenty-nine, was born in Memphis, Tennessee, and had arrived in Boston two years previously. The *Post*'s Jack Grant was twenty-four years old and from Ottawa, Canada. He had served his apprenticeship at the *Moncton* (New Brunswick) *Times*.

George Graham was a relatively fresh face at the *Boston Globe.* He had worked there for only two years. Graham was English by birth and emigrated when he was five years old, in 1860. He had apprenticed at the *Bridgeport Farmer.* Between 1873 when he was setting type for the *Bridgeport Standard,* and 1884 when he arrived at the *Globe,* Graham worked in nine different states.[7]

Graham had "a beautiful motion" at the case, according to a reporter, "rapid and with a smooth grace that is very pretty." His fluid skill—"he seems to be touching the type with the tips of his fingers"—could nonetheless let him down. On the morning of day four he "made an out," allowing Crosby to catch up, and "the immense audience cheered and cheered again." That night, however, Crosby returned Graham's favor of the morning, himself making an "out." His betting buddies grieved.[8]

Racing crowds at Austin and Stone's were enthusiastic and emotional. Before day four's events, the museum's master of ceremonies, "Professor Hutchings," presented the men with some morale boosts from the boys back at their shops. Graham got a bouquet from his "comrades in the 'alley.'" Rallying round, Cross's mates gave him a "handsome floral emblem in the shape of a composing stick."[9]

Typesetting races had rarely been garden parties. Fast-lane typeracing usually happened where men could become boisterous away from polite society. Swifts at Austin and Stone's, however, found themselves amid pretensions to bourgeois decorum. By midweek nothing had disturbed the sporting tranquillity. As the *Globe*'s reporter put it, the men were on friendly and cordial terms, and there had been no "unpleasantness." Behind their backs, however, things could get unpleasant indeed. On Wednesday night, for instance, Jack Grant suffered "a contemptible trick." During the seven o'clock heat, Grant discovered someone had sabotaged his second typestick, resetting an important thumbscrew gauge. Referee J. H. West, noting that each of the others had set twenty-four lines as Grant struggled with his stick, awarded the luckless fellow an equivalent number of lines. The contestants collegially went along with this.[10]

Finally, on Friday Crosby came a cropper on a pair of outs and a bad line ending. To the consternation of his many fans, Crosby broke the word *neglect* after the letters *ne* instead of after *neg*. The combination of errors dropped him into third place and allowed Cross to jump into second. The tension waned. Graham was home free. By Saturday's finishing heats, placing a bet with a Crosby supporter "was a thing of the past."[11]

Still, great crowds turned out for the finale. The competition obviously struck a chord with the casual museum goer. The general public, whether wagering or merely curious, rose to the tension of the races and in turn contributed to the room's electricity. Ordinarily, the men raced amid "perfect silence" from the crowd, "but at the close Bedlam seemed let loose." George Milbank, the manager of Austin and Stone's claimed never to have seen anything like the attendance. "I shall have to take the paper off the wall," he said, "if many more come in." Museum owner Stone agreed that as a commercial venture, it had been great business.[12]

Throughout the week, the competition drew sizable numbers of printing's artisanry. Colleagues of the four men, familiar with shopfloor athletics, provided expert commentary and kept the energy level high. Graham, on his way to victory, impressed everybody. "Graham's style was the favorite among the many members of the craft present." By Saturday's final day, the room was filled with printers. Indeed, one onlooker wondered who was left to mind the store. "Judging by the crowds of typos to be seen," said the *Globe*'s reporter, "one would think that every available 'sub' had been engaged to get out the Sunday papers." Well-known printers "by scores," he said, "together with numbers from surrounding cities and towns" had formed cheering sections.[13]

Holding his lead to the end, Graham won the tournament.

"COPY ALL OUT!"

The Globe, as Usual, Leads All Competitors.

George Graham Takes First Prize at the Type-Setting Tournament.

Crosby Second, Cross Third and Grant Last Man.

The six-day type-setting contest, under the management of Austin & Stone, closed last night at 10 o'clock, Graham being the winner of the first prize. The lead he gained during Friday was too much for Crosby to overcome, but the contest throughout has been so close, and the men so evenly matched, that had it not been for the unfortunate "outs" made by Crosby, the result would have been very doubtful up to the close. Below we give portraits of the four competitors:

GEORGE GRAHAM

Boston crowds flocked to watch George Graham win the New England Championship.
(From *Boston Globe*)

With his victory came a "solid gold Waltham hunting case watch," thirty dollars, and "tremendous applause" from those present at the victory presentation. The effort drained him. Called upon to speak, "Graham expressed his thanks as best he could for emotion." Melvin Crosby rallied to finish second. His reputation, unlike Graham's, preceded him, and his support was consistent and effusive. The "magnificent bouquet" his composing room mates presented him at the finish was the eighth such he had received. Crosby also won a gold Waltham, simpler in design than Graham's, while Cross's third-place timepiece was silver. The top three finishers each won an additional thirty dollars. Grant, trailing the field, won a cash award and the crowd's "great enthusiasm."[14]

The Women's Race

The women's race, which opened the following Monday morning, built on that "great enthusiasm." The publicity before the men's race had made the women an afterthought. Indeed, the museum's rigged-out setting—a newspaper composing room—was men's territory, and while familiar to the women, it bore little resemblance to their own book composing rooms. More to the point, the popularity of the competition had taken everyone by surprise. The men had been a hit, and the women inherited that momentum. "To say that Austin & Stone's Museum was crowded at the opening of the ladies' six-day type-setting tournament," declared the *Globe,* "would give only a faint idea of the immense number present." Far from diminishing, "the interest taken in the competition last week," claimed the reporter, "bids fair to be exceeded during this."[15]

Building on inherited enthusiasm was a challenge; the men's race was a tough act to follow. The women, however, confronted something far worse. Their styles, manner, and techniques became completely and disconcertingly identified with their predecessors. Throughout the week, they would be referred to in terms of the men. Each of the fastest three of the four women—Francis, White, and Kenney—was consistently compared to the man whose typesetting cases she had inherited. Thus Francis's working manner was oddly reminiscent of Crosby, White's uncannily the same as that of Cross. A day into the women's competition, Kenney, "already . . . a great favorite," resembled Graham: "The same methodical and calm motions in picking up the type, and her coolness during the twenty-minute heats, are remarkable."[16]

Moreover, the women used phony names. Newspaper convention required the substitution of "Miss" for the first names of competitors. Nonetheless, this imprecision compounded some further chicanery. At the conclusion of the week's racing, three of the four women announced that they had raced under assumed names, *noms de metier*. Kenney, the eventual winner, had raced as "Miss Kenni." In real life, "Davis" and "Hammond" turned out to be White and Hartford. Francis remained Francis, presumably because people already knew who she was. The others were so lightly known that disclosure came as a surprise.[17]

The unfamiliarity of the racers gave their matches a generality the men's did not share. Certainly the women raced each other, and judging from the reactions of the crowd, the ebb and flow of their competition was every bit as exciting as that of the men. By the second day, however, onlookers recognized that the women were a quartet, racing the men. The women's race was never a simple horserace, and their relative anonymity deepened this impression. Whoever these women were, at the finish the Great Hall was once again filled with male compositors, now no longer rooting for their shopmates but earnestly interested in seeing how well the thing could be done. "No mistake," mused one, "they can set type."[18]

Opening day was a strain. Francis broke out early and led White and Kenney through Monday's early heats. She had learned her trade in Maine before coming to Boston, where "for several years" she had worked at Rockwell and Churchill's book office. Francis was experienced—onlookers put her age at thirty—but she was no more ready for a mob scene than any of the others. Huge Washington's Birthday crowds traumatized young women unused to spotlights. "It was a trying day to the nerves of the young ladies, who had never appeared in public before, and it took all the persuasion of courteous Manager Milbank to hold them to the work." By the next morning's ten o'clock first heat, the women "looked somewhat careworn," but "soon settled down to their work."[19]

Francis began to stumble during Tuesday's daytime sessions. She set the most type but had "a great number of turned letters and a few typographical errors." She lost six lines in corrections. Neither Kenney nor Hammond erred, while White lost three lines to errors. White, like Francis, was plainly fast. "In decided contrast to her rivals," a *Boston Herald* reporter noted, "her face was bent over her work with the most earnest determination as her hands flew over the case." She had learned her trade in New Hampshire before moving to Boston, where she worked "for some time." After this sojourn, White hit the road, working as a typesetter in New York and Springfield, finding other jobs in "other cities." She had been back in Boston "but a few weeks," working at Getchell's book office. "The young lady is very unassuming and a very intelligent talker, and her record is certainly a surprise to numbers of the printers of the city." She was, thought a *Globe* reporter, "about" twenty-three.[20]

After the second day, Francis retained a narrow cumulative lead over Kenney and White, who were tied. Tuesday evening, as had been the case throughout the day, Francis and White set more type, but Kenney's errorless work allowed her to catch up, and by the end of Wednesday's third day, Kenney trailed Francis by only 100 ems.

A racing pattern had developed. Each day Francis and White set a frenetic pace and piled up a lead, only to be beaten in proofs by Kenney and her maddening consistency. Kenney, "in her graceful way," did not seem to be performing as fast as the others, "but among the audience could be heard numbers saying that she was the coming winner." Members of the printing craft in attendance were amazed "at the fact that of Miss Kenni setting type for the three days without sufficient errors in any heat to cause the loss of a single line."[21]

L. J. Kenney simply never made mistakes. Born in West

Newbury, Massachusetts, she had learned to set type at the *Woburn Advertiser.* For seven years she had alternated her working life between Alfred Mudge's book office, where she "studied under the amiable Joe Coleman" and Boston's *Commercial Advertiser,* where apparently she read proof. She seemed, the *Globe* assured us, "a very affable and good-tempered young lady, always with a smile upon her face." She was twenty-four years old.[22]

On Thursday Kenney finally overtook Francis. Thursday had also been the most exciting day for the men, it being the day that the three leaders became grouped to within four lines of each other. Among the women, Kenney, as usual, was perfect. "The result caused great excitement, for Miss Kenni, the 'Graham' of the contest, had now wrested the coveted lead from Miss Francis, while Miss Davis had crept up very close to No. 1, and little Miss Hammond had improved in her average score."

By this time, Francis knew she must at all costs avoid "the terrible turned letters" that were proving her undoing. Certainly she did not lack support. After Thursday's first heat, the museum's Professor Hutchings, as he often had done with the men, presented Francis with "a beautiful bouquet" from her Rockwell and Churchill book room associates. An attached note wished her well and hoped she would do them proud as their "representative championess." Francis "was quite overcome for a few moments."

Like most, a *Boston Advertiser* reporter thought Francis was "undoubtedly superior to the others." A colleague at the *Herald* thought he knew what ailed her: she was confounded by unfamiliar type. Standard type carried a single groove or "nick" on the side of the letter to aid compositors in proper alignment. The letters the women handled bore two nicks "which are simply a snare to the compositor." Francis, the most experienced compositor and fastest, was surely thrown off her stride by the double nicks and as a result suffered from turned letters. Whatever the case, Francis responded well to her support. Bearing down, she would lose but one line to error in the second forty minutes.[23]

But by the end of the fourth day, "Miss Kenni had set an equal number of lines to Graham's splendid record of Friday and had surpassed his record of the fourth day, being only one line behind the famous score of the Saturday of last week, when both Graham and Crosby set 4350 ems." On Friday she tried to squeeze a couple of lines by breaking the words "upon" and "into" on their syllables and paid the price when Proofreader Burns called her error. Kenney easily withstood her only deduction of the week.[24]

THE MEN BEATEN.

Close of the Contest of Lady Compositors.

Miss Kenni Captures the Handsome and Valuable Gold Watch,

Miss Davis the Silver One, and Miss Francis the Last Take.

"Well, they are daisies," "No mistake, they can set type." "I could not believe the scores published until I came and saw the girls," and other similar expressions were to be heard yesterday, when the contest of the last day began at Austin & Stone's Museum. All is over now, and the ladies have succeeded in beating the records made by the men. Each day they either broke or tied the previous scores, until at the close all three of them led by a handsome number of ems. Miss Kenni has performed her work in a remarkable manner, not only with regard to speed, but setting her type each day so cleanly that the lines of each heat did not contain errors enough to cause her over thirty seconds correcting, so that, with the exception of the unfortunate division of the words "upon" and "into," on Friday morning, her record for "no deduction" was unbroken.

One week following the men's championship, Bostonians watched L. J. Kenney beat George Graham, the freshly crowned champion. (From *Boston Globe*)

"An immense crowd filled every available space" for Saturday evening's finale and the presentation of prizes. In the end, the top three women had surpassed the men at every stage of the six-day event. Kenney had beaten Graham by 950 ems. White, in second place, beat him by 650 ems. Francis, fading to third, nonetheless finished ahead of the men's winner by 475 ems. At the conclusion of racing, the museum's Professor Hutchings presented the prizes. "In his usual happy manner," Hutchings gave Kenney "a handsome hunting-case gold Elgin watch" worth, he was quick to state, forty-eight dollars. White received a silver watch and accessories, valued at twenty-five dollars. In third place Francis got eighteen dollars' worth of pearl-mounted French opera glasses. In addition to the merchandise, each of the women received a cash prize of thirty dollars. Finally and smiling grandly, Professor Hutchings awarded young Hartford a "consolation prize," two crisp ten-dollar bills.[25]

Women's Work and the ITU

Francis was a union woman. "Upon her breast," observed a reporter, she wore "the gold pin, or emblem, of the Knights of Labor." In this, both Francis and Austin and Stone's were following regulations. According to the rules, all contestants were members of "typographical unions." Boston women printers found their voice and home in the Knights of Labor. In 1870, following the lead of Augusta Lewis's Women's Typographical No. 1, a "Mrs. Lane" had urged the same course on Boston's Local No. 13 of the International Typographical Union. According to union archives, Boston printers had resisted, and "the scheme did not materialize." Over the next sixteen years, member locals of the ITU reluctantly opened their doors to women, but as of February 1886, Boston's Local No. 13 had not.[26]

In Boston as everywhere else, the heart of printing union membership remained newspaper compositors. Women therefore worked in other kinds of printing establishments—the job shops or book printers available and open to them. Francis, Kenney, and White worked at three Boston book and job printers, Rockwell and Churchill, Mudge, and Getchell, respectively. During 1884–86 these establishments were where the Knights of Labor found them. Few women would ever crack Local No. 13, Boston's haven of elite journeymen.[27]

Printers called book work "straight matter," the setting of columns of text that required no typographic embellishments, no headline fitting or tabular work. It called on fewer skills than jobs requiring more page makeup, and it gratified many journeymen therefore to consider it a lowly effort, "women's work." Swifts, of course, raced at setting straight matter. Moreover, in their daily tasks shorter lines were all that differentiated most journeymen's newspaper work from that of book composition. Veteran printers nonetheless disdained book office employees. The perception included even Kenney, the eventual winner at Boston. "This lady is not particularly a fast setter, as the judgment of the composing room would go," claimed the *Herald*'s correspondent, "but she has a very clever idea of what a compositor should be, and . . . can hold her own on straight work." Above all, book compositors often worked for less than union scale. When newspaper employees looked at book house people they saw a simple source of scab labor. The fact remained, however, that at the time of the Boston's races, fully one-fourth of the city's compositors were women.[28]

Men, of course, belonged not to the Knights of Labor, but to Boston's Local No. 13 of the ITU. For such men, Boston Knights might easily represent dual or competing unions, a situation normally anathema to trade unionists. Boston's printers, however, like most ITU member locals, regarded them as New York's printers had regarded Women's Typographical No. 1—an unavoidable, if sometimes annoying, by-product of their own solidarity.

In the 1880s the Knights of Labor both created and profited from a rising tide of working-class enthusiasm. The crossover appeal of typesetting races fed on this enthusiasm. Museums such as Austin and Stone's caught this wave of popular appeal and sponsored events that offered shopfloor printers the high profile of public amusement. The Knights thereupon allowed women to join their game.

"Daisies"

Women found more to be desired at Austin and Stone's race setting than had the men. For starters, they faced a gallant conspiracy. Normally, when printers encountered female competence, they assumed that the bar had been lowered, the standards relaxed. The easiest way to sustain this judgment was to ensure it. Gentlemen, even race referees, deferred to ladies and demanded less of them. Still, nothing in any news report from Austin and Stone's spoke of a single instance of special treatment.

The contrary, in fact, was true. The women confronted flaws in the "identical" racing conditions from the outset. The men had begun racing the week before with "tolerably full cases of type." No one bothered to replenish these, certainly identical, cases. On Monday's opening day, the women "began on the cases as the men left them." This meant that they were forced to "set out the bottoms of the cases, and in some instances [had] only half a dozen letters left in some of the boxes." The women therefore lost time fishing tiny letters out of virtually empty type boxes. Before Tuesday's second day of racing the women attentively distributed their own type.[29]

Then there was the background noise. Banished while the men competed, the monkeys reappeared. "During the day," reported the *Globe,* "the monkeys Jack and Fido, which had been removed from the cage adjoining the frames during the last contest, were replaced in their old home." No one protested. It "did not seem to annoy the ladies in the least." Nothing seemed to, and here they certainly differed from the men. Once over their opening day jitters, the women were less nervous throughout.[30]

There were other distinctions, such as L. J. Kenney's situation. The men carried the solid credentials of steady shopfloor wage earners. Kenney, born locally, had learned and first plied her trade in Woburn, Massachusetts. Lately, however, she had worked intermittently. "During the last three years," the *Globe* reported, "from sickness and other causes, she has worked but little at the business, and her performance during the week is the more remarkable." In other words, Kenney, who that week managed to set more type faster than anyone else in Boston, was an unemployed part-time compositor.

Of the eight men and women who competed at Boston, only one was out of depth. The young woman the crowds knew as "Miss Hammond" turned out to be a youngster named Alice May Hartford. Hartford had "a very pretty style, entirely her own," but as she dropped farther and farther behind, that description seemed to be putting it kindly. "Miss Hammond was . . . admired for her pluck in working against such fearful odds and with scarcely a hope of overtaking any one of them," commented the *Globe*, "but the young lady works along, nothing seeming to disturb her." What Hartford seemed most like was an apprentice, and sure enough, she turned out to be sixteen years old. Before the Boston tournament, Hartford had worked at her trade for all of "a few months," having learned it at the *Charlestown News*. By Wednesday's third day, "Miss Hammond had now given up all hope of overtaking any of the leading ladies, but her happy face was to be seen at her frame each heat, nothing disturbing her." This finally was printing's stereotypically inept female.[31]

In fact, the skill of the women impressed crowds and astounded their brethren. From the start, the women seem to have drawn nearly as well as the men. By the end of Monday's Washington's Birthday holiday, the women had worked in front of more than 11,000 people passing through the museum. Daily attendance thereafter surely diminished, especially during the daytime heats, but big crowds persisted. On Thursday night it stormed in Boston, and the Friday morning heats were lightly attended. By Saturday morning the issue was no longer in doubt, and attendance once again was sparse, "the friends of the young ladies evidently waiting until the closing contests should take place, most of them being of the opinion that, bar accident, Miss Kenni could not be overtaken."[32]

Friends of the young women were merely happy. Working printers were impressed. "I could not believe the scores published until I came and saw the girls," said one. Many merely shook their heads, less patronizingly than before: "Well, they are daisies." The surprises had begun early. At the end of the first day's heats, the women had collectively outperformed the men. By evening of day two, "a great number of printers" had joined the "usual crowds gathered around the frames." At week's end, it was as obvious as it was unbelievable that the women were going to outperform the men. By the end of Friday night's last races, "a great number of well-known typos were on hand, and the greatest silence was kept by all during the heats in progress." The crowd roared when the totals were added to the running score. "The announcement on the blackboard evidently was a surprise to many, who seemed scarcely to believe that the records of last week could be beaten."[33]

In particular, the men found the stamina of the women remarkable. By Thursday, "each of the ladies showed signs of the terrible strain upon them of the hard work of the three days." But so had the men. The women worked in the same short bursts of twenty minutes as had the men, seven times each day. Total working time amounted to two hours and twenty minutes. The heats, however, were spread over twelve hours, and preparations and meals kept them on location for at least thirteen hours a day. If the men could handle this, it seemed the women resolved to handle it as well. According to the *Boston Globe,* "The men, without exception, during the previous contest, considered it one of the hardest week's work they ever did, and the ladies so far have pluckily shown a determination to beat the records, if possible."[34]

Women had long insisted that they could perform with the men in most of the workrooms of a printing plant, certainly composing rooms. Men, especially union men, insisted they could not. Some reasons were traditional and silly: women were careless; women lacked the patience to decipher badly handwritten copy. Above all, women could not take the routine grind. The women might last a day or two, but by midweek, "many a member of the craft was willing to bet . . . that the ladies would succumb to the strain upon them." They did no such thing. L. J. Kenney and her colleagues scored better than the men at the end of their first twenty minutes, and they continued to do so at every stop throughout the week.[35]

The End of an Event

However personally gratifying to L. J. Kenney, as a gender triumph, her victory at Boston proved as short-lived as Augusta Lewis's earlier union organizing. Lewis herself was gone, now the wife of a New Haven newspaper publisher. She was already a monument, a representative union woman toward whom men could point with virtuous pride. Without Lewis's charismatic leadership, the ITU had swallowed the membership of Women's Typographical Union No. 1 into its own rank and file. In short order, much the same legacy befell Kenney and the women of Boston.

The women's race ended the Boston competition; the fact of it happening at all curtailed racing generally. Austin and Stone's typesetting races of 1886 proved a novel focus for gender rivalry, an experiment in head-to-head compositional skill. No one intended this. Indeed, the women were an end-of-column afterthought in all prerace publicity. The Boston event became a public amusement that, in the eyes of union printers, very nearly got out of control. The races simply should not have been close, but few were in a position to know that they might be. A women's race so publicly competitive with men could not have happened until typeracing emerged from the shopfloors and saloons of printing's working class and entered the public halls of dime museums.

Entertainment provided a path by which printing threatened to leave a producing subculture and its sponsoring agencies, union and shopfloor, and enter a wider world of a consuming middle class. Boston's Local No. 13 responded with alacrity. Discussions to admit women into the union began days after the race, and admission came four months later. According to a union archivist, "The admission of female compositors was taken up at the March meeting, and bore fruit at the June meeting, when President Pym blushingly initiated twelve young ladies and gave them some 'fatherly' advice." Unable to control what it did not sponsor, Boston's printing union acted quickly. It opened its doors and ended public racing. And it reclaimed a male hegemony.[36]

Union women quickly discovered more marginality, men in

masculine enclaves perpetuating "two classes" of worker. Men outnumbered the women, of course, in any union gathering, but worse, they polluted them past caring. "If women came to meetings in the same proportion as men," complained the printer Belva Mary Herron, "they would still form a little group in a large roomful of men; they would have little influence; and would find the atmosphere little to their taste, for it is likely to be black with tobacco smoke." Certainly, said Herron, women were "most unlikely to speak freely, and take an active and unembarrassed part in gatherings where men are in the majority." For their part, men felt themselves "abused and imposed upon, if obliged, out of respect to women, to give up the privilege of smoking at regular meetings." Like politicians, Herron went on, "the men wrangle and draw out the discussions to unconscionable length, and the women, taking little part in the discussion, naturally become tired and depart in disgust."[37]

The ranks of women would thin dramatically. The number of women in the printing trades peaked in the three decades following the Civil War. From slightly short of 4 percent of all printers and publishers in 1870, over the next twenty years the proportion of women in printing, presswork, and lithography grew to 10 percent. By the turn of the century, however, the proportion of women in printing was in sharp decline. "Men are displacing women in printing and publishing in the long run," the printing historian Jacob Loft declared in 1944. Printers would forever congratulate themselves on their contributions to gender equality, but by 1900 the International Typographical Union had weathered a crisis, and its women were in retreat.[38]

Women had sought equality in the labor market at least since the Civil War. Led by labor leaders such as Augusta Lewis, women insisted they could competently set type. Perhaps they were even better at it than men. Men found a dozen arguments to deny it. How could they know for certain? They could race. But once that question was answered, women would never race again.

7 | Mr. Mergenthaler's Revolution

TYPESETTING RACES, ALL THE RAGE IN THE SPRING
of 1886, ceased by that summer. As early as late March, Philadelphia held what proved to be the last "national" handsetting tournament. Thousands of Philadelphians and all of the local newspapers attended the city's tournament, held at Bradenburgh's
Ninth and Arch Street Dime Museum. "Rapid newspaper composing," gushed the *Philadelphia Inquirer*, "has been elevated to
a fine art," and no one had raised it higher than Alexander Duguid,
Philadelphia's champion. On March 27, 1886, the *Cincinnati Enquirer* Swift set more type by hand faster than anyone ever had or
ever would. Across the ocean, even Englishmen paid attention.[1]

But in little more than a decade, typesetters racing on new
Mergenthaler machines would become astonishingly faster than
these Swifts. It took a *Baltimore Sun* Linotype operator named

William Henry Stubbs less than ten minutes to match an hour's effort by the handsetting journeymen. Between 1886 and 1899, hot-metal Linotypes rearranged a world of printing. Not least among alterations, the Linotype immediately changed the ancient jargon of its trade. Printers stopped calling fast typesetters Swifts. Fast typos ceased rushing. Speedy shopfloor workers became "lino men," new printers who could "hang an elevator," or, in other words, operate a machine fast enough to jam its mechanism. Then, within a year of Stubbs's Linotype performance, the International Typographical Union (ITU) prohibited racing altogether.[2]

Racing ended, and with its demise came a rebuilt, heavily male printing industry. The Linotype quickly made racing Swifts irrelevant, their world obsolete. New machinery thinned great herds of handsetting journeymen. At the same time, the numbers of women printers, which had grown steadily through the mid-1880s, began a long decline. Women had both spurred and profited from the modest proliferation of early, pre-Linotype typesetting equipment such as the Alden Typesetter. But unlike earlier manufacturers of typesetting equipment, the Mergenthaler company had not designed an easily operated machine. The Linotype was heavy, dirty, and loud. Union men controlled its use. As a result, the Linotype reduced the ranks of women even faster than those of the men. Women became as irrelevant as Swifts, and neither worked the new composing rooms of the Linotype.

The Philadelphia National Championship of 1886

Philadelphia always considered itself at the forefront of printing excellence. Merely to mention Benjamin Franklin was to honor the city's artisanal heritage. After the Civil War, Robert S. Menamin became the latest of the city's prominent printers. As the editor of *Printers' Circular,* Menamin was, until his death in 1887, a respected voice of the nation's printers. Little passed him unnoticed. In February 1870 he was as transfixed as anyone in the trade when news arrived of George Arensberg's racing achievement, and he immediately invited Arensberg for a demonstration. The invitation amounted to an audition, and Arensberg responded quickly. Soon, on May 10, *Printers' Circular* sponsored a formal typesetting match that the Velocipede, by now employed at the *Philadelphia Sunday Mercury,* promptly won. When, fifteen years later, interest grew in organized typeracing, Philadelphians eagerly got in line.[3]

C. A. Bradenburgh's Dime Museum hosted the Philadelphia tournament of 1886. Like all other such museums, Philadelphia's mixed mild doses of edification with surefire entertainment. As usual at Ninth and Arch, for example, the "Elastic Skin Man" would be on hand as the printers gathered, and in case the turnstiles slowed, the museum laid in a bill of vaudeville acts. Compositors at Bradenburgh's competed with each other, and with Stoddart's Grand Operatic Minstrel Show, Hughey (the "rajah of fun") Dougherty, and Nala Damjanata, "the Beautiful Hindoo Princess and Snake Charmer."[4]

For all that, the museum did its best by the printers. Before the races, as was now formulaic among museums, Manager Bradenburgh turned his Curio Hall into a workroom of a large daily newspaper. "As the newspaper composing room is but little known to the outside public," commented the *Philadelphia Press,* "this will be a good opportunity to see how the thousands of little metal pieces are put together to produce the printed page." For this, the museum turned to R. S. Menamin. Menamin's Printers' Warehouse provided the cabinets, cases, typesticks, and all the rest of a composing room's paraphernalia. Philadelphia's *Evening Call* supplied the type. The *Call*'s type would be 6-point "nonpareil," slightly smaller than the minion Swifts often used. Alex Shane of the *Philadelphia Record* read proof.[5]

Bradenburgh's mission, then, was instructive as well as diverting. "Thousands of people who are strangers to the secrets of the composing and press rooms," declared its publicity, "will gladly welcome this opportunity to see the deft-fingered champions of the typographical world present the moulded thoughts of the writers of the day in plain English print." As attuned to the bottom line as museums anywhere, Bradenburgh's also offered Professor Irwin, "assisted by Miss Sadie," and his "troupe of Living Fairies."[6]

By the Monday afternoon of March 15, Bradenburgh's "composing room" was ready, and at one o'clock the usual New York headliners, Barnes of the *World* and McCann of the *Herald*, joined Alexander Duguid of the *Cincinnati Enquirer* in challenging a Philadelphia contingent of the *Times*'s Peter Thienes, James Washington of the *Inquirer*, and James J. Nolan of the *North American*.

Joseph McCann jumped into the early, first-day lead. Two months earlier, at Chicago's inaugural "national championship," McCann had frozen at the start, effectively losing the race to William Barnes. McCann's fast start therefore surprised some onlookers. Barnes, in fact, quickly passed McCann for the lead on the second day of racing. He was far showier than McCann, as smooth and stylish as McCann was jerky and abrupt. "The printers were pleased and amazed at the ease, swiftness and delicacy with which Barnes handled the little pieces of metal," reported the *Record*. "He stands close to the case and holds his stick easy, so as to be ready to follow the right hand when it goes to the remote corners of the case." He was tall and spare and was oblivious to the crowds. Typeracing was a young man's game, and at forty-two Barnes was experienced to the edge of elderly.

McCann, twenty-nine, was short in stature and as energetic as Barnes seemed gracefully languid. McCann's right arm pumped at the typecase like a piston. He was blazingly fast, but he made more mistakes than did Barnes or the others. The early line at Bradenburgh's favored Barnes, but back in December McCann had beaten Barnes in a big New York match. He was, after, all the "ex-champion," noted the *Philadelphia Record*, and between the two it would be "nip and tuck."[7]

Philadelphians flocked to the races. As always, the bets flew. Public museums attracted thousands of ordinary people, a new kind of miscellaneous public, some of whom came to wager, some merely to mill about. According to the *Inquirer*, the mix at Philadelphia proved annoying from the start. "There was a great crowd in attendance, and some of the typos complained of interference in their work by the spectators."[8]

Most early money was on either Barnes or McCann. Alexander Duguid, however, was the dark horse winner. A newcomer at Philadelphia, Duguid defeated both favorites by rallying furiously on the last day of racing. McCann had reclaimed the lead on the fourth day, and he continued to hold it until Duguid's charge. On the final afternoon of the tournament, Duguid "put on a little extra steam," passed McCann, and led for the first time. He had averaged 2,259 ems an hour that afternoon, the fastest speed ever. That evening he finished even faster, averaging 2,277 ems per hour, "beating his previous record, and any heretofore attained anywhere."[9]

At Philadelphia's national championship, Alexander Duguid set type faster than anyone ever had, or would.
(From *A Collation of Facts Relative to Fast Typesetting,* New York: Concord Co-operative Printing Company, 1887)

Duguid had come to Philadelphia without the public exposure of his New York competition. "Duguid showed signs of nervousness the first day," commented the trade journal *Printers' Circular,* and started slowly. Philadelphia's tournament demanded "considerable nerve and endurance" of its participants, especially "when the many annoyances, such as the conversations of the crowds of people and the bustle incident to a general exhibition hall, are taken into account." For all of that, the inexperienced Duguid managed to stay within reach of the leaders.[10]

Duguid's triumph was not an upset. It is tempting to see a "former farm boy" in the Ohioan, a "bush league entrant" who "proceeded to show up the old boys." Duguid, however, had not wandered in off the street. Philadelphia was his first sanctioned match, but Duguid had worked a case at the *Cincinnati Enquirer*, a big newspaper and one with a sizeable composing room racing reputation. The *Enquirer*'s famous 1877 composing room all-star "Big Ten" was only slightly before Duguid's time. In a local match in late December, Duguid had set 2,093 ems of solid minion. This performance alerted the trade, and Chicago had invited him to its tournament, but he declined because Kohl and Middleton's Museum scheduled races on Sunday. Philadelphia went out of its way to accommodate his scruples. Bill Barnes knew all about Duguid; he suspected he was faster even than McCann.[11]

Like McCann, Duguid was twenty-nine years old. Local reporters described a man of "medium height and solid build." Less smooth than Barnes, Duguid's style nonetheless caused type "to fairly jump from the case into his stick." He learned his trade at the *Toledo Blade*, where he apprenticed in 1873. Philadelphia newspapers called Duguid a "model typo," and he seemed that and more. Duguid thought that "total abstinence" from both tobacco and alcohol was "conducive to good health, and good health is indispensable to rapid typesetting." Indeed, Duguid's rectitude tended to identify him as readily as his skills. "Duguid is the compositor who neither chews or smokes tobacco, drinks intoxicating liquors or participates in contests on the Sabbath." Printers, by reputation, did all of these things. Duguid was worth lining up to see.[12]

Dime museums knew that people also wanted to watch the local talent. This meant Peter Thienes, James J. Nolan, and James Washington, each of whom stood ready at the start. A fourth Philadelphian, W. H. Crane of the *News*, missed the opening afternoon sessions and never caught up. The hometown entrants lacked sanctioned track records. As the *Philadelphia Inquirer* pointed out, they had their reputations "and consequent good salaries."[13]

Local opinion thought highest of Thienes. He was thirty years old and had worked in Cincinnati at the *Times* and *Star,* as well as at the *Baltimore Herald,* before joining Philadelphia's *Times.* Thienes built his reputation on notably clean work. In two weeks of racing, Thienes spent only thirty-two minutes in corrections, a third as many as McCann, for instance, and ten minutes fewer than Barnes. Timekeeping and proofreading were crucial in type-racing. The Bradenburgh Museum's referee was William H. Foster, foreman of the composing room at the *Evening Call.* Widely respected, Foster was past president of Philadelphia's local typographical union and a national ITU officeholder. Thienes and the others at Philadelphia worked from identical printed matter, a luxury when a compositor's ability to unravel bad handwriting was a job requirement. For each minute spent correcting mistakes, proofreader Alex Shane deducted 25 ems—one line of type—from a compositor's gross total. Thienes won the city championship gold medal and finished fifth behind the imported stars.[14]

The remainder of the hometown contingent fell behind early and stayed there. James Washington had arrived at the *Philadelphia Inquirer* three years earlier from his native England and membership in the Manchester Typographical Union. Washington was thirty-two years old, as was James J. Nolan. Nolan had joined the staff of the *North American* in 1876. According to the *Inquirer*'s reporter, "Mr. Nolan first saw the cheering sunbeams . . . in the city of Dublin, Ireland." Nolan, who shared those Irish sunbeams with Joe McCann, also shared his size. "Though not very tall," the *Inquirer* mused ambiguously, "he has a big local reputation as a fast worker." Washington and Nolan, along with the tardy Crane, brought up the rear.[15]

The tournament had begun without one of its star attractions. Two months earlier, the *Chicago Evening Journal*'s Thomas C. Levy had provided much of the Chicago meet's excitement when he rallied fiercely to finish third before the hometown crowd. Thanks to his closing rush, Levy became Chicago's local champion, and it earned him a trip to Philadelphia. "Bangs" Levy—Philadel-phians quickly learned his nickname, the meaning of which has been lost—could race with the fastest, but he also brought along the best in shopfloor swagger. Levy got to Philadelphia a day late, and while race officials allowed him a makeup session, he could finish no better than fourth. Bangs, however, found solace. He found, according to Philadelphia's *Sunday Times*, Nala Dam-janata, the snake charming maiden who shared the bill. The journeyman typo and "the Hindoo princess" were an instant item. "What more fitting than that a 'print' should fall in love with a princess?" asked the *Sunday Times*.[16]

William Barnes saved his own moves until the last day of the tournament. As he had done in Chicago, Barnes first set type from reversed cases, and then awed the crowd by setting blindfolded, copy being read to him by Thienes. Barnes made only six mistakes during his blindfolded effort at Philadelphia. "These are the most difficult feats ever performed by a compositor," marveled a re-porter. Barnes's tricks were well considered; his abilities in these things had been widely ballyhooed, and crowds came expecting to be astonished.[17]

Head-to-head racing naturally fascinated audiences. The dol-lar value of what the Swifts accomplished impressed people, as well. At the end of an evening's racing, as Barnes put down his typestick, a *Times* reporter caught a conversation: What did the champion make? someone asked. A "practical printer, who was standing near" answered 6,186 ems.

"Darn your ems. I want to know how much money he earned."
"Well, let's see. 6,186 at 40 cents a 1,000 would be $2.47."
"How long did he work?"
"Three hours."
"Three hours! I wish I was a printer. I work eighteen hours a day and only get $2. I ain't quick at figuring, but if that champion worked as long as I do he would make about $15 a day."
"You have to allow for distributing the type," the printer started to say, "and that will . . ."

"Never mind, my friend. I can't wait to hear any more. I've got to go to work at five o'clock tomorrow morning."

"And the man of inquiring disposition hurried away," concluded the *Times*. "He is a car conductor."[18]

The "great type-setting contest for the championship," announced the *Printers' Circular,* is the "sensation of the month, typographically."[19] By the tournament's second week, however, the typesetters needed everything in Bill Barnes's bag of tricks. Stoddart's minstrel show had moved into the museum, drawing crowds away from the sweaty Swifts. "The clicking of the types was lost yesterday in the sound of the bones and the rattling of the tambourine in the theatre," reported the *Press.* "The minstrels proved a rival attraction, and people calmed the excitement caused by watching the typos by listening to the merriment of the artists in cork."[20]

Finally it was over, and Philadelphia crowned a new "national champion." Onlookers found it "difficult to imagine that the nerves and muscles of any man will be brought hereafter to such a pitch of skill and endurance as to surpass this exhibition of swiftness." On Monday night, March 29, Manager Bradenburgh awarded the prizes, stage center "in the presence of an immense audience, who loudly applauded." Those prizes were medals, created by the local jeweler C. P. Herold. Duguid's championship award bristled with diamonds, while second place through fifth got versions in gold, silver, and bronze. Jeweler Herold had displayed these gaudies throughout the tournament in his Chestnut Street shop windows. In addition and as usual in such matches, the men won the wage their totals would have fetched in ordinary shopfloor work. And, of course, Bangs and the "Hindoo" princess had each other.[21]

Then an odd thing happened. As spring of 1886 became summer, typeracing, the printing pastime that had emerged from obscurity into a widespread public amusement, simply stopped. Just months before, in January, the promoter J. R. Davis had envisioned a national typeracing tour moving through the dime museums of

Chicago, Philadelphia, New York, and Boston, maybe others. Successfully launched, the project quickly foundered. Pittsburgh's Chalet Museum held a local tournament in late March, and Indianapolis's New Iron Zoo followed in early April, but museum-sponsored high-stakes racing ended at Philadelphia.[22]

Its brightest star, of course, Joseph McCann, had begun the tour with a pair of losses and faced fading prospects. Years later, McCann mildly complained of mistreatment at Philadelphia. While it was true that Alexander Duguid had smashed his sprint record, McCann set more overall type at Philadelphia and lost to Duguid only in proofs, in corrections. As it happened, the type at Philadelphia had been identical to that used in Cincinnati and un-familiar both to McCann and to Barnes. "It was the same size type used on the *Cincinnati Inquirer*, where Mr. Duguid worked and which he had been handling for years," explained McCann. "A man who had never handled it before would find it very difficult to calculate in spacing and correcting, especially when every sec-ond counted in a speed of 2,200 ems an hour." According to Mc-Cann, "In making a record one must be able to calculate, coming to the end of a line, what size spaces to use, and in correcting he must with his eye tell whether a letter or word will come in to avoid overrunning." Often, he said, "I would hair space to get in a letter or word but it would not come in, and thus that much time was lost, as I would have to overrun."[23]

In the end, however, playing with house type did not undo Mc-Cann. The introduction of the Linotype, newly online at the *New York Tribune*, did that. Journeymen compositors were no more prepared for the Linotype than they had been for the challenge of women typeracers. In 1885, a few months before the Philadel-phia tournament, the *Inland Printer* had dismissed reports of the new mechanical typesetter, calling those reports "rubbish" circu-lated by "smart alecks of the New York press." The April issue of *Inland Printer* reported "an item . . . going the rounds of the press" that spoke of a keyboard machine that set whole lines of type at once. Moreover, the thing, unnamed in the *Inland Printer* report, cast its own type, which the operator then melted down and used all over again, sidestepping the entire issue of type distribution. Could this possibly be? It seemed unlikely to the *Inland Printer.* Joseph McCann was surely a beauty and no mistake, was he not?[24]

The Winner Was Whitelaw Reid

The working printers who read the *Inland Printer* may have considered a linotype machine unlikely, but their owners and managers did not. In their view, slow and bungling typesetters far outnumbered typeracing Swifts, wonders that they were. Printing businessmen employed far too many people, regardless of speed or skill, at extremely intensive tasks. Most printing employers were therefore eager to the edge of desperation to find a reliable device that might reduce their complete dependence on journeymen compositors.

It was certainly true of Whitelaw Reid. Unlike his predecessor Horace Greeley, a man who was enormously respected by printing's rank-and-file, Reid identified little with the world of journeymen Swifts. Greeley had served an apprenticeship in the trade, built the *New York Tribune* only after spending years at the typecase, and subsequently honored fellow artisans as they did him.

Reid's own "apprenticeship" contrasted sharply with that favored by his boss. He had graduated from Miami University in Oxford, Ohio, and began his career not on shopfloors but as a city desk journalist at the *Cincinnati Gazette.* The Civil War offered Reid a chance to hone both reportorial and editorial skills, and in 1868 those skills led him to Greeley's *New York Tribune.* A short year later, Reid was the newspaper's managing editor. When Greeley died, in 1872, Reid became principal proprietor and editor in chief. He remained, more or less, at the newspaper throughout a life of political power brokerage, statesmanship, and candidacy for high public offices.[25]

In the mid-1860s, Greeley's composing room had employed men of substantial reputation. Few journeymen could match the Swift Ben Glasby, for instance, or Hugh Morton. But Swifts fled Reid's *Tribune.* Unlike Greeley, Reid was a corporate executive,

not a master printer. His employees, whatever else they represented to him, were balance sheet entries. Collectively, their wage
constituted an ongoing variable of the cost of production. Reid
might have tried to absorb this expense by, for example, finding
ways to increase sales, but instead he consistently chose to reduce
costs. To accomplish this, his *Tribune* innovated more widely than
most newspapers. Independent news stringers, for instance,
quickly became costly, so in 1881 Reid formed a cartel that pooled
the resources of a dozen smaller news-gathering agencies. The Associated Press, as he called it, subsequently provided a more reliable flow of information, and by monopolizing it for its membership, reduced costs.[26]

"Reid was no less concerned with handling news than with
gathering it," says his biographer, and so he constantly looked for
faster, more efficient ways of getting it into his paper and onto the
street. He had already installed the fastest printing press available,
the new perfecting double cylinder rotary press developed by the

As Swifts mounted their biggest races, Whitelaw Reid installed the
Linotype at the *New York Tribune.*
(Courtesy, Chicago Historical Society; ICHi-35062)

venerable equipment firm of Richard Hoe. In 1873 he thought he was the first to do so.[27]

Fast, new printing presses increased the *Tribune*'s productivity. Speeding up pressroom performance, however, proved less challenging than similarly accelerating the paper's composing room. While enormous presses delivered printed pages at a dizzying rate, setting *Tribune* type remained the slow handwork typical throughout the printing trades. Beginning in the early 1880s, Reid sought a mechanical solution that would set the kind of brisk pace in his composing room that high-speed rotary presses did in the pressroom. He installed a machine called the Burr Typesetter.

The Civil War had slowed experimentation in mechanical typesetting. In 1855 John F. Trow's New York printing firm had been the first to install commercially useful composing machines. Trow's typesetters had been renditions of a model patented by William Hazlet Mitchel. Two years later, just as Timothy Alden was introducing his earliest machine, Maine's W. H. Houston patented yet another keyboard model. Innovation then lagged amid the fighting, but with the end of the war, printers renewed their interest in the possibilities offered by automatic composing machines.

In the late 1860s many big city printers used low-wage typesetting personnel in combination with composing machines and found it an attractive alternative to rooms full of skilled but expensive union journeymen. In 1867, as the *New York World* was exploring a system of gendered equipment, the New York printing company of Gray and Green bought the patent rights to W. H. Houston's typesetter. Gray and Green, like the *World*, had discovered a way to cut composing costs while expounding a social ideal. Within a year, the Gray and Green company had arranged to print Susan B. Anthony's *Revolution,* the distinctive voice of American feminism. The firm subsequently built and installed twelve Houston machines, renamed the Green Typesetter, on its Manhattan shopfloor.[28]

Gray and Green Printers did not survive the depressed economy of the early 1870s. In 1875 Henry A. Burr, a hatmaker, bought their business, including, of course, the typesetting equipment. Burr promptly renamed the machine, and the Green typesetter, formerly the Houston, became the Burr. When Whitelaw Reid bought his first typesetting equipment, the machines he bought were Burr Typesetters. In 1883 the *New York Tribune* was employing at least two Burr machines.[29]

The *Tribune* composing room thereupon used Burr machines throughout the 1880s. Burr typesetters, individually, were dedicated to single type sizes. At the *Tribune,* Burr operators used a brevier model to set portions of the editorial page and a second machine to produce minion-sized type for most foreign letters. Each machine set portions of the eighth page, the Local Miscellany section, of the paper. It amounted to an extensive commitment, and the *Tribune* was likely the only daily in the country attempting it.[30]

There were, of course, reasons for this. Mechanization often seemed to cause as many problems as it solved. Burr machines used special type and broke much of it. Worse, the equipment mechanism itself repeatedly malfunctioned. And difficulties were not limited to the machines. The *Tribune's* mechanized shopfloor constantly offended labor leaders. None of these problems deterred Reid. The machines, he insisted, saved money in the composing room.[31]

Relentlessly innovative, Reid from the start looked beyond his Burr machines to better ones. That search led him to the Linotype. "He was more realistic in appraising its possibilities," says Reid's biographer, "when he first saw the complex and cumbersome invention of Ottmar Mergenthaler."[32]

Printing unions were likely to impede the cost-cutting efficiencies of mechanized composition. Whitelaw Reid easily resolved to break those unions. In Reid's view, typesetting machines and handsetting journeymen offered identical product. Swifts were sometimes fast and often careful, and they were proud of being both. They were not, however, cheap. Neither were they all that easy to order around, and indeed, they, like most journeymen, felt free to wander from the premises, having arranged substitutes. This, too, was normal, a practice of long standing among unionized printers. Reid naturally wanted a fast typesetter's speed in his composing room because he needed maximum output, but the efforts of fast individuals among scores of slower ones afforded only marginal gains in production. Reid needed speed consistent with a dependable supply of modestly capable, competent, and cheap workers. His composing room strategy combined a ceaseless search for machinery with hardline adversarial union negotiation.[33]

Not surprisingly, Whitelaw Reid's *Tribune* antagonized a generation of union printers, and Reid himself became anathema to the brethren of New York's Big Six. Beginning in 1877, Reid operated his composing room as an open shop, hiring without regard to union membership, indeed demanding his employees forswear such affiliation. Putting it gently, workingmen widely deplored Reid's policies. For the next fifteen years, Reid's *Tribune,* alone among New York newspapers, withstood the strikes and boycotts of New York's Local No. 6 of the ITU. Unique among New York City's morning dailies, the *Tribune* was set by nonunion typesetters.[34]

The Coming of the Linotype

All typesetting innovation triggered a shopfloor paradox. While few printers would spend holidays setting type, many were proud of their skills, and by 1886 journeymen bristled at an equation that linked their skills with those of a machine. "It is all very well to say that the compositor's art is mechanical," commented the Swift William Barnes, but if that were so, he would be easier to replace. "In all machines the same operations are repeated from time to time," explained Barnes, "whereas the apparatus for composing may be at work for years and may not once perform exactly similar motions for five minutes together." Inventors simply cannot devise "a piece of mechanism that can think," argued Barnes, "and the numerous efforts to secure this phenomenon proves the sure foundation on which the compositor's art is based."[35]

Among compositors, Barnes's point was an article of faith. Neither union officials nor shopfloor journeymen therefore paid much attention to machinery before the mid-1880s. According to

George A. Stevens, historian of New York's Local No. 6, union officials ignored machines "during the long period that was devoted
by inventors in experimentation." Machines needed too much
manpower—setting, justifying, distributing—for maximum effi-
ciency. Therefore, "their utility was of a doubtful character and
was never seriously regarded by employers," Stevens said, and
added, "neither was there any apprehension among journeymen
as to the possibility of their general introduction." The earliest
record of union reaction to machines was June 3, 1883, when No.
6 appointed a committee of three "to visit the machine typesetters and endeavor to organize them."[36] That machine was the Burr
typesetter. As of the mid-1880s, the union had not gotten around
to setting a wage scale for operators of typesetting equipment.[37]

Ottmar Mergenthaler's "blower" Linotype slugcasting machine. As rendered in the pages of *Inland Printer,* this 1886 model was the earliest
viable Linotype.
(From *Inland Printer*)

Like the other machines, early Linotypes regularly malfunctioned. In fact, large printing plants began employing a new type of printing worker, a compositor/machinist. Other inventors were focusing on simplicity and ease of operation. Ottmar Mergenthaler instead tackled typesetting's distribution difficulty, the time spent in mindlessly recycling letters, and solved it by sidestepping distribution altogether. Instead of setting and replacing individual pieces of type, the Linotype machine, as its name suggested, cast whole lines. A Linotype machine worked not with single types, but from a magazine, or container, of brass matrices for casting characters of a font of type. The operator installed this magazine atop the machine. Strokes at a keyboard accessed individual typemolds that then slid into proper alignment. Jets of lead from an adjacent pot of molten metal filled these and cast a single, fused row, or "slug," of type. Instead of distributing single characters after printing, an operator simply melted these lines of type. Line justification remained a problem, but when the Mergenthaler corporation incorporated J. W. Schuckers's recently invented sliding wedge spacebands, the result was a justifying linecaster that allowed the "Merg" to pull away from the field in the U.S. typesetter wars. By 1892 twenty-three American newspapers were running some 300 Linotypes.[38]

In the mid-1880s, however, such a contraption seemed far from an overnight answer to printing's prayers and, in fact, no better than any other machines. In New York City the Linotype was only one of several possible "automatic" typesetters. Moreover, the Linotype inspired the same sorts of doubt as the others. As late as 1890 the English authority John Southward put the Linotype squarely in the lengthening line of museum pieces. "We months ago decided to cease manufacturing it," he quoted Mergenthaler officials as saying. It was "another addition to the melancholy list of failures during the past seventy years." Southward was misinformed, but the slugcasting revolution had been many years in the making, and many more would pass before every print shop in the land bought a Lino.[39]

End of an Era

Possessing unmatched compositional prowess, Swifts had seemed irreplaceable. Still, if he thought about it, a Swift such as William Barnes might have understood that his efforts transcended ordinary expectations, that his speed confounded standard definitions of shopfloor performance. Racing in Philadelphia, as in Chicago and elsewhere, had created stars. Bradenburgh's headline racers extended working-class heroics to something approaching fame and celebrity. Some who spoke narrowly for the printing trades tried to reclaim the men as industry models and ethical paragons, but the mixture—grinding toil and show business—seemed at odds with itself. Printing brethren had often reacted ambivalently to racing, and many remained cautious in their praise of fast typesetters. *Inland Printer* tried to make role models of the Swifts, urging apprentices to "persevere till you do succeed," as McCann, Barnes, and Arensberg had done. But *Printers' Circular* consistently demurred. Marvelous as they were, thought Editor Menamin, Swifts turned the heads of working stiffs. Young compositors should know that it is far better to be "slow and accurate" than "swift and bungling."[40]

Still, journeymen printers loved to strut their stuff, and for the rank-and-file a typesetting match was literally a day at the races. Union leaders, however—printing's policymakers—frowned. On May 9, 1886, the Board of Delegates of New York's Local No. 6, officially condemned typeracing. According to union spokesman Thomas Condon, "the system lately introduced of museum typesetting matches is certain to have a bad effect on the trade at large." For years, unionized printers had resisted all management movements toward production quotas. Union printers had insisted on controlling the pace of their work, and while willing to set minimum productivity standards, union strategists were uninterested in publicizing how much faster they could go. Suddenly, in glaring public, a handful of Swifts were making perfectly competent shopmates seem dilatory. New York's Big Six thereupon urged the ITU convention "to vote to condemn such exhibitions in the future."[41]

Traditionally, Swifts had defined themselves in terms of their union. The ITU and its locals provided the structure of their lives, the framework of their deeds. Within that framework, Swifts might become "free spirits," in Alexander Lawson's phrase, "typographic entrepreneurs." The shopfloor subculture of the Swifts honored troupers such as Harry Cole. "Old 'Arry" was "a true friend, a sincere enemy, a strong labor advocate" and an ideal among journeymen.[42]

In luring William Barnes and Joseph McCann from their composing rooms, dime museums fouled this water. Outside the boundaries of union hall, shopfloor, and saloon, typographic entrepreneurship became something like apostasy. Shopfloor sponsors easily felt betrayed when museums stole their meal tickets. Foreman Geary at the *New York Herald* took it personally. "Geary never forgave me," recalled a rueful McCann. And general shopfloor solidarity remained an issue past the personal relationship between Geary and McCann.[43]

In a new context, a Swift's prowess became disruptive. Once it had been expressed fraternally, communally, but now it threatened to destabilize a working relationship between unions and employing printers. Rank and file compositors admired Swifts because they were good printers, by which the journeymen usually meant that they were fast. Before typesetting machinery, speed was, of course, what employers were interested in, as well. Swifts, however, worked only secondarily for an employer. Journeymen printers achieved their status and thereby qualified for their employment by meeting union standards, not those of employers. Composing room union foremen interceded between working journeymen and employing printers. They hired their staffs, Swifts among the rest, on behalf of ownership. Therefore, when George Arensberg or Joseph McCann abandoned the *Times* or the *Herald* to hit their road to stardom, they damaged foremen far more than their employing newspapers. The shopfloor defined Arensberg's prowess, as it defined that of Harry Cole or Joe McCann or Bill Barnes. Speed had not made these men good employees; it made them heroes. When unions convened annually in plenary session, journeymen went elsewhere to race, to wager, and in the process to reinvigorate their calling. Public typeracing—arena events—diminished that calling. Removed from a context of shopfloor and union hall, speed and prowess made a different kind of sense. Mannis Geary had been right. Dime museums had violated the blended, communal world of the Swift.

The Linotype machine thereupon altered everything. Its arrival ended the world of the Swift and slammed the door on women, Swift or not. Intricate printing would require hand composition for many more years, but to race at it implied that its essence remained speed. Very quickly the swiftness of the Swifts became anachronistic, their races as arcane as caber tossing, performed to gatherings of eccentrics.

Prowess, however, now remained as an essential category or ingredient of a renewed, masculine craft. The post–Civil War Alden typesetter, predecessor to the successful Linotype, had arrived as a "feminized" device, but by 1890 the Mergenthaler Linotype no longer carried that connotation. Typesetting equipment that had once been "demasculinized" had become "remasculinized." Machine composition once again became men's work. In the process, women printers were absorbed within existing unions and their numbers dwindled.[44]

It helped that the Linotype was filthy. Molten metal slugcasters were noisy and dirty, and their type magazines were heavy to lift. Unlike other contending typesetters, Mergenthaler's invention occasionally spurted wayward and dangerous jets of hot lead. Open pots of molten metal necessarily smelled bad. It therefore easily fit the meager expectations of shopfloor journeymen. When, after 1890, printing shops routinely installed the Mergenthaler machine, union printers had established control over machine training and operation. Slugcasting became the work of newly trained men. Older Swifts fell to the wayside, and women were almost completely eliminated. "Sources of competing cheap labor," claimed labor historian Jacob Loft, "were eliminated by mechanical compositors."[45]

The Stubbs Race

After 1890 racing returned to the shopfloor, occurring more or less spontaneously among handsetting old-timers. In 1888 and again in 1890, Chicago's trade magazine *Inland Printer* sponsored local contests. Both races matched Leo Monheimer and Peter Thienes, veteran competitors of the big championships of the mid-1880s. Both men had finished fifth in their biggest races, Monheimer at Chicago's national championship and Thienes at Philadelphia, and the results continued to rankle. In November 1888 the men tangled again, matched this time in a six-hour affair hosted by the *Inland Printer,* a race Monheimer won. Two years later, the persistent Thienes again challenged Monheimer, managing this time to win. As usual, both Monheimer and Thienes had migrated throughout the decade. Indeed, the nomadic Thienes had changed cities, moving from the *Times* of Philadelphia to Chicago's *Evening Mail,* Joseph Hudson's old paper. Monheimer shifted to the *Chicago Herald* from the *Daily News.* Although *Inland Printer* judged their efforts "creditable on the whole," neither man surpassed the records set by Joseph McCann and Alexander Duguid. Unlike the earlier public extravaganzas, these races played solely to printers, "between two and three hundred members of the union being present during the contest."[46]

Chicago's journeymen cheered and bet and generally enjoyed themselves at the Monheimer-Thienes matches. But races that two or three years earlier had been headline grabbers, overnight had become emblems of printing's good old days. On a similar shopfloor at the *New York Tribune,* a young printer named Lee Reilly was showing the trade how subsequently the task would get done. In the winter of 1893, Reilly became the first star of Linotype typesetting. During a week in late December, Reilly set and corrected 411,200 ems of nonpareil in six consecutive eight-hour nights. Reilly averaged 8,567 ems an hour, a week's work for a handsetting journeyman. The great Swift Alexander Duguid had once averaged 1,937 ems over a period of twenty-one hours, a blistering pace not ten years before. The trade journal *Union Printer* called Reilly's effort an "unparalleled feat," which put it mildly.[47]

A portrait of young Reilly suggested a fresh-faced earnest modernity. His photograph, reproduced by the new halftone technique, contrasted sharply with line engravings of the mustachioed Leo Monheimer. The contrasting renditions of the pair indicated a chasm that Reilly had negotiated but that Monheimer, himself only twenty-nine years old, had not. According to the *Union Printer*, it had been "a great many years since a record has either been made or broken in our business." The magazine seemed somehow to consider mid-1880s typeraces among printing's incunabula episodes. "McCann, Barnes, and Duguid," said the *Union Printer*, "have held the only records ever made that were considered worthy of a place on the pages of books devoted to records." But those records, "meritorious events under the old regime," paled before the deeds of young Reilly. His performance amounted to "a larger 'string' than any one man ever got up in the same length of time before," reported the magazine, "and when contrasted with the 'records' of hand composition, it leaves no doubt of the fact that typesetting machines have passed from the 'theory' stage to the stage of 'condition.'"[48]

Then, on October 3, 1899, thirteen years after the last of the great handsetting races, a journeyman printer named William Henry Stubbs simply obliterated the Swifts' records. That day in the composing room of Philadelphia's *Times*, Stubbs won $700 in bets and bragging rights to a new "world record" in speed composition. Stubbs, a Linotype operator at the *Baltimore Sun*, set 66,717 ems of corrected nonpareil type in five hours and thirty-three minutes and averaged 12,021 ems an hour, new records for Linotype speed and accuracy. The race, a scheduled seven-hour event, ended early when the challenger, William Duffy, trailing badly and fading, retired. At the end, Stubbs was running his machine at 93 lines per minute, or 15,000 ems an hour. This was astonishing speed, daunting to the *Philadelphia Inquirer*'s Duffy

and well in excess of the existing record of 10,800 ems, set four years earlier by a *St. Louis Post-Dispatch* Linotype operator.[49]
No one had called Lee Reilly a Swift. Six years later, in 1899, the prowess of William Henry Stubbs also became differently expressed. At the end of the century, when Stubbs demolished their old records, the *Inland Printer* credited the machine, not its operator. Speed tests, according to the magazine, were useful only insofar as they indicated the limits of the equipment, how fast a Linotype machine could go. Stubbs, after all, was faster by half than Lee Reilly, but the *Inland Printer* thought that "so far as the linotype is concerned its speed is far greater than any operator's ability to manipulate the keyboard." Stubbs was now fulfilling both management's hopes and its requirements, an equipment jockey running corporate machines as fast as they could go. And what of Joseph McCann? He had married Mary McDermott in 1891 and moved to Washington, D.C., to become a Government Printing Office proofreader.[50]

No "bracers," William Stubbs cautioned, no "nervines." Tonics and stimulants of every kind fell out of favor on the new shopfloor. A Linotype operator, according to the new record setter, must have a sound education and live the clean life. Alex Duguid would certainly have agreed. Greatly admired among shopmates, Duguid nonetheless remained a choirboy. Most printers paid lip service to purity and eagerly shared their workbreak bracers. Now, though, workplace deportment was changing as equipment demanded subtle new skills. In particular, Stubbs pointed out, a fast Linotype keyboard operator needs "nicety of touch." That little machine phrase contained a cultural profundity. According to the *Inland Printer,* the Linotype dictated sobriety. Besides, machines stayed put; Linotypes limited job mobility. Tramping ceased. Linotype work was straight matter, with none of the "heads, leads, and slugs" that fattened a compositor's piecework pay envelope. A lino operator was expected to average 5,000 ems an hour. The collegial, convivial 1,000-em day became a thing of the past.[51]

The New Culture of the Linotype

The Linotype was usefully fast. As important, however, it disciplined an industry. Early Linotypes at the *New York Tribune* were as faulty as any other contending machine. It would require huge financial commitment and a printing cartel led by *Tribune* editor Whitelaw Reid to see the Lino to fully successful acceptance. It also required a social revolution that accompanied the technological revolution.[52]

Typesetting machines most altered the rhythms of those compositors who worked on morning newspapers. These had been the Swifts, the night warriors, the men who worked through the small hours getting out the metropolitan dailies. They worked by the piece, and their wage depended entirely on the quantity of their work. They were the fastest, the best. Such men reported to work in the afternoon to distribute their previous day's standing type, to refill their cases and prepare them for the evening's work. At some point in the late afternoon, they broke for a period of "such recreation as was possible" before returning at seven o'clock for the start of composition. It "was often near dawn of the succeeding day before they reached their homes." With travel, it might be sixteen-hour workday. Life was a grind for an ordinary journeyman in the world of the Swifts.[53]

"The old system was demoralizing," said one printing foreman. "A man would come down at one or two o'clock to distribute his type, then go out for a time before commencing the night's work. . . . Now he leaves home just in time to land him in the office at seven o'clock, gets in his eight hours, and goes home." Veteran compositors on the eve of Philadelphia's 1899 Linotype match no longer found printers very interesting. Linotype work "is so routine in its character that the compositor is very much in the nature of a human clock, doing the same thing in the same way day in and day out." The machine, according to Hugh Wallace in the *Inland Printer*, "has done away with the chaff and chatter, discussions, friendly and otherwise, which were a feature of distribution time." There was more work to do, less time to do it, and more pressure to get it done. The Linotype made automatons; men themselves became machines. Compositors, he found, were taking up side interests. Printers who once read the *Inland Printer* for composing technique, now read it for tips on hobby photography. Working-class heroes had not been expected to have hobbies.[54]

The speed of the Linotype, although astounding, nonetheless had a limit. William Stubbs in fact could outrace his equipment. Indeed, an operator's ability to do that—to hang his machine—became a standard. The Mergenthaler Linotype Corporation in concert with an assortment of employing printers envisioned racing as a way to measure the competency of workmen. Five years earlier, New York's union printers had declared a minimum Linotype standard of 18,000 ems for an eight-hour day. In 1899, to the delight of print managers everywhere, Stubbs could approach that total in an hour. Prowess of this kind might soon replace journeyman status as a measure of competency. When operators subjected themselves to corporate speed tests, their skill pointed toward production quotas. To combat these trends, the union hobbled its own speed. When the International Typographical Union convened its annual meeting at Milwaukee in 1900, a new section was added to the ITU General Laws. "No member of the International Union," declared the union, "shall engage in speed contests, either by hand composition or on machines."[55]

By the time William Stubbs won at Philadelphia, journeyman compositors worked in a new printing world. After 1890 and the proliferation of typesetting machines, employers could no longer tolerate often willfully slow-paced piecework compositors. Wage work changed shopfloor rhythms formerly based on piecework rates of payment. Before mechanized typesetting, scores of union men had found ready work as composing room substitutes. Indeed, many "subs" scarcely looked for full-time jobs at all. Surrounded by scores of colleagues, men could dally at their tasks; among pieceworkers a leisurely pace hurt mainly the leisured. Machines, however, needed to stay busy, and their use demanded a dependable, sober, and generally reformed worker. The substitute compositor, formerly ubiquitous, vanished. "The three-weeks' spree has to be cut out," said the *Inland Printer.* Observance of the holiday printers called Saint Monday ceased.[56]

The pattern of power shifted as well. In 1886 Philadelphia's newspapers reported Alex Duguid driving down the stretch, working "almost like a piece of perfect machinery." Almost, it soon would seem, like William Stubbs. By 1899, by the time the Linotype made everyone fast, the Swifts were gone. At the end of the century, the typographers, men such as Daniel Berkeley Updike and William Morris and Bruce Rogers, were redefining workplace expertise, replacing speed and skill with taste and refinement. In the process, they shifted the locus of power and prestige from shopfloor and union to studio and salon. Honor in printing turned away from its workmen and toward design.[57]

8   Art and the Swifts: Shopfloor Design from Harpel to Rogers

LATE-NINETEENTH-CENTURY JOURNEYMEN PRINTERS represented what the printing historian Alexander Lawson calls "the ultimate triumph of the ordinary compositor." Before giving way as "typographic entrepreneurs," these artisans "could fully control at the frame the design of the printed word," and they dominated their trade. By contrast, typesetting workers to follow became Linotype operators, compositor-machinists who emerged amid a declining working-class culture of the Swifts.[1]

A second set of newcomers showed up on shopfloors, as well. These were stylists, people of aesthetic refinement, who directed the printing enterprise without performing its labor. The industry called them printer-architects, and they introduced new notions of effective and attractive typography.

In time, the trade would call this new printer a graphic

designer, and his emergence coincided with the decline of the typeracing Swift. Bruce Rogers became the best known of these. Rogers's arrival, in 1895, on the shopfloor of the Houghton Mifflin Company's Riverside Press signaled a gravitational shift in printing, as art and design specialists began supplanting plain compositors in the shopfloor hierarchy. But design itself didn't start with Bruce Rogers. Before Rogers there were "layout men," among them Oscar Harpel. *Harpel's Typograph* was the aesthetic bible of late-nineteenth-century compositors.

Harpel's Typograph

In 1870 two names reverberated within the composing rooms of American printers. Early that year, George "the Velocipede" Arensberg had galvanized the world of journeyman compositors by setting more than two thousand ems of type in a single hour, an astonishing milestone. Overnight, Arensberg's name became legendary among rank-and-file printers. Ten months later, in December, Oscar Harpel announced the imminent publication of his *Typograph,* a book of typographic design that was singular in the trade. In the quarter century following the Civil War, George Arensberg epitomized the skillful American shopfloor printer, and Oscar Harpel supplied his artistry.

Harpel's Typograph was a printing stylebook, something of a novelty among utilitarian printers. Harpel operated a Cincinnati job printing firm, and he printed the prosaic calling cards and raffle tickets of a commercial world. Job printing in Cincinnati, however, was special. Located on the Ohio River, the major waterway west, Cincinnati was a printing hub, at midcentury a market driven by the tickets, timetables, and advertising brochures of riverboat and railroad trade.

Cincinnati's jobbing trade emphasized eye-catching design and extensive color printing. Thomas Lynch's *Printer's Manual* of 1859 had preceded Harpel's stylebook, and in 1892 John Earhart's *Harmonizer* would follow it. Both men were Cincinnati printers, and each emphasized color work. The *Typograph* therefore fitted into an existing job-printing tradition. In fact, the *Typograph* did not address book printing considerations. In Cincinnati, Harpel's printing designs addressed different issues, and in this sense he might not be considered a graphic designer at all.[2]

In 1870 Oscar Harpel published *Harpel's Typograph,* a style authority that quickly became required reading among journeymen printers.
(From Oscar Harpel, *Poets and Poetry of Printerdom*)

Oscar Harpel, however, harbored ambitions. He wanted a comprehensive printing book and he wanted to sell a lot of them. The *Typograph* consequently incorporated at least three genres: it was a letterform specimen book, a printer's instruction manual, and a guide to operating a successful printing business. Previous publications, often house organs generated by equipment firms and type foundries, specialized and exemplified each of these separate focuses. Although it bore a kinship to these, the *Typograph* was never merely Harpel's way of drumming up trade. Books from job printing companies such as his ordinarily contained samples of typefaces available to customers, as well as examples of printing the firm felt it did well. Harpel certainly drew upon local Cincinnati specimens, but the *Typograph* expressed a typographic generality that aimed well beyond the Ohio Valley.

The *Typograph* opened with some detailed descriptions of printing practice. Harpel instructed his reader on subjects ranging from proofreader's marks to the manner of making printing

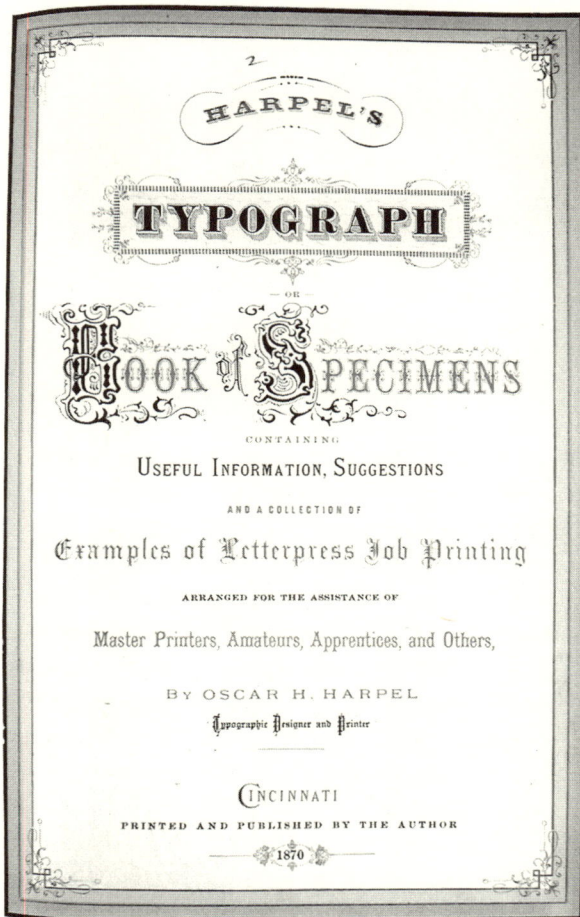

The title page of *Harpel's Typograph.*
(From Oscar Harpel, *Harpel's Typograph, or, Book of Specimens*)

press rollers. Many printers offered such advice, dating back to 1683 and the original of the genre, Joseph Moxon's *Mechanick Exercises,* and Harpel drew from the standard nineteenth-century canon: Lynch's *Printer's Manual* dated to 1859, John A. Wilson's *A Treatise on English Punctuation* was in its twenty-fifth edition, Thomas MacKellar's *The American Printer: A Manual of Typography* appeared in 1866. Like most such guidebooks, the *Typograph*'s advice expected shopfloor proprieties that real journeymen printers universally ignored. Harpel, for instance, counseled type distributors never to toss metal types back into the typecase—never "pepper" the boxes. Rather, they must "lightly lay the letters lengthwise in their respective boxes and with the faces toward you."[3]

Journeymen compositors, however, did not read the *Typograph* as an instruction manual. Almost no one distributed type Harpel's way, because it was far too slow, and most typesetters claimed it made the letters subsequently difficult to pick up. The average compositor read the *Typograph* for inspiration, to find out how they might turn artisanry into art. The *Typograph* was the first manual devoted to "artistic" shopfloor considerations that might rise above daily typeslinging. Oscar Harpel had handed the everyday journeyman a guidebook to typographic wizardry.

Harpel's typography was nothing if not eclectic. The late nineteenth century was printing's high tide of typographic display. Harpel embodied the aesthetic, and if he did not invent it, he was the prime publicist of a style. Rustics and gothics and fat-faced Egyptians—all coexisted in an eye-catching assortment of printing types that was emblematic of the age. Broadfaced text type, he thought, "harmonized" well with gothics and the lower case of "neat antiques." Any of these would, at the same time, contrast pleasingly with "sloping letters."[4]

The Harpel style dictated fancy rules, or linework, along with its typeface displays. The *Typograph* was filled with ornate scrolls. "Rulework is really the only branch of the printing business where a printer of artistic inclinations has an opportunity to show his good taste," claimed an *Inland Printer* contributor. Outfitted with a modest kit of tools, the ordinary journeyman could follow any flight of fancy. Virtually all print shops were equipped with a mitering machine, rule cutters, curving machines and a vise, said the layout artist "A. R. A." in *Inland Printer,* "so that all that is necessary for a printer to supply himself with is about three good files, tweezers, knife, small plyers, an old key or a saw set (which I find the best tools for kinking or waving rule)." Compositors could be artists: "we do not have to rely entirely upon the products of the typefoundry to enable us to ornament our work." The result was a syncopated combination of rattails and swirls that, along with typography, further defined the age.[5]

Custodians of taste in later generations would tear their hair over this ornamentation, which they considered a vulgar mess. The Harpel style bespoke an egalitarian century. Its art attended commerce; its artists were tradesmen compositors. The combination made the product a preeminently democratic one. Printers wrestled with the implications of this. Better than most observers, they understood a thin line between "good" printers and bad ones, and they could recognize results that matched the difference. Customers, however, wanted fancy printing, and their demands often compromised a printing firm's standards.[6]

Printers such as Oscar Harpel declared a printed piece ugly in one of two ways. Technically, it might be badly printed—overinked, possibly, or its words irregularly spaced. Conversely, its design elements, however carefully chosen, might offend the eye. Harpel found technically inferior printing repellent—that went without saying. Defects of design, however, were matters of taste or, in printing shops, negotiation. Most printers considered artful printing to be printing of great adornment. Immoderate use of curlicues and devices likely was unfortunate, but Harpel considered unprofitable labor a far graver sin. Ornate printing was simply hard work, and he thought a printer should avoid it "unless it is amply paid for." Harpel resisted "useless composition" that incorporated "elaborate border and flourish work, and curving type lines and rules into a bad imitation of engraving." Such printing was neither bad nor wrong, and in skillful hands it was, in fact, splendid. Generally, it wasted a workman's time. It was a "nuisance and a positive bar to the profitable prosecution of a job."[7]

Harpel thought gifted artists made art. While his *Typograph* contained model design work, Harpel very nearly told everyday compositors that most of them might just as well forget emulating it. Far too many attempts at shopfloor artistry necessarily resulted in imperfection. Good design depended entirely on the compositor. If that person was "artistic," beauty prevailed, but "for ordinary purposes," the talents and tools of everyday journeymen were "extremely unadaptable as well as troublesome." Still, Harpel had published a book on splendid design, and his comments served to enhance that art, not condemn it. Find a good printer, he said, and pay him. Harpel advocated "the most elegant and *artistic* effects that can be produced, *if it is paid for.*"[8]

The publication was an event. In September 1870, *Printers' Circular* previewed the "forthcoming" *Typograph*. Judging from the "beauty of the specimen sheets," the trade magazine promised a surefire winner. The *Typograph* offered "practical advice upon matters of special interest to the craft, and information which has been the result of much experience in the many details of the profession, as well as of careful thought upon its acquirements." Harpel would go beyond normal "generalities" of the trade to the "special details which have been held among the secrets of the profession." He had used his own facilities, said Harpel, but he had been careful to consult "others of our most successful typographers." The *Typograph* would be a universal shopfloor manual, a textbook to the trade.[9]

Oscar Harpel promised this much and more. He wanted the *Typograph* to be a coffee-table book. He would define an entire nation's aesthetics, not just those of its printing shops. In a prepublication advertising campaign, Harpel recommended the *Typograph* as "an ornament to the centre-table." It was "an exhibit to the general public," Harpel said, and contained the "latest information and the freshest ideas" in typography. The book would be of interest to "all who are in any way interested in the progress of Typography."[10]

Unhappily, Harpel encountered a hitch. "I have met with quite a misfortune," Harpel informed the *Printers' Circular*, "just as my book was almost completed, and the main bulk of it in the binder's hands." Cincinnati had suffered a late autumn downpour and the bindery had leaked. Consequently, four eight-page signatures of the *Typograph* were ruined "by rain that beat upon them." Harpel had to reprint those sheets, and worse, their forms required re-setting, as well. This was "pretty bad," Harpel reported, "as several of the pages were very troublesome." He had printed one of the signatures in five colors.[11]

The calamity delayed distribution of a completed *Typograph* for a month and a half. In February, however, *Printers' Circular* reported delivery, and the book, "which we have already applauded on trust," the trade paper remarked, had "justified all our praises." The *Typograph* was indeed a picture book, filled with specimens of stationery letterhead, business cards, advertising display, and the rest of the nineteenth century's ephemera. "To printers, so fine a collection of specimens of job work will be exceedingly welcome," sang *Printers' Circular*, "and to those interested in the art, the book will present a striking proof of the immense variety, as well as the remarkable excellence, of American typography."[12]

Picking favorites in such an exceptional volume seemed "in-vidious," *Printers' Circular* thought, but "Mr. Stillman's picture of the returning dove, executed with a ruling-machine, must attract especial consideration as a triumphant application of machinery to art." Moreover, Oscar Harpel's own page of ornamental colored borders was "exceedingly tasteful and creditable." The volume was "handsomely bound in an appropriate style." Overall, declared the journal, *Harpel's Typograph* was "fully entitled to the distinction of its aristocratic red edges.[13]

Oscar Harpel hoped for a best-seller. He wanted "to inaugu-rate a better understanding of the tasteful utility as well as artis-tic scope of typography in the present day." He nonetheless tar-geted the journeyman printer, offering a "practical handbook and guide," best for novices, but good for everyone in the trade. A *Ty-pograph* nearby was an ideal way for a printing manager to illustrate what he wants of his workmen. Whether from "lack of ability or carelessness in arrangement," ordinary printers became trapped in their substandard designs. By using the *Typograph,* good craftsmen might encourage "bungling workmen." Together, the printer "culls the best of it, and distances his weaker rival in the advance to financial success. . . . All engaged in the business of printing should take advantage of every avenue leading to better information and practice in its accomplishment, if they would reach the higher results of this progressive art."[14]

It had cost Harpel a year of "unremitting labor and superintendence" to hatch his book. He had used "the choicest and latest productions of the foundries" in its reproductions. He printed its 300 pages on special high-grade paper. He included sections of infolded sheets. He spared no embellishment. To culminate his effort, Harpel offered a special limited edition. He printed 250 copies of the *Typograph* on "tinted paper," and he bound the edition in varieties of calfskin and Turkey morocco antique. The limited edition fetched $10.50. The price scarcely covered it, sighed a weary Harpel. "The expense of the *Typograph* has been greater than was at first anticipated," he said in his preface. A second edition was "very doubtful."[15]

Art and the Journeyman Compositor

The Harpel "look" represented an industry standard. Oscar Harpel called himself a "typographic designer and printer," but in his equation, printing skills subsumed artistry. Neither Harpel nor his readership readily distinguished high art from routine design, which at the century's end was a normal distinction for a different typographical generation. Among artisans, the *Typograph* spoke to journeymen printers who equated excellent workmanship with beauty. It allowed compositors to enlarge their authority as professionals of the printed page.[16]

The *Typograph* itself easily joined a handful of other books as an essential literature of America's printers. In 1870, the year the *Typograph* appeared, Robert Menamin published Luther Ringwalt's authoritative *Encyclopedia of Printing.* Theodore L. DeVinne's

Printers Price List, an effort to rationalize printing's costs, came out at the same time. Printers recognized each as an essential addition to the libraries of the trade. *Proof-Sheet,* for instance, a trade paper and specimen page from the Philadelphia type founding firm of Collins and M'Leester, included Harpel's *Typograph* in its list of currently available printing books, along with DeVinne's book and Ringwalt's encyclopedia. In most lists, they joined John Wilson's *Treatise of Punctuation* and Thomas MacKellar's *American Printer* as the requisite bibliography of the industry. Before the 1883 introduction of *Inland Printer,* Menamin's trade journal, *Printers' Circular,* was the representative voice of America's working printers. Its glowing recommendation of the *Typograph* ensured the attention of an industry, and from its pages Editor Menamin offered a list identical to that of Collins and M'Leester's *Proof-Sheet.* The *Typograph* had joined the canon of the trade.[17]

The book also became a typeracing prize, no better gauge of stature within the ranks. In 1874 a Washington, D.C., Swift named W. W. McCollum took home the *Typograph* for finishing third in a race hosted by the Washington *Republican.* It was an apt award for a competitor specially commended for clean proofs of "superior excellence."[18]

The "Harpel approach" defined an industrywide typographic trend, one to which type suppliers eagerly contributed. In April 1886, *Inland Printer* called the attention of the industry to "recently concluded arrangements with the leading typefounders in the United States, by which their latest productions will appear monthly in our pages." Type foundry catalogs thereupon offered brass rules of every kind, endless assortments of dingbats, and rule-bending devices to assist the creative spirit. "Employers who desire to keep up with the times," suggested *Inland Printer,* should take note. If they did not, their employees certainly would. So encouraged, remarked the printing historian Alexander Lawson, "what was to hold back an itchy-fingered comp as he examined the master's gorgeous examples, page after page?" The Harpel model "fed the creative urge of compositors bored with sticking just nonpareil or brevier."[19]

The typographic result became a wonderfully exotic printed page. A profusion of brass rules and typographic ornaments accompanied display typefaces of myriad designs, all of it driven by a shopfloor democracy of journeymen compositors. Oscar Harpel had set loose the working typo with complete artistic freedom at his case, at least from the viewpoint of his peers. "Go into any job office, large or small, and you will find printers with some pretensions as to rulework," claimed the *Inland Printer,* "even in the newspaper offices can be found the individual who, in a modest way, will resort to some original and appropriate design in rule when he gets the opportunity."[20]

Launched in October 1883, *Inland Printer* proved popular throughout the industry and subsequently provided this artistic vision its professional showcase. *Inland Printer,* however, was never an art magazine. Another journal freshly hatched in 1883, *Art Age,* spoke to printers seeking especially high aesthetic standards. But from the start *Inland Printer* billed itself "an operative journal, conducted by workmen." Early editions of the magazine welcomed particularly well-composed printing specimens. Soon its pages featured full-page samples of far-flung shopfloor artistry. The magazine offered cash prizes—originally fifteen dollars; in time twenty-five dollars—for the best of these submissions, usually awarded quarterly. A five-member awards committee judged the recently published examples of all submitted specimens and selected the winners.[21]

From its inception, the editors of *Inland Printer* provided commercial printing a stylistic forum missing in other printing journals. In the view of the magazine's awards committee, fine printing combined five elements. Conceptually, a design's eye-catching originality counted for a great deal. At the same time, printing was a useful art, and "practicability" mattered. The committee also kept a sharp eye on a pair of craft considerations. Printing was preeminently grid work, straight lines at right angles. The introduction of curved rules and slanted lines established difficulty as they introduced novel designs. Curves and joints therefore became the committee's third and fourth areas of judgment: a prizewinner's

curved rules ought to be impeccably symmetrical, and those
mitered rules should join perfectly. *Inland Printer*'s fifth consideration, general excellence, thus mirrored an industry's commitment to an end-of-century rule-bending craze. Prizewinners featured wildly radiating rules and snazzy borders over classically
proportioned, elegantly spare typography.[22]

Samples of typographic wizardry flowed into the *Inland Printer*
from all across the nation. M. F. Dougherty, a compositor at

The Chicagoan A. R. Allexon repeatedly won *Inland Printer*'s design
competitions with entries such as this.
(From *Inland Printer*)

Chicago's J. M. W. Jones Printing Company, offered original designs and generally fine presentation. In March 1886 the awards committee announced that his advertising and letterhead work for the comedians Harrison and Gourlay had won first prize. F. Russell of New York City became a winner, as did Harry DeWitt of Chicago. George Moore of Beverly, Massachusetts; James Hough of Guelph, Ontario; A. V. Haight of Poughkeepsie, New York; and James Shier of Denver all won design prizes.[23]

Inland Printer surely intended this regional outreach and welcomed diverse sources. Indeed, by autumn 1886 the repeatedly offered excellence of Chicago's A. R. Allexon was beginning to vex the awards committee. Although far less publicized than a racehorse Swift, Allexon possessed skills at display composition that made him their fine art counterpart. A compositor at the Chicago job printing company of Shepard and Johnson, Allexon had won four times, and the committee suggested "he should be debarred from participating."[24]

Over the years the production values of *Inland Printer* itself changed. Those standards had always been high, of course, especially compared to older magazines such as *Printers' Circular* or house organs like *Typographic Messenger* or the *Proof-Sheet.* The predecessors of *Inland Printer* offered straightforward columns of text, an occasional engraving, minimal coloration, and generally pedestrian design. *Inland Printer* quickly incorporated industry innovations ranging from halftone reproduction of photographs to serially unique covers, many of them by the young illustrator Will Bradley. It also launched a further competition among compositors. By 1890 the magazine was awarding a range of medals worth up to $100 for the preceding year's best multicolored submissions.[25]

By the 1890s, giddy with the possibilities of shopfloor design, many competitors had ceased setting type altogether. Fred B. Crewe's 1890 competition specimen was a stag's head composed entirely of bent brass rules and bits of metal from the sorts case. Fred Crewe worked at the job printing office of the *New York World,* the same organization that four years earlier had been home to the acclaimed Swift William Barnes. They may have been

Fred B. Crewe's 1890 competition specimen was a stag's head composed entirely of bent brass rules and bits of metal from the sorts case. (From *Inland Printer*)

shopmates, Crewe and Barnes, and possibly friends, but their skills could not have differed more widely. Barnes once outperformed a field of typeracing competitors while setting type blindfolded, listening to dictated copy, and making but three mistakes in the process. Crewe's meticulous stag's head and Barnes's immaculate blindfold text were the extremes of a late-nineteenth-century journeyman's craft. Speed and accuracy defined everything Barnes attempted. To Barnes, taking time to bend rules into the likeness of a deer must have seemed insane.

Layout Men

Exemplified by cocksure Swifts, late-nineteenth-century American printers fairly reveled in their craft. Journeymen displayed great skill, and through their unions, many sensed a small

[BLINDFOLD WORK.]
ONE HOUR AND A HALF.—[1,635 EMS.]

By WILLIAM C. BARNES, March 27, 1886, Philadelphia National Tournament, nonpareil, solid, 17⅜ ems to lower-case alphabet, 28 ems wide, no break-line, full-sized cases, emptying his own sticks; conditions of spacing, National Rules. (The copy was dictated by Mr. Thienes, one of the contestants, and constitutes a portion of Barnes' total score in the tournament; the proof contained but seven errors, which are allowed to remain in this reprint):

distance before us, and neither very thickly wooded nor very bushy; but no bear was to be seen, although our eye could penetrate the woods for at least two hundred yards. After the first disappointing glance around we thought bruin might have mounted a tree, but such was not the case, as on looking everywhere nothing could be seen of his black body, and we were obliged to bonclude that he had run out of sight in the brief space of time we occupied in ascending the little bank. As we were once standing at the foot of a large sycamore tree on the borders of a long and deep pond, on the edge of which, in our rear, there was a thick and extensive cane-brake, we heard a rushing, roaring noise, as if some heavy animal was bearing down and passing rapidly through the canes directly towards us. We were not kept long in suspedse, for in an instant or two a large bear dashed out of the dense cane, and plunging into the pond without having even seen us, made off with considerable speed through the water towards the other shore. Having only bird-shot in our gun we did not think it worth while to call

his attention to us by firing at him, but turned to the cane-brake, expecting to hear either dogs or men approaching shortly. No further noise could be heard, however, and the surrounding woods were as still as before this adventure. We supposed the bear had been started at some distance, and that his pursuers, not being able to follow him through the almost impenetrable canes, had given up the hunt. Being one night sleeping in the house of a friend, who was a planter in the state of Louisiana, we were awakened by a fervant bearing a light, who gave us a note which he said his master had just received. We found it to be a communication from a neighbor, requesting our host and ourself to join him as soon as possible and assist in killing some bears at that momeno engaged in destroying his corn. We were not long in dressing, and on entering the parlor found our friend equipped. The overseer's horn was heard calling up the negroes, some were already saddling our horses, whilst others were gathering all the cur-dogs of the plantation. All was bustle. Before half an hour had elapsed four stout negro men, armed with axes and knives, and mounted on strong nags, were following us at a round gallop through the woods, as we made directlp for the neighbor's plantation. The night was none of the most favorable, a drizzling rain rendering the atmosphere thick and rather sultry; but as we were well acquainted with the course, we soon reached the house, where the owner was waiting our arrival. There were now three of us armed with guns, half a dozen servants and a good pack of dogs

William C. Barnes made only seven mistakes setting this passage at competition speed, but his staggering skill was out-of-date.
(From *A Collation of Facts Relative to Fast Typesetting*, New York: Concord Cooperative Printing Company, 1887)

but meaningful autonomy. They had wondrous new equipment. Typesetting machines constituted a mixed blessing, of course, but the type foundries were turning out the designs and devices—curved rules, splattered dewdrops, scrollwork borders—that once compositors themselves devised. Those same foundries provided choices from among myriad typefaces. The state of their art encouraged an entire trade in fantastic and ornate display. Spokespersons for the arts and crafts movement hated the hectic style and declared most printers tasteless or blind.[26]

They were only partly right. Good taste in printing soon would be defined in ways other than those of journeymen printers. Those journeymen, however, were nothing if not alive to the artistic nature of their craft. Strangely, amid their successes, printers constantly fretted about the decline in aesthetic standards and repeatedly condemned printing's "travesty on good taste." Paradoxically, tasteful printing was not at the heart of their concern. Tawdry workmanship was what they feared and loathed. Having condemned stylistic barbarity, printers proceeded to reward notably well-done examples of precisely that bad taste.[27]

Late-nineteenth-century printers thought they were upholding standards, not degenerating. They understood that compositors once bent their own rules and fashioned their own displays because they had to. By the 1880s, however, things had "entirely changed." Type foundries were more than happy to sell printers what they once fashioned for themselves. What followed, according to *Inland Printer*, was an unschooled misuse of artistic devices that too easily came to hand, a "recklessness" that led to an "endless profusion" of typographic gadgetry. Used "promiscuously," these designs were "unmeaning and offensive to good taste."[28]

"To produce a good job does not necessarily mean to besmear it with a lot of hieroglyphical nothings, which have no meaning or none of the attributes of an ornament, just because there is room for them," commented a writer in the new journal *Artist Printer*. "The truly artistic printer is the one who possesses a natural taste for harmony, and who can make his white spaces and margins as effective as his type lines or his borders." Printers knew this; they understood expertise. After all, they had honed their skills through years of applied training. Likely, more of the same would make them better printers. Trade journals such as *Inland Printer* urged journeymen to learn design. "The man who can not only set up a job, but who can also design one, is the *coming man* in the letterpress business."[29]

If ordinary compositors expected to retain autonomy at their cases, haste was of the essence. Already, the industry was being bidden to make distinctions between the designer of the printed piece and the compositor who would execute that design. "The design function as far as it relates to the composing room is planned to be in the hands of one man," declared an expert in composing room management. The "layout man" formulates the copy for the job "so completely that the man who sets the type and makes it up can do his work in but one possible way." Typography was well on its way out the shopfloor door.[30]

This introduced an irony. Book compositors at the end of the century produced books that would become objects of highest art, but in so doing these workers relinquished all claims to the shape of their pages. "Absolutely nothing," experts told composing room managers, "is left to the discretion of the compositor." Other people would make the design decisions.[31]

Graphic Designers

In 1895 Riverside Press in Cambridge, Massachusetts, hired a youthful typographic artist named Bruce Rogers. In time Rogers became the best in his business, and Houghton Mifflin's book designs gained world renown. Rogers's typeface designs, notably Centaur, became equally famous throughout the English-speaking world. He was the first "graphic designer."[32]

In the mid-1890s, however, he was not merely new on the Riverside shopfloor, he was a new kind of printer. Not yet called graphic design, the modernized skills, sensibility, and sophistication Rogers brought to Riverside vastly extended the domain of the shopfloor's layout men. More than these, Rogers seemed to be a new sort of person, an employee to be sure, but a professional amid wage earners. In college at Purdue University, Rogers had studied art, not printing. He needed diagrams to find his way around a typecase; he could neither ink a press nor dampen its paper. George H. Mifflin's new printer possessed no production skills whatever.[33]

Turned loose on the shopfloor, Rogers seemed like an intruder. Riverside Press, in many ways a model book printing plant, was notable for its great size. In the 1880s and 1890s, its composing room employed between forty and fifty men, perhaps fifteen women, and a half dozen apprentices. In the summer and fall of 1883, Riverside employed twenty proofreaders. Thirty press operators worked in Riverside's pressroom, assisted by three dozen press feeders and six apprentices. Such a shopfloor was short on aesthetes, particularly those devoid of job skills, and it doubtless unsettled the young Rogers.[34]

George Mifflin, however, had hired Rogers to design books, not produce them. In 1900 Mifflin and his typographer introduced a new line of Houghton Mifflin books, exquisitely rendered limited editions called the Riverside Press Editions. The project would establish Rogers's reputation. The first of these, the *Sonnets and Madrigals of Michelangelo* and the second, Omar Khayam's *Rubaiyat*, represented Rogers's beginning efforts at "direct supervision of type composition, presswork, and binding." Actually, Rogers began work on the *Rubaiyat* first. The tale was dependably popular, a warhorse of excellence, a standard publication of "fine" printing at the time. Production crawled, however, as bottlenecks quickly developed in the composing room. For the *Rubaiyat,* Rogers had turned up a small quantity of a typeface called Brimmer, "a vigorous, transitional face that he found in a corner of the Riverside composing room." Riverside compositors had only enough Brimmer to set four pages at a time. Workmen set those four pages, electroplated them, distributed the type, and began again.[35]

Many of those printers found Rogers's "fancy jobs" too precious for the shopfloor. Composing office and pressroom personnel treated him as a pariah, and he left his own small workspace with trepidation. Shopfloor colleagues complained of his snail's pace and that he used "homeopathic fonts of type" nonetheless in demand elsewhere. For his part, Rogers "disliked intensely" the smell of printing ink and benzine, and he hated the noise of the presses. Their constant "double pneumonia, double pneumonia, double pneumonia" drove him crazy.[36]

Doubtless Rogers also detested the dull routine of setting type. The smallness of daily composing room decisionmaking—minute matters of thin spaces, line breaks, and punctuation—somehow fell beneath him. As an art director, however, an overseer, Rogers surely monitored those choices and vetoed those decisions. He was too closely attentive to detail to do otherwise. Lacking what he felt was a suitable typeface for *Geofroy Tory* incarnated as a Riverside Press Edition, Rogers proceeded to invent a font that came to be called Riverside Caslon. He began with foundry Caslon as a base, combining twelve-point capitals with fourteen-point lower-case characters. Rogers then worked on every letter in the font with a graver, slightly wearing at the type in order to increase its depth of color. He reduced the fit of the type as well, in order to bring the characters closer together. Riverside electrotypers then made matrices of the proofed characters from which Monotype typecasters produced individual types for hand composition. Care of this kind was not the behavior of a person who handed manuscripts to a shopfloor compositor, worthy artisan, and hoped for the best.[37]

With one or two exceptions, Rogers found shopfloor employees at Riverside tolerable, little different from those in other job offices. At Riverside Rogers did not have "the mechanical difficulties of bookmaking to contend with personally." Generally, he considered the Houghton Mifflin firm "one of the ultra-conservative kind and with the exception of Mr. Mifflin, the senior partner, not in the least bookish." Happily, Mifflin backed Rogers's projects: "it is only by his approval that I am allowed to have full swing in these special editions." According to Rogers, nobody at Riverside questioned the details of his designs. Among compositors or pressmen, of course, those details could be production nightmares. Still, shopfloor personnel apparently never challenged Rogers's projects. The manufacture of his books elicited "apathy," never mutiny. "The two or three workmen I have (not always the same ones) are interested enough usually," said Rogers, "but they are not under my direct control, and the foremen generally consider the whole scheme foolish and a mere fad." Nonetheless, "it requires my closest supervision to have the composition and printing as well done as it is." Rogers, it seemed, had everything he needed at Riverside except "enthusiasm."[38]

Still, the shopfloor was no place for Rogers. By 1903 Riverside Press had renovated a small storage outbuilding and turned it into a design studio. Called the "Studio," Rogers's new workspace came equipped with "the elder pressman Dan Sullivan," and together they set about making more Riverside Press Editions. By 1903 Riverside Press had installed typesetting equipment, originally Thorne machines, but "the main part of the composition is done by hand." Riverside remodeled and refitted Rogers's old building on the river bank for the purpose. The Studio exuded an antique feel: large, heavily mullioned windows, brick walls, open-timbered roof. The pre-machine feel of Rogers's "working quarters" was matched by an old-fashioned approach to the entire process. "The only machines are the heavy hand presses upon which occasional volumes of the Riverside Press Edition are printed, for many of these books are printed wholly by hand, and often they are printed directly from the types, and not from electrotype plates." The special workshop gave Rogers "larger opportunities for investigation and experiment."[39]

This was a long way from the world of the Swifts. During the closing third of the nineteenth century, those artisans had lost control of their craft. A short ten years separated the typeracing debut of Joseph McCann and the day Bruce Rogers found work at the Riverside Press. New printers such as Rogers, Updike, Goudy, and Dwiggins retrieved classic design for American typography. By the turn of the century, a change had occurred that was unthinkable in George Arensberg's day. Artists in graphic design were telling shopfloor compositors how to do their work.

9 The Death of a Velocipede

ON SEPTEMBER 15, 1884, A PRINTER NAMED WILLIAM
Thompson died. He had been foreman of the ticket room of
Chicago's J. M. W. Jones Printing Company. Born in Canada,
Thompson had migrated south to work for the Chicago firm of
Cameron and Amberg. After a "number of years," he left the Mid-
west to join a brother in Denver. In time his brother died, and
Thompson returned to Chicago, where he found work with the
Jones company, a well-established job printing firm. Thompson
held his job for the rest of his working life, until early 1884, "when
failing health compelled him to relinquish his trust." Thompson
went again to Denver, hoping that city's climate might help, "but
the fell disease, consumption, had fastened its fangs too certainly
to be thus shaken off." He returned once more to Chicago, home,
to die. "His many noble characteristics of head and heart," the

trade journal *Inland Printer* reported, "endeared him to a large circle of acquaintances, by whom his loss is deeply deplored." So ended, it would seem, a long and busy life. Thompson was thirty years old.[1]

Printing lives were short. Almost everything we know of the endings of those nineteenth-century lives is statistical. Few obituaries survive. Typographical unions typically kept mortality data throughout the last half of the nineteenth century. The figures indicated that printers aged more rapidly than other Americans, and they died sooner. Presumably, elite compositors, those whose accomplishments found fame, shared the fate of their colleagues.[2]

A journeyman printer's world in 1870, the world of the Swift, was different from that world in 1900. "Formerly," occupational disease expert Alice Hamilton reported in 1917, "it was taken for granted that printing should be for the most part carried on in small, low, dark, crowded rooms, with dust-encrusted floors, dim windows never opened, and furniture covered with the accumulated dust of years." An 1868 printing plant could be remarkably toxic even before journeymen contributed their own unhealthy habits. That malodorous world was rapidly passing by the turn of the century, and the Swifts were already gone. George Arensberg died in the summer of 1886, seven short months after watching Joseph McCann and William Barnes wage war on his legend. The Velocipede died as he had lived, in the world of Swifts.[3]

The Shopfloor Deathtrip

"Considering the high class of labor employed in this trade," a U.S. Department of Labor study reported, which required decent education, "especially among hand compositors," the provisions for cleanliness in most printing plants were "surprisingly inadequate, sometimes really wretchedly neglected and dirty." Thirty years before this report, a printing shopfloor would simply have assaulted the senses. The smell, especially, would have been distinctive past modern comprehension. All printers recommended a well-ventilated workplace, but despite such agreement, shopfloor ventilation was often bad. Throughout the nineteenth century, compositors worked under harsh gaslight, or perhaps through the vapors of whale oil or kerosene. Late in the nineteenth century, printers thought "good old-fashioned oil" provided the best lighting (newfangled electricity, which tended to pulsate, was the worst). Gaslight was hot and bright, but specific. Shadows existed everywhere. Compositors feared eyestrain and liked plentiful light, arranged to reduce glare. A gaslamp, however, might consume the oxygen of five men, so by a midwinter dawn, composing rooms were miasmic.[4]

Toilets were notably breathtaking. Sanitation measures therein contended with printshop standards born of an era of inking balls, the suppleness of which derived from nightly urine soaks. Ink balls were gone by midcentury, but the single and universal water closet towel remained, standing, propped like a board. Horse manure made loading docks and the interior courtyards of the larger firms smell like barnyards. Throughout the shop, workers caught whiffs of benzine, of ink, of the body odor of many men, of cigars, of spittoons, of missed spittoons, spilled beer, flatulence. As went the wisdom of the trade, compositors should wash their hands regularly and bathe often, surely once a week. The workplace ought to be kept "comfortably warm," sixty degrees in winter—at least. Still, whatever the sources of heat and light, a printing establishment might be as dim as an opium den. It was a male sanctuary, a place of low comedy, often scatological.[5]

Isolated, any of this might have been merely offensive. But printers, of course, died in these conditions, on average almost a decade faster than the rest of the population. According to the records of the New York Typographical Society, a sick benefit association that dated to 1818, a printer in 1850 was 28 years old when he died. By 1868 printers lived to be 35. Twenty-five years later, printshop lives lasted 38.78 years. In 1905 the International Typographical Union paid death benefits for 567 members, who had died at an average age of 46.48 years. By 1920 printers were living to be slightly older than 53.[6]

By modern standards most thirty-year-old printers resembled middle-aged men. In 1886, when they struggled for national championships, the Swifts Joseph McCann and Alexander Duguid were twenty-nine years old, and it is easy to assume they were youngsters at the case. Approaching thirty, however, McCann and Duguid, and for that matter the Chicagoan William Thompson, had worked half their lives. Other examples abound. In 1886, in an Albany, New York, printing shop, five out of six compositors were in their early- to mid-30s. All had at least fifteen years of experience; each had established a solid career. Thirty-year-old Thomas Willard had begun working when he was thirteen, and despite being a seventeen-year veteran, he remained the firm's youngster. Charles H. Staats had been on the job for twenty-five years and was only thirty-six.[7]

If printing lives were short, they were shortest among big city Swifts. These were the nighttime compositors, fast and accurate under the deadline pressure of morning newspapers. "The poor health and short life of night-workers are proverbial," declared the *Inland Printer* in 1886. Heroic journeymen all, Swifts nonetheless paid a terrible price. In the view of one commentator, theirs was a world of "hollow-chested, dyspeptic, consumptive-looking men," sick in the manner one "so often finds in the newspaper offices of our large cities." Skilled as he might be, the night compositor usually complained of being "all broke up" as he "stripped himself for one more night's agony under the hot gaslight of the composing room of one of our great morning papers."[8]

Compositors spent their days and nights leaning over typecases, breathing lead dust under oxygen-robbing gaslights. The chronic illnesses of lead poisoning were therefore constant shopfloor threats, and they offered a variety of symptoms. At the very least, compositors complained of "a dull, heavy, languid feeling." The digestive systems of victims malfunctioned. Workers became pallid. Afflicted persons weakened generally, but earliest in the fingers, hands, and wrist. This led to a condition called "wrist drop" or "hang wrist" that made an individual useless for work. Weakness then spread from the shoulders and legs to encompass the whole body, a plight known in the trade as "printer's paralysis."[9]

Printers often spoke of "lead colic," a particular reaction to lead poisoning that produced acute abdominal pain and rugged constipation. Sufferers might develop a tell-tale bluish "lead line" on the gums. If he inhaled enough lead dust, a compositor might develop a chronic lung disorder. In time, brain cells thus starved of oxygen produced dementia.[10]

But printers usually succumbed to respiratory disorders, not mental derangement. Most often, they died not of lead poisoning but of tuberculosis, the disease they knew as "consumption."[11] This led to some confusion among health researchers. The obvious symptoms of lead poisoning—colic, convulsions, lead-lined gums—were all "very rare" on the shopfloor. "No one," the U.S. Department of Labor reported, "claims that acute lead poisoning is common among printers." Nonetheless, printers knew they worked in uniquely dirty places. Gaslight fumes or those from solvents such as benzine were unhealthy, and everyone reckoned lead poisoning somehow at the bottom of printing's high death rate. Tuberculosis, however, was a contagious disease, spread when a healthy individual inhaled the tubercle bacilli of an afflicted shopmate. Tuberculosis victims transmitted their disease by coughing, sneezing, or spitting. Pulmonary tuberculosis, a gradual weakening of the respiratory function, was the most common print shop form.[12]

The hacking cough and wheezing a compositor called "catarrh," then, might be a product of either toxic lead or the tubercle bacillus. No two physicians would agree on the sources of such symptoms. In either case, however, printing firms found few remedies beyond better ventilation. Throughout the late nineteenth century, trade publications urged compositors to wash more frequently, especially their hands. They also told journeymen to stop sticking pieces of type in their mouths, a remarkably difficult habit to break. Compositors often ate on the job, a practice *Inland Printer* deplored. "A hurried stand-up meal is frequently taken in offices where men nearly always work at high pressure," observed the journal. Compositors should stop the habit because it was "next to impossible to prevent the type-dirt getting into the system." Beyond these suggestions, there was little anyone could do to avoid the toxic effects of handling metal type.[13]

Tuberculosis was a contagion that could be tracked not solely to the metals requisite to the trade, but also to moral deficiencies on the parts of journeymen. By the turn of the century, therefore, the health committee of New York City's Local No. 6 of the International Typographical Union could claim that the low incidence of colic—two cases in a sampling of 203 compositors—pointed to a waning toxic metal threat. According to the group's secretary, "no other signs or symptoms were found that would suggest the possibility of lead poisoning."[14]

However, Local No. 6's investigation turned up thirty cases of tuberculosis itself, thirty more of pleurisy, and twelve cases of emphysema or "suspected" tuberculosis. Fully a quarter of those printers studied suffered from some form of "catarrh," an irritation of the mucous membranes of respiratory passageways. By dismissing the relevance of lead dust to this problem, by understanding "colic" to be lead poisoning's sole configuration, turn of the century occupational authorities managed to call composition a "wholesome" job. By printing standards, the two cases of colic ranked lead poisoning with acne in its incidence as less threatening than hemorrhoids.[15]

Remedies

Respiratory diseases among compositors seemed part of the landscape. Cures, even effective treatment, eluded most physicians. Printshop lungs full of lead dust seemed as unavoidable as a coal miner's black lung. Physicians could not cure lead colic. Doctors sent afflicted workers to bed "at once." Rest and good diet was the treatment—and a poultice of linseed meal laced with thirty drops of laudanum. It went on the abdomen.[16]

Be it stomach cramps or shortness of breath, printers tended to address issues of personal hygiene and the need to change habits. "To prevent tuberculosis you will have to urge in and out of season temperance in spitting, temperance in drinking, and cleanliness, as well as shorter hours and ventilation," said Paul Kennaday on behalf of New York's Committee for the Prevention of Tuberculosis. Printers themselves quickly isolated spittoons, as ubiquitous as they were noisome, as certain sources of any ailment. All parties called for the "maintenance of cuspidors."[17]

To many, a shorter workday was an obvious answer, a reform the industry as a whole might sponsor. Journeymen themselves thought that shorter working hours lengthened their lives. Fewer hours spent in a bad environment surely helped. Predictably, printing managers resisted work-curtailment measures until 1906, the year legislation created the eight-hour workday. That legislation came after an ardent half-century's struggle, and after piecework labor had long since given way to the time clock and the hourly wage. Boston compositors in 1848 worked twelve hours a day, seven days a week. They toiled in foul, smoky, badly lighted workrooms. "Working on piece," they might wait hours for late-arriving New York mailboats or European liners on "steamer night." "Is it any wonder," asked a Boston printer, that printers once died when they were twenty-eight?[18]

As a last resort—after cleaning toilets, heating wash water, scouring spittoons, and venting bad air—union printers could farm out their derelict members. In 1892 the International Typographical Union constructed a printers' rest home in the pure mountain air of Colorado Springs, Colorado. In short order they filled it with an industry's consumptives.

Remarkably, it was always tempting to blame these victims, to find the source of a compositor's ill health not in foul workplaces but in a moral deficiency. "Nature," claimed *Inland Printer,* offered an antidote for the illnesses of printers. That cure was "simply the proper amount of muscular exercise, coupled with regularity and a reasonable quota of fresh air." This seemed very much like saying that printers would be healthier if they would stop printing. Indeed authorities acknowledged the difficulty of finding the time and place to accomplish this. Still, there was no alternative. "We must take time," *Inland Printer* insisted.[19]

This of course lifted the problem out of miasmic workplaces

and handed it to the journeymen. Working compositors were unlikely to sleep regularly, take long walks, and smell flowers. They
were apt instead to reach for "nervines" or a therapeutic boost
from the corner saloon. Authorities insisted they were foolish to
do so. "Phosphatic or so-called brain and nerve food," claimed one
writer, were "much to be reprobated." They provided inadequate
substitutes for a good diet. Occasionally, stimulants provided
timely "adjuncts" for a compositor, but "a man might as well expect to work indefinitely upon the stimulation of alcohol" as routinely to rely upon them.[20]

Naturally, if perversely, alcohol remained the booster of choice.
Shortly after the turn of the century, a third of one hundred
Chicago printers interviewed "freely admitted they used alcohol
to excess." The glory years of the Swifts, "the halcyon days of the
printing business," paradoxically produced what Joseph McCann
described as "demoralization." Later in life, McCann remembered
long nights and intense heat. An exhausted compositor, thought
McCann, was especially vulnerable to a "nervous condition" that
was "superinduced" by the need to produce columns of text under
deadline. The system "made wrecks of thousands of young men."
And after work they eagerly shared "the convivial cup."[21]

Drinking further confounded the etiology of printing diseases.
Early symptoms of lead intoxication seemed confusingly similar
to those of tuberculosis, and alcohol masked both. A U.S. Department of Labor study indicated that habitually excessive
drinkers often complained of the same symptoms described by
lead poison victims: gastric distress, morning vomiting, foul taste
and breath, constipation, stomach pains, muscle cramps, trem-
bling hands, weak grip, premature aging. Alcohol and toxic lead,
the study concluded, constituted a "vicious circle." Alcohol weakened a printer's resistance to lead intoxication, as the poison in-
tensified the effects of alcoholism.[22]

Habits changed hard, especially the defining behavior of Swifts.
As early as 1886 *Printers' Circular* thought it saw decline in the
ranks of print trade dissolutes, increasing sobriety among journalists "and to some degree in the composing room." Alexander

Duguid, that model of sobriety, two months earlier had won the Philadelphia typesetting championship. Like Duguid, observed *Printers' Circular,* "most of the men" in that competition were sober sorts.[23]

The Death of a Velocipede

They had been heroes. "The glory of the composing room is gone forever," Alexander Duguid remarked in 1895, "and soon will be but a reminiscence as it fades before the everyday, practical typesetting machine." Nine years had passed since Duguid's own glory at Philadelphia's national championship. "Who does not recall the good old days when a man could joke and talk and laugh all night long and set type just the same?" Now, thought Duguid, "the rattle and bang, the rumble and din of the machine shop takes the place of conversation, and the operator is alone among his fellows." Handwork vanished and time clocks replaced the piece system. "The old-time independence is gone," Duguid said. "We are workingmen now, and realize that our trade has lost much of its distinctive features and become commonplace."[24]

The world of the Swifts had vanished. "Every printer will remember the youthful days when his ambition was to set the biggest string on the paper," Duguid said, "and hope was high in his breast that he might be considered a 'swift.'" A handful achieved the dream and none were faster than Alex Duguid, but no one eclipsed the legend of the Velocipede, George Arensberg.[25]

Arensberg died on July 28, 1886, in New York's Bellevue Hospital, almost on cue. He died as younger Swifts gathered at their grandest races. Newspapers reported that he was "now broken down in health, although still working occasionally in the composing room of the New York *Times.*" A *New York Herald* reporter, on the scene for the McCann-Barnes match, spied him quiet in the background. Arensberg was there to watch, "glad," it seemed, "to be out of the trouble." He died as the *New York Tribune* installed its original bank of Linotypes. According to the *Printers' Circular,* Arensberg was "a man generally liked in the fraternity, although he has been little heard of in recent years." Perhaps this was so, but they remembered him across the Atlantic. In September 1886 the Velocipede earned an obituary in London's *Printers' Register*.[26]

According to the *New York Times*, Arensberg succumbed to "a complication of disorders." Friends called it an "early death," but he had been a printing legend since he was twenty and seemed an elder statesman. "Well, boys," Arensberg said, "I haven't long to stay in this world; but I tell you I've had a heap of fun, and I'm ready to go." The greatest of them all had not raced in fifteen years. He was thirty-seven years old.[27]

Afterword

THE VELOCIPEDE DIED, AND SOON THE SWIFTS WERE gone, displaced by the demands of a new technology. Now, at the onset of the twenty-first century, many expect the computer-driven "digital age," having ended traditional typesetting, to eclipse it all, an entire 550-year "age of print." The demise of the Swifts can be seen as one prologue in this drama.

But journeymen in the late nineteenth century themselves confronted a variation on an old and recurrent theme. Centuries before the Swifts, Johannes Gutenberg's moveable metal type radiated from Mainz to unhorse the monks and end a scribal culture. Fast forward, and only yesterday it happened again. In 1987, in a special exhibit space off their building's entryway, the Compugraphic Corporation of Wilmington, Massachusetts, proudly displayed its workhorse photocomposition machine, the Editwriter

7500 typesetter, ubiquitous from coast to coast. Ten years earlier, the machine had not existed; ten years later it was a museum piece. The forerunner of that machine, Mergenthaler's Linotype, had lasted some seventy-five years, and in both instances equipment obsolescence meant technological unemployment for legions of operators.

Changes in technology challenged workforce institutions as well as the workers themselves. Traditional printing had required the hand labor of many compositors. Their sheer numbers meant that printing's trade organization, the International Typographical Union (ITU), became *their* union, at the expense of pressmen and the various other printing trades, each of which organized its separate union. When in the mid-1880s typesetting machinery confronted their industry, union printers managed to retain control of training programs and subsequent use of those machines. The International Typographical Union, in other words, remained printing's artisanal gatekeeper.

Because the compositors of the ITU were overwhelmingly men and would remain so, workplace feminization stalled. The male constituency of the union subsequently benefited, but women printers generally did not. After 1890 and into the twentieth century, printing underwent a workplace risorgimento, a "re-masculinization." In Britain, the numbers of women on mid-nineteenth-century shopfloors steadily increased into the twentieth century, albeit more trickle than tidal wave. In the United States, however, women printers were in retreat everywhere by 1900. Union printing's evolving gender apartheid, which resembled its institutional racism, ensured task segregation well into the twentieth century.

Not until the 1970s did women gain the widespread access to printing shopfloors that circumstances immediately after the Civil War had promised. In the second half of the twentieth century, the challenge to print compositors became computer-driven photocomposition. This time, unlike the 1880s, the ITU lost control of the equipment. The oldest and once mightiest union in the land folded in 1986.

Alongside machines and women, Swifts winced at a third challenge, the redefinition of competence implied by the introduction of graphic design personnel. Nineteenth-century compositors set themselves apart from the mass of working-class society. Certainly they were manual workers, but that work demanded physical effort combined with literate judgment. Printers who considered themselves elite artisans reacted badly to graphic designers bearing detailed typesetting instructions. "You are making hod carriers of us," one complained.[1]

Hod carriers they would remain, serving professional graphic designers as builders served architects. Journeymen compositors would never regain elite status. In 1992 the eminent typographer Robert Bringhurst updated the compositor's diminished condition. Digital methodology helped "bring editing, typography and type design back to the close relationship they enjoyed in the golden age of letterpress," Bringhurst thought. Still, "everything the writer, type designer, editor and typographer do is still contingent on the skills and methods of the printer, and printing often remains a world apart." That world, Bringhurst warned, "remains . . . a commercialized, standardized and highly industrial process, and, unless tenaciously guided, "will readily erase the typographer's personal touch."[2]

For all the change that had come to text composition, printing seemed eternal. The Internet developer Matthew Butterick, for instance, thought that typographic texts would survive the onslaught of visual stimuli. "Text rules the digital frontier," Butterick claimed, "because it is compact to load, easy to create, familiar to use, and compatible with all computing platforms." The World Wide Web would, he felt, remain text driven, because "though it's less flashy than pictures, sound, and video, [text] offers the best bang for the bandwidth." It therefore followed that "if text is alive and well, so should typography be: after all, there can be no visual representation of text without type."[3]

It was easy enough to think back from Windows or Macintosh to the days of hot metal type. One hundred years ago, the choice of a Linotype machine or a Monotype caster was a proprietary commitment. As Matthew Butterick reminded us, a hot metal caster "was a sort of operating system for type, and the matrices were the software that worked with it." You chose a system and stuck with it. So it went, through phototypesetting and early digital typography, where proprietary systems meant proprietary fonts, and type design firms from the American Typefounders Company through Adobe Systems Inc. dictated the forms texts could take.[4]

As printing entered the twenty-first century, proprietary control faced uncertainty. Gutenberg's gift once expanded a civilization of history and literature, of geography, of literacy and the printed word. By the year 2000, this culture seemed under siege, challenged by alternatives of performance and technique, television, and computer-enhanced information. Electronic institutions, notably television and the Internet, diminished both the spatial and temporal dimensions of the world and its history and geography. The change seemed revolutionary.

Printing, of course, did not vanish. In fact, among many practitioners, the Swifts' kind of printing had not even changed. Fine printing, the specialized effort of traditional, letterpress craftspeople, produced books of extraordinarily high quality and value in inverse relation to any marketplace relevance to the effort. This kind of printing emerged in the last decade of the nineteenth century in reaction to the perceived lackluster products of industrialized printing. Spokesmen for the private press movement, closely identified with the Kelmscott Press of the Englishman William Morris, were pointedly disgusted with the artisanry of journeymen Swifts. The point of view persisted. At the end of the twentieth century, at the "end of print," a new generation of men and women rediscovered hand typesetting, handmade paper, and printing on the letterpress. Thanks to the personal computer, a middle class once barely able to differentiate roman type from italic gained a working familiarity with typefont families.[5]

In the end, the lessons of the Swifts are about more than printing. Briefly, typesetting races became a popular spectator amusement. Thanks to dime museums, journeymen Swifts became stars of a popular culture, and printing joined a developing consumer amusement market, one that seamlessly clustered authentic, actual activities with the performed renditions of those activities. Eventually, this sort of thing blurred distinctions among headline news events, commerce, and exhibition. The phenomenon ranked among the most fascinating aspects of postmodern American culture.

Glossary

Big Six. Nickname of New York City's Local No. 6 of the International Typographical Union.

Blacksmith. An incompetent compositor. Also "shoemaker."

Bogus. Makework for otherwise idle compositors. Also "horse."

Bourgeois. A size of type, approximately 9-point by modern measurement. Pronounced "burjoyce."

Brainery. Editorial rooms of a newspaper.

Brevier. A size of type, approximately 8-point by modern measurement.

Chapel. The name for the collectivity of a shopfloor, assembled to mete out assignments, rewards, and punishments. Its elected leader was called the "father" of the chapel.

Comp. A person who sets type; a compositor. Also "dabster" and "crab."

Companionship. A work pool assembled for large jobs, especially when the task involved different kinds of work.

Dabster. A person who sets type; a compositor. Also "crab."

Devil. The shopfloor "boy" of all work, usually an apprentice.

Distribution. Returning used type to its proper place in a typecase.

Estate. A journeyman's vested job at a printing plant. A kind of tenure.

Em. A unit of typographical measurement. A space equivalent to the square of a given point size. See *Quadrat.*

En. Half of an em.

Fat. Easily set copy, perhaps poetry. A particularly wide typeface was fat type, or "stud horse."

Form. Type and associated material, often a page, locked together and made ready for the press.

Galley. A metal tray into which composed type is placed for storage and proofing before "makeready."

Jeffing. A dice-like game played with metal "em quadrats."

Jerry. Raucous taunting or derisive shopfloor noises.

Jour. A journeyman printer.

Justification. Word spacing that spreads the series of words in a line evenly to both edges of a measure.

Leading. Metal strips used to separate lines of type. Pronounced "ledding."

Makeready. Tightening, positioning, and otherwise preparing a form for the press.

Measure. The length of a line of type.

Minion. A size of type, approximately 7-point by modern measurement.

Nonpareil. A size of type, approximately 6-point by modern measurement.

Out. In setting type, a word or phrase inadvertently omitted.

Pi. Mixed, jumbled, or miscellaneous type. Accidentally dropped type is "pied" type.

Pica. A printer's unit of measurement. There are six picas in an inch.

Piecework. A traditional criterion of payment. Ordinarily printers received the weekly sum of their actual daily output, their "string." Employers paid printers by the piece until an hourly wage became standard at the turn of the twentieth century.

Point. A printer's unit of measurement. There are twelve points in a pica.

Quadrat. A piece of spacing metal less than type high. Usually shortened to "quad." See *Em.*

Rat. A printer willing to work for less than union scale.

Reglet. Strip of wood, thicker than metal leads, used in spacing.

Rusher. An alternative name for a Swift, a fast "dabster."

Signature. A bindery term for a gathering of pages to be sewn into place alongside others.

Sit. A printer's "situation." His job.

Sorts. Miscellaneous type symbols, such as the ampersand, which are not letter characters.

Stick. A "typestick." The hand-held metal device for receiving individual types. Also a "pan."

Sticking. The act of setting type by hand.

Stone. Broad table surface on which a printer prepared type for the press.

Straight matter. Copy to be set into undifferentiated columns of type, as books or newspapers.

String. The amount of a compositor's daily billable labor, derived from the length of a string wound around his standing block of type.

Three-em space. More accurately, a 3-to-the-em space. The thickest spacing material for separating words in a line of type. A 4-em space was slightly thinner, a 5-em space thinner still, and a thin space thinnest of all.

Tramp. A traveling printer.

Traveling card. A union-issued card attesting to a carrier's competence and standing.

Two-thirder. An apprentice who sought a journeyman's appointment before completing his term of indenture. A lightly trained printer.

Typo. A compositor, a person who sets type.

Notes

Introduction

1. *New York Herald,* 16 December 1885, 9.
2. Irvin S. Cobb, *Stickfuls: Compositions of a Newspaper Minion* (New York: George H. Doran Company, 1923), 31–32.
3. Linotype operators tested their machines by running a finger down the first two rows of keys. The result, a slug of set type reading "etaoin shrdlu," was analogous to the word "qwerty" at the left hand's top row of a typewriter layout.
4. Alexander Lawson, *The Compositor as Artist, Craftsman, and Tradesman* (Athens, Ga.: Press of the Nightowl), 9.

1. A Gutenberg Legacy

1. The words compositor and typesetter are not quite synonyms. Composition implied skills sufficient to arrange a pleasing, readable page. Occasionally, therefore, printers differentiated between compositors, who could do this, and mere typesetters, persons of limited skills, perhaps apprentices, who were capable of little more than stringing together lines of metal words.

2. *American Dictionary of Printing and Bookmaking* (New York: Howard Lockwood & Co., 1894), 308. Below the edge of their imposing stone, or table, players shook five quads, perhaps seven, and threw them onto the surface in the manner of dice. Each quad had a nick, a marking for type alignment, on a single side, all others blank, smooth. Contestants counted the number of nicks the cast caused to face upward. The winner after three rounds (or more) stood aside, while the rest tossed to determine the reverse, the player with the fewest nicks upward. This contestant lost the entire bet, freeing all the other players, and the loser paid the winner. An average winning throw (three rounds and nine throws) was a seven. They called it "the witch." Nine was excellent. Nomenclature and conditions varied. Contestants repeated a "false throw," one resulting in stacked quads, which was known as a "cock." A "Molly" (or a "Miss" or a "Mary" or a "Susan") was a blank toss, no slot showing.

3. See Bruce Laurie, *Artisans into Workers: Labor in Nineteenth-Century America* (New York: Noonday Press, 1989), 35–36. See also W. J. Rorabaugh, *The Craft Apprentice: From Franklin to the Machine Age in America* (New York: Oxford University Press, 1986).

4. Laurie, *Artisans into Workers,* 35.

5. Ava Baron, "An 'Other' Side of Gender Antagonism at Work: Men, Boys, and the Remasculinization of Printers' Work, 1830–1920," *Work Engendered: Toward a New History of American Labor,* Ava Baron, ed. (Ithaca, N.Y.: Cornell University Press, 1991), 50–55. Historians have used various criteria other than literacy for defining and understanding printing's "aristocratic" status. These would include wage levels compared to a wider working class, indices of group consciousness, and degrees of self-governance in the workplace. Following Friedrich Engels's *Condition of the Working Class in England,* English Marxian historians such as E. J. Hobsbawm have found the notion of a conservative labor aristocracy important in understanding non-revolutionary industrial capitalist regimes. It provides the focus of Patrick Duffy's *The Skilled Compositor, 1850–1914: An Aristocrat among Working Men* (Aldershot, U.K.: Ashgate Publishing Ltd., 2000), chapter 3 and *passim.*

6. Ava Baron, "Questions of Gender: Deskilling and Demasculinization in the U.S. Printing Industry, 1830–1915," *Gender & History* 1, no. 2 (1989): 183. See also Mary Biggs, "Neither Printer's Wife nor Widow: American Women in Typesetting, 1830–1950," *Library Quarterly* 50 (1980): 431–52.

7. Baron, "An 'Other' Side of Gender Antagonism at Work," *Work Engendered,* 49.

8. Michael Schudson, *Discovering the News: A Social History of American Newspapers* (New York: Basic Books, 1978), 15.

9. Ibid., 14–31.

10. Michael Winship, *American Literary Publishing in the Mid-Nineteenth Century* (Cambridge, Mass.: Cambridge University Press, 1995), 11.

11. *American Dictionary of Printing and Bookmaking,* 548.

12. Ibid.

13. James Moran, *Printing Presses: History and Development from the Fifteenth Century to Modern Times* (Berkeley, Calif.: University of California Press, 1973), 113–21.

14. *American Dictionary of Printing and Bookmaking,* 549.

15. James W. Carey, *Communication as Culture: Essays on Media and Society* (Cambridge, Mass.: Unwin Hyman, 1988), 204.

16. Schudson, *Discovering the News,* 45.

17. Elizabeth Faulkner Baker, *Printers and Technology: A History of the International Printing Pressmen and Assistants' Union* (New York: Columbia University Press, 1957), 12.

18. Philip Gaskell, *A New Introduction to Bibliography* (New York: Oxford University Press, 1972), 214–30.

19. Dixon Wecter, *Sam Clemens of Hannibal* (Boston: Houghton Mifflin Company, 1952), 200.

20. Richard E. Huss, *The Development of Printers' Mechanical Typesetting Methods, 1822–1925* (Charlottesville, Va.: University Press of Virginia, 1973), 39. See also Richard E. Huss, *Dr. Church's "Hoax": The Inventions of a Yankee Genius* (Lancaster, Pa.: Graphic Arts Inc., 1976).

21. *American Dictionary of Printing and Bookmaking,* 549.

22. Including, of course, the Paige Compositor, a complex device with a famous champion. Mark Twain financed the Paige, which failed miserably but thanks to Twain was a famous mistake. See Corban Goble, "Mark Twain's Nemesis: The Paige Compositor," *Printing History* 36: 2–16.

23. William S. Pretzer, "Tramp Printers: Craft Culture, Trade Unions, and Technology," *Printing History* 12:4–5.

24. David Montgomery, *Workers' Control in America: Studies in the History of Work, Technology, and Labor Struggles* (Cambridge, Mass.: Cambridge University Press, 1979), 12.

25. The organization called itself the National Typographical Union until 1869, when it incorporated several Canadian locals. It thereupon became the International Typographical Union, by which name, for clarity, we will refer to it throughout.

26. George A. Stevens, *New York Typographical Union No. 6: A Study of a Modern Trade Union and Its Predecessors* (Albany, N.Y.: J. B. Lyon Company, 1913), 205. Delegates jeffed for pride of number. Indianapolis won, becoming ITU Local No. 1.

27. Seymour Martin Lipset, Martin Trow, and James Coleman, *Union Democracy: The Internal Politics of the International Typographical Union* (Garden City, N.J.: Doubleday Anchor Books, 1962), 37–47.

28. Schudson, *Discovering the News,* 68.

29. William C. Barnes, Joseph W. McCann, and Alexander Duguid, *A Collation of Facts Relative to Fast Typesetting* (New York: Concord Cooperative Printing Company, 1887), 52.

2. The Arensberg Wager and the Swifts

1. Clipping of *New York Sun,* 20 February 1870, in Joel Munsell, "Printers Scraps: Feats of Fast Typesetting," volume 11 of bound scrapbooks containing newspaper clippings, marginal notes, and assorted ephemera. Rare Books and Manuscripts Collection, Butler Library, Columbia University, 146. See also Barnes, McCann, and Duguid, *Fast Typesetting,* 38. The book, compiled by three of the best-known Swifts, is a record of match results and manual of technique.

2. Barnes, McCann, and Duguid, *Fast Typesetting,* 19–20.

3. *American Dictionary of Printing and Bookmaking* (New York: Howard Lockwood & Co., 1894), 231. See also Munsell, "Printers Scraps: Feats of Fast Typesetting," 147, and Luther J. Ringwalt, ed., *American Encyclopaedia of Printing* (Philadelphia: Menamin & Ringwalt, 1871), 168.

4. Joel Munsell, "Printers Scraps: Feats of Fast Typesetting," 146. See also Ringwalt, *Encyclopaedia,* 168.

5. Barnes, McCann, and Duguid, *Fast Typesetting,* 23.

6. Ibid., 50–52.

7. Harry W. Baehr, Jr., *The New York Tribune since the Civil War* (New York: Dodd, Mead & Co., 1936), 183.

8. Barnes, McCann, and Duguid, *Fast Typesetting,* 7.

9. Providence Typographical Union, *Printers and Printing in Providence, 1762–1907* (Providence, R.I.: Typographical Union No. 33, 1907), 35.

10. Printers usually called such people "stonemen," because they performed their makeready work at large, heavy tables, called "stones." A stone, the heavy table on which printers set up their pages, by midcentury was made of iron, but alluded to a time when such tabletops were, in fact, flat stones. A typical type cabinet contained a dozen or more drawers, segmented trays full of type that compositors removed entirely and installed at their workplace. The proper term for these trays or drawers was typecase.

11. So it went at the *Providence Journal,* a typical city daily. *Printers and Printing in Providence,* 34.

12. Joseph W. McCann, "Old Time 'Swifts,'" in *Convention Souvenir,* publication of the International Typographical Union, 60th Session, Providence, R.I., August 10–15, 1914.

13. Robert Darnton, *The Great Cat Massacre and Other Episodes in French Cultural History* (New York: Vintage, 1985), 81.

14. Ibid., 81.

15. *Printers and Printing in Providence,* 35.

16. *Inland Printer* (September 1887): 813; July 1887, 686.

17. Theodore Low DeVinne, *The Printers' Price List: A Manual for the Use of Clerks and Book-Keepers in Job Printing Offices* (New York: Francis Hart & Company, 1871), 47; *Inland Printer* (September 1887): 813.

18. *Inland Printer* (September 1887): 813.

19. John Tebbel. *Between Covers: The Rise and Transformation of American Book Publishing* (New York: Oxford University, 1987), 49–50; Riverside Press, *The Riverside Press* (Cambridge, Mass.: Riverside Press, 1911), 2.

20. Howard P. Chudacoff, *The Age of the Bachelor: Creating an American Subculture* (Princeton, N.J.: Princeton University Press, 1999), 35–36 and passim.

21. McCann, "Old Time 'Swifts'," *Convention Souvenir;* Barnes, McCann, and Duguid, *Fast Typesetting,* 52.

22. *Inland Printer* (April 1890): 593.

23. Ibid., March 1886, 331; *Printers' Circular* (December 1870): 415; *Inland Printer* (March 1886): 331.

24. *Inland Printer* (March 1886): 331.

25. *Printers' Circular* (February 1870): 42.

26. Lawson, *Compositor,* 14.

27. *Printers' Circular* (February 1870): 450; Barnes, McCann, and Duguid, *Fast Typesetting,* 54.

28. Elliott J. Gorn, *The Manly Art: Bare-Knuckle Prize Fighting in America* (Ithaca, N.Y.: Cornell University Press, 1986), 139. See also Ann Fabian, *Card Sharps, Dream Books, & Bucket Shops: Gambling in 19th-Century America* (Ithaca, N.Y.: Cornell University Press, 1990), 41. Shopfloors and union halls, along with saloons, therefore provided journeymen Swifts with the institutional scaffolding of an occupational subculture. Within and among these institutions printers spoke the language of their trade and through common apprenticeship identified with an ancient tradition at the case. The resulting beliefs and behaviors created a subset of a larger bachelor culture among journeymen Swifts in late-nineteenth-century America. See, for instance, Chudacoff, *The Age of the Bachelor,* 12–14.

29. Pretzer, "Tramp Printers," 3–16.

30. Quoted in ibid., 3.

31. Barnes, McCann, and Duguid, *Fast Typesetting,* 39.

32. *Philadelphia Inquirer* (15 March 1886): 2.

33. Pretzer, "Tramp Printers," 9. Pretzer finds four distinct periods of tramping. For all its supposed antiquity, full-time tramping seems to have typified the American printing industry only in a forty-year period after the Civil War.

34. Barnes, McCann, and Duguid *Fast Typesetting,* 38–39. In 1852 Pittsburgh's printing union became founding member Local No. 7 of the National Typographical Union, the first national labor union in the United States.

35. Ringwalt (*Encyclopaedia,* 168) himself expressed surprise at Dawson's figure. He comments: "This being so incredible a performance—although published in the newspaper—I inquired of Mr. Dawson . . . who asserts that it was an honest 22,022 ems, done in a day of something more than ten hours; he thinks thirteen hours." See also Barnes, McCann, and Duguid, *Fast Typesetting,* 54–58.

36. Ibid. See also Ringwalt, *Encyclopaedia,* 169.

37. Ibid.,168; Munsell, "Printers Scraps: Feats of Fast Typesetting," 149.

38. Ringwalt, *Encyclopaedia,* 168.

39. Barnes, McCann, and Duguid, *Fast Typesetting,* 57; 33.

40. *New York Sun,* 20 February, 1870. Clipping in Munsell, "Printers Scraps: Feats of Fast Typesetting," 148. All quotations pertaining to the Arensberg Wager derive from this source.

41. Barnes, McCann, and Duguid, *Fast Typesetting,* 20. Twenty-four ems was the width of a newspaper column, twelve or thirteen picas.

42. *Typographical Messenger,* January 1870, 4; ibid., 20; *Printers' Circular* (April 1871): 64.

43. *The Proof-Sheet* (May 1871): 92; *Printers' Circular* (May 1871): 112; June 1871, 161; Barnes, McCann, and Duguid, *Fast Typesetting,* 20–21.

44. *Printers' Circular* (July 1871): 210; Boston Typographical Union, *Illustrated Historical Souvenir,* 1898, 98.

45. *Printers' Circular* (December 1877): 227.

46. Ibid.

47. Barnes, McCann, and Duguid, *Fast Typesetting,* 23, 38.

48. Boston Typographical Union. *Leaves of History: From the Archives of Boston Typographical Union No. 13* (Boston: Boston Typographical Union, 1923), 24.

3. The Gendered Machine of Timothy Alden

1. Alden Typesetting and Distributing Machine Co, *The Wonderful Type-Setting and Distributing Machine* (New York: Alden Typesetting and Distributing Machine Co., 1863), 10; Goble. "Mark Twain's Nemesis," 2–16; Barnes, McCann, and Duguid, *Fast Typesetting,* 58.

2. *New York Times,* 11 August 1862, 5.

3. *The Wonderful Type-Setting and Distributing Machine,* 10; Corban Goble, "Rogers's Typograph Versus Mergenthaler's Linotype: The Push and Shove of Patents and Priorities in the 1890s." *Printing History* 35: 26–44.

4. Goble, "Roger's Typograph Versus Mergenthaler's Linotype," 8.

5. *New York Times,* 11 August 1862, 5.

6. The standard source on nineteenth-century typesetting machines is Huss, *The Development of Printers' Mechanical Typesetting Methods, 1822–1925.* John Southward, *Type-Composing Machines of the Past, the Present, and the Future* (Leicester, U.K.: Raithley, Lawrence & Co., De Montfort Press, 1891) and John S. Thompson, *History of Composing Machines* (Chicago: Inland Printer Co., 1904) are important early commentaries.

7. *The Wonderful Type-Setting and Distributing Machine,* 7.

8. *New York Times,* 11 August 1862, 5; *The Wonderful Type-Setting and Distributing Machine,* 4, 8, 9. Nonetheless, Mr. Welch, testing the machine, managed two typographical errors. On page 10 of the pamphlet, the word

remarked is rendered "remaked," and the page contains one instance of a missing closing quotation mark.

9. Huss, *The Development of Printers' Mechanical Typesetting Methods, 1822–1925,* 52.

10. Stevens, *New York Typographical Union No. 6,* 192–94.

11. Ibid., 421–40.

12. Ibid., 326.

13. *New York Times,* 11 August 1862, 5.

14. *The Wonderful Type-Setting and Distributing Machine,* 10–11.

15. Ibid., 11.

16. *New York Times,* 13 July 1868, 8.

17. Ibid. More than twenty years later, the Swift William Barnes claimed Leaning was "highly spoken of by those who worked with him as very rapid." Barnes, McCann, and Duguid, *Fast Typesetting,* 58.

18. Ibid. The "Skyrockets" piece, a single column inch of three sentences, is on page 4 of the June 30, 1864, edition of the *New York Herald.* It is a warning against using certain fireworks on July Fourth: "The sticks of the rockets are liable to impale the spectators or to act like firebrands upon the surrounding houses." The type—same style, same size—is brighter than the type surrounding it, probably because it is newer.

19. Charles C. Yeaton, *Manual of the Alden Type-Setting and Distributing Machine,* (New York: Francis Hart and Company, 1865), 220. Yeaton's *Manual,* a particularly fine example of mid-nineteenth-century printing and binding, is surely among the grandest industrial prospectuses ever produced.

20. Ibid., 221.

21. Ibid., 222.

22. Ibid., 223.

23. Ava Baron, "Women and the Making of the American Working Class: A Study of the Proletarianization of Printers." *The Review of Radical Political Economics* 14 (Fall 1982): 31; see also Ava Baron, "Contested Terrain Revisited: Technology of Gender Definitions of Work in the Printing Industry, 1850–1920," in *Women, Work, and Technology: Transformations,* eds. Barbara Drygulski Wright(Ann Arbor, Mich.: University of Michigan, 1987), 62–65.

24. Gray, "Organizational Struggles of Working Women in the Nineteenth Century," *Labor Studies Journal* 16 (Summer 1991): 23.

25. *New York Times,* 13 July 1868, 8.

26. *American Artisan* 7 (22 July 1868): 24.

27. Goble, "Mark Twain's Nemesis: The Paige Compositor," 2.

4. Augusta Lewis and Women's Typographical Union No. 1

1. Historians tend to regard Lewis as a participant in the life of Susan B. Anthony. Kathleen Barry's *Susan B. Anthony: A Biography of a Singular Feminist* (New York: New York University Press, 1988) reflects this attitude. Among labor histories, see Philip Foner's *Women and the American Labor*

Movement: From Colonial Times to the Eve of World War I (New York: The Free Press, 1979). Eleanor Flexner's *Century of Struggle: The Woman's Rights Movement in the United States* (Cambridge, Mass.: Belknap Press of Harvard University Press, 1959) and Ellen Carol DuBois's *Feminism and Suffrage: The Emergence of an Independent Women's Movement in America, 1848–1869* (Ithaca, N.Y.: Cornell University Press, 1978) place Lewis in a feminist context. See also Barbara L. Gray, "Organizational Struggles of Working Women in the Nineteenth Century," 16–34.

2. Letter dated 13 April 1911 in Stevens, *New York Typographical Union No. 6,* 432; Eleanor Flexner, "Augusta Lewis Troup" in Edward T. James, ed., *Notable American Women,* Vol. 2, 478. See also *Typographical Journal* 57 (October 1920): 408–409. This obituary seems written by family committee. The writer wants to praise Lewis's memory by linking her with famous figures such as Susan B. Anthony, and so she becomes her "friend." Paradoxically, such a treatment sells Lewis short. She knew famous people, all right; she carried an important fight to Anthony.

3. See, for instance, Rorabaugh, *The Craft Apprentice,* 76–96. See also Ava Baron, "Questions of Gender," 178–99.

4. Gray, "Organizational Struggles of Working Women in the Nineteenth Century," 23.

5. *Typographical Journal,* 408; *American Artisan and Patent Record,* 7 (22 July 1868): 24; *Printer's Register,* 6 October 1868, 261.

6. In addition to Stevens, *New York Typographical Union No. 6* and Walter A. Tracy, *History of the Typographical Union* (Indianapolis, Ind.: International Typographical Union, 1913), see International Typographical Union, *A Study of the History of the International Typographical Union, 1852–1966,* Vol. 2(Colorado Springs, Colo.: ITU, 1967); Gray, "Organizational Struggles of Working Women in the Nineteenth Century," 18.

7. Ibid., 19–20.

8. The episode is a defining moment in the women's movement and widely discussed. See Foner, *Women and the American Labor Movement,* 146–47.

9. *Revolution* 2 (11 February 1869): 90; Stevens, *New York Typographical Union No. 6,* 426.

10. Barry, *Susan B. Anthony,* 213; Foner, *Women and the American Labor Movement,* 141.

11. *Revolution* 1 (24 September 1868): 182; Foner, *Women and the American Labor Movement,* 142.

12. DuBois, *Feminism and Suffrage,* 141–42.

13. *Revolution,* 1 (24 September 1868): 182.

14. Ibid. (1 October 1868): 197.

15. Ibid.

16. Ibid.

17. Ibid.

18. Ibid.

19. *Printers' Circular* (February 1867): 161.

20. Munsell, "Printer's Scraps," 146.

21. This is essentially the argument Ava Baron makes in several monographs on women and printing. Women printers, says Baron, suffered less from a manipulative marketplace capitalism than they did from a more fundamentally oppressive patriarchy. Baron, "An 'Other' Side of Gender Antagonism at Work," in *Work Engendered*, 50–55.

22. *Revolution*, 1 (24 September 1868): 182; ibid. 1 October 1868: 197.

23. Huss, *The Development of Printers' Mechanical Typesetting Methods, 1822–1925*, 83; Foner, *Women and the American Labor Movement*, 150–51.

24. *Revolution* 2 (9 September 1869): 154; Foner, *Women and the American Labor Movement*, 151.

25. Gray, "Organizational Struggles of Working Women in the Nineteenth Century," 30.

26. Among many accounts of this ruckus, see David Montgomery, *Beyond Equality: Labor and the Radical Republicans, 1862–1872* (New York: Random House, 1967), 398–99.

27. Ibid., 399.

28. Stevens, *New York Typographical Union No. 6*, 431–32; Barry, *Susan B. Anthony*, 216; Foner, *Women and the American Labor Movement*, 136.

29. Stevens, *New York Typographical Union No. 6*, 433–34.

30. John McVicar, *Origin and Progress of the Typographical Union: Its Proceedings as a National and International Organization, 1850–1891* (Lansing, Mich.: D. D. Thorp, Printer and Binder, 1891), 48.

31. Ibid.

32. Ibid., 49.

33. Ibid.

34. DuBois, *Feminism and Suffrage*, 125; *Revolution* 1 (24 September 1868): 182; Foner, *Women and the American Labor Movement*, 151.

35. Tracy, *History of the Typographical Union*, 251; DuBois, *Feminism and Suffrage*, 152; Stevens, *New York Typographical Union No. 6*, 437–38.

36. Flexner, *Century of Struggle*, 135; McVicar, *Origin and Progress of the Typographical Union*, 53. By June 2, 1879, the ITU convention found itself unable to prevent southern locals from denying legitimately issued union traveling cards. It was, according to McVicar, a calamity foreseen ten years earlier "owing to the unjust and impotent conclusion in the case of L. H. Douglass." It was also the session that prohibited the extension of exclusively women's local unions. Women's issues, as those of black men, subsequently were left to local option, a federated system that effectively ended the presence of either on shopfloor or union hall; ibid., 73–74.

37. Tracy, *History of the Typographical Union*, 254–55.

38. Stevens, *New York Typographical Union No. 6,* 433–34.

39. ITU, *A Study of the History of the International Typographical Union, 1852–1966,* 237; Tracy, *History of the Typographical Union,* 254–55.

40. Stevens, *New York Typographical Union No. 6,* 433.

41. Tracy, *History of the Typographical Union,* 255.

42. *Printers' Circular* (January 1872): 464.

43. Ibid., 465.

44. Tracy, *History of the Typographical Union,* 253–54.

45. *Printers' Circular* (January 1872): 457; ibid., June 1872, 135; ibid., August 1872, 215; ibid., January 1872, 457; ibid., 465. Augusta Lewis married Alexander Troup, former secretary/treasurer of the ITU, whom she had met when he negotiated the founding of Women's Typographical Union No. 1. Beginning in 1872, Troup published a New Haven daily newspaper, the *Evening Union.*

5. Joseph McCann Takes the Swifts to the Show

1. Minutes, Dublin Typographical Provident Society, Trinity College Library, Dublin, Ireland. 14 May 1881.

2. Minutes, Dublin Typographical Provident Society, 28 May, and 9 July 1881; Charles H. Potter II, *Typeline,* Summer 1991), 1. *Typeline* is a newsletter of the U.S. Government Printing Office employees. Charles H. Potter II is McCann's grandson. The McCann Archive is in his possession, at Washington, D.C.

3. See McCann's collection of union cards, including those of Boston for the fall and winter of 1882–83. See also his handwritten note indicating a return to the *Herald* in April 1883, immediately after returning from Boston. McCann Archive.

4. *Inland Printer* (April 1900): 67. Summarized in Huss, *The Development of Printers' Mechanical Typesetting Methods, 1822–1925,* 23–24.

5. Barnes, McCann, and Duguid, *Fast Typesetting,* 28–33; *Inland Printer* (May 1886): 505.

6. McCann, "Old Time 'Swifts.'"

7. Ibid.; Barnes, McCann, and Duguid, *Fast Typesetting,* 39.

8. *New York Herald,* 5 June 1885.

9. Ibid.; Barnes, McCann, and Duguid, *Fast Typesetting,* 39.

10. Ibid., 140–42; *Inland Printer* (October 1885): 64.

11. *New York Herald,* 16 December 1885, 9.

12. Ibid.

13. Ibid.; Gorn, *The Manly Art,* 143.

14. Barnes, McCann, and Duguid, *Fast Typesetting,* 22, 26; the reference book was Luther Ringwalt's *American Encyclopaedia of Printing,* published in 1871.

15. McCann, "Old Time 'Swifts'"; A. H. Saxon, *P. T. Barnum: The Legend and the Man* (New York: Columbia University, 1989), 308.

16. Tracy, *History of the Typographical Union*, 283–320.

17. Stevens, *New York Typographical Union No. 6*, 309, 416.

18. *Printers and Printing in Providence, 1762–1907*, 54–56, 93.

19. Stevens, *New York Typographical Union No. 6*, 311–16.

20. For the Knights' broadened mission, see Robert E. Weir, *Beyond Labor's Veil: The Culture of the Knights of Labor* (University Park: Pennsylvania State University Press, 1996), *passim*.

21. *Printers and Printing in Providence*, 94. The year 1884 was a turning point for the national organization of the ITU in several ways. It instituted some structural changes, alterations that significantly increased its power. The establishment of a defense fund, a mortuary benefit, and an old-age pension fund channeled union funds to the central administration. Control of the disbursement of these funds to members of local unions empowered the national organization and subsequently proved to be a watershed in the federal composition of the ITU. Jacob Loft, *The Printing Trades* (New York: Farrar & Rinehart, Inc., 1944), 187.

22. Barnes, McCann, and Duguid, *Fast Typesetting*, 29.

23. *Rochester Morning Herald,* 2 March 1886, 7; *Rochester Democrat and Chronicle,* 2 March 1886, 7; *Inland Printer* (April 1886): 419; *Rochester Morning Herald,* 2 March 1886, 7.

24. *Rochester Democrat and Chronicle,* 2 March 1886, 7; *Inland Printer* (April 1886): 419.

25. Such a convergence is central to the cultural analysis of the 1880s developed in Weir, *Beyond Labor's Veil*, 17.

26. J. R. Davis to Joseph W. McCann, 23 December 1885. McCann Archive.

27. *Chicago Tribune,* 10 January 1886, 3; *Inland Printer* (January 1886): 237; Neil Harris, *Humbug: The Art of P. T. Barnum* (Chicago: University of Chicago Press, 1973), 33. See also, David Nasaw, *Going Out: The Rise and Fall of Public Amusements* (New York: Basic Books, 1993); Andrea Stulman Dennett, *Weird & Wonderful: The Dime Museum in America* (New York: New York University Press, 1997); and Brooks McNamara, "'A Congress of Wonders': The Rise and Fall of the Dime Museum," *Emerson Society Quarterly* 20 (3rd quarter 1974): 220.

28. Chudacoff, *The Age of the Bachelor,* 132.

29. Dennett, *Weird & Wonderful,* 41–42.

30. Ibid., 41.

31. *Chicago Tribune,* 10 January 1886, 3.

32. Ibid.

33. Ibid., 12 January 1886, 3.

34. Ibid., 13 January 1886, 3. Contestants worked from identical extracts from Henry George's *Progress and Poverty. Chicago Tribune* (12 January 1886): 3.

35. *Inland Printer* (February 1886): 299.

36. *Printers' Circular* 20, no. 11: 206; Barnes, McCann, and Duguid, *Fast Typesetting*, 43.

37. *Chicago Tribune,* 12 January 1886, 3.

38. Ibid., 14 January 1886, 3.

39. *Inland Printer* (October 1890): 54; *New York Times,* 14 January 1886, 5; *Chicago Tribune,* 12 January 1886, 3.

40. *Chicago Tribune,* 13 January 1886, 3.

41. Ibid., 14 January 1886, 3; ibid., 15 January 1886, 5. He did these tricks at competition speed. Barnes's reversed-case half-hour total was 966 ems; his hour-long total was 1,822 ems. Blindfolded, he set 1,005 ems in one hour. See Barnes, McCann, and Duguid, *Fast Typesetting,* 26, 42.

42. *Chicago Tribune,* 13 January 1886, 3; ibid., 12 January 1886, 3.

43. *Inland Printer* (May 1885): 334; *Chicago Tribune,* 12 January 1886, 3.

44. *Chicago Tribune,* 15 January 1886, 5.

45. Barnes, McCann, and Duguid, *Fast Typesetting,* 40; *Chicago Tribune,* 12 January 1886, 3; ibid., 15 January 1886, 5.

46. *Chicago Tribune,* 13 January 1886, 3; ibid., 15 January 1886, 5.

47. Ibid., 12 January 1886, 3; *Inland Printer* (January 1885): 167; ibid., May 1885, 334; *Chicago Tribune,* 13 January 1886, 3.

48. *Chicago Tribune,* 14 January 1886, 3; ibid., 15 January 1886, 5.

49. *Chicago Tribune,* 15 January 1886, 5; ibid., 18 January 1886, 3.

50. *Inland Printer* (February 1886): 299–300.

51. McCann, "Old Time 'Swifts,'" 5.

52. *Chicago Tribune,* 18 January 1886, 3.

53. *Chicago Tribune,* 18 January 1886, 3; *Printers' Circular,* 20, no. 11: 206; Barnes, McCann, and Duguid, *Fast Typesetting,* 26; *Chicago Tribune,* 18 January 1886, 3; ibid., 18 January 1886, 3.

54. *Inland Printer* (January 1885): 167; McCann, "Old Time 'Swifts.'"

55. Ibid.

56. Receipt, C. Martin, Practical Tailor, Dublin, Ireland, 29 August 1886. McCann Archive.

57. *Printers' Circular* (June 1871): 162.

58. *Inland Printer* (May 1886): 466; ibid., March 1886, 333.

59. *New York Times,* 12 January 1886, 5.

60. J. R. Davis to Joseph W. McCann, 16 February 1886, McCann Archive; *Inland Printer* (February 1886): 300.

6. Fast Women

1. Barnes, McCann, and Duguid, *Fast Typesetting,* 28.

2. Biggs, "Neither Printer's Wife nor Widow," 448; *Inland Printer* (October 1884): 16.

3. *Boston Globe,* 14 February 1886, 11.

4. Ibid., 18 February 1886, 5; *Boston Post,* 18 February 1886, 4.

5. *Boston Globe,* 16 February 1886, 2.

6. Ibid., 17 February 1886, 5.

7. Barnes, McCann, and Duguid, *Fast Typesetting,* 44.

8. *Boston Globe,* 19 February 1886, 5; *Boston Advertiser,* 18 February 1886, 8.

9. *Boston Advertiser,* 18 February 1886, 8; *Boston Herald,* 19 February 1886, 4.

10. *Boston Globe,* 19 February 1886, 5.

11. Ibid., 20 February 1886, 3. Customs change. Current American practice breaks the word *neglect* as Crosby broke it. *Boston Globe,* 21 February 1886, 3.

12. *Boston Globe,* 20 February 1886, 3; ibid., 21 February 1886, 3.

13. *Boston Globe,* 20 February 1886, 3; ibid., 21 February 1886, 3.

14. *Boston Globe,* 21 February 1886, 3.

15. Ibid., 23 February 1886, 2.

16. Ibid.

17. *Boston Globe,* 28 February 1886, 6. Furthermore, the speedy young "Miss Davis" was actually a slightly more seasoned Mrs. White.

18. Ibid.

19. *Boston Globe,* 28 February 1886, 6. Neither would we know White's given name.

20. *Boston Herald,* 28 February 1886, 11; *Boston Globe,* 28 February 1886, 6.

21. *Boston Globe,* 23 February 1886, 2; *Boston Globe,* 25 February 1886, 5.

22. *Boston Herald,* 27 February 1886, 2; *Boston Globe,* 28 February 1886, 6.

23. *Boston Advertiser,* 24 February 1886, 8; *Boston Herald,* 27 February 1886, 2; *Boston Globe,* 26 February 1886, 5.

24. *Boston Globe,* 27 February 1886, 5.

25. Ibid., 28 February 1886, 6.

26. Ibid., 23 February 1886, 2; ibid., 14 February 1886, 11; Boston Typographical Union, *Illustrated Historical Souvenir,* 94. Susan B. Anthony, lately offensive to both the National Labor Union and the International Typographical Union, was another recently recruited Knight. According to the organization's historian, Robert E. Weir, both Susan B. Anthony and Elizabeth Cady Stanton held membership cards in the Knights of Labor. Weir, *Beyond Labor's Veil,* 7.

27. For an overview of mid-1880s working-class Boston, see Jama Lazerow. "'The Workingman's Hour': The 1886 Labor Uprising in Boston," *Labor History* 21 (1980): 200–220.

28. *Boston Herald,* 27 February 1886, 2. Ava Baron. "Contested Terrain Revisited," 69.

29. *Boston Globe,* 24 February 1886, 5.

30. Ibid., 23 February 1886, 2.

31. *Boston Globe,* 23 February 1886, 2; ibid., 25 February 1886, 5.

32. *Boston Globe,* 28 February 1886, 6; ibid., 27 February 1886, 5; ibid., 28 February 1886, 6.

33. *Boston Globe,* 28 February 1886, 6; ibid., 24 February 1886, 5; ibid., 27 February 1886, 5.

34. *Boston Globe,* 26 February 1886, 5.

35. Stevens, *New York Typographical Union No. 6,* 426; *Boston Globe,* 28 February 1886, 6.

36. Boston Typographical Union, *Illustrated Historical Souvenir,* 111.

37. Belva Mary Herron. "Unionization for Women: The Typographical Union," in *Root of Bitterness: Documents of the Social History of American Women,* ed. Nancy F. Cott (New York: Dutton, 1972), 338, 342.

38. Loft, *The Printing Trades,* 70–71.

7. Mr. Mergenthaler's Revolution

1. *Philadelphia Inquirer,* 15 March 1886, 2; *Paper & Printing Trades Journal,* London 55 (June 1886): 12.

2. See, for instance, Maggie Holtzberg-Call, *The Lost World of the Craft Printer* (Urbana, Ill.: University of Illinois Press, 1992), 82.

3. In 1873 Menamin and Luther J. Ringwalt published the *American Encyclopaedia of Printing; Printers' Circular* (April 1871): 2; *The Proof-Sheet* (May 1871): 92. See also Barnes, McCann, and Duguid, *Fast Typesetting,* 20–21.

4. *Times,* Philadelphia, 21 March 1886, 8.

5. *Philadelphia Press,* 16 March 1886, 3; *Times,* Philadelphia, 14 March 1886, 8; Barnes, McCann, and Duguid, *Fast Typesetting,* 29. Proofreaders are rarely household names. The *Philadelphia Inquirer* called the man Irvin A. Shane, and *Times* thought his name was Alex Shaw. *Philadelphia Inquirer,* 15 March 1886, 2; *Times,* Philadelphia, 21 March 1886, 8.

6. *Times,* Philadelphia, 14 March 1886, 8; *Philadelphia Inquirer,* 15 March 1886, 5.

7. *Philadelphia Record,* 17 March 1886, 4.

8. *Philadelphia Inquirer,* 17 March 1886, 5.

9. *Printers' Circular* (March 1886): 1. Duguid and McCann averaged more than 2,000 ems an hour over eleven days in succession. See also *Printers' Circular* (April 1886): 21.

10. *Printers' Circular* (March 1886): 1.

11. Lawson, *The Compositor as Artist, Craftsman, and Tradesman,* 11; *Philadelphia Record,* 17 March 1886, 4.

12. *Philadelphia Record,* 17 March 1886, 4; *Philadelphia Inquirer,* 15 March 1886, 2; ibid., 29 March 1886, 8; Barnes, McCann, and Duguid, *Fast Typesetting,* 16.

13. *Philadelphia Inquirer,* 15 March 1886, 2.

14. Ibid., 15 March 1886, 2.

15. Ibid.

16. Quoted in *Inland Printer* (April 1886): 433.

17. *Philadelphia Record,* 17 March 1886, 4; *Printers' Circular* (March 1886): 1; see also Barnes, McCann, and Duguid, *Fast Typesetting,* 29.

18. *Times,* Philadelphia, 19 March 1886, 3.

19. *Printers' Circular* (March 1886): 1.

20. *Philadelphia Press,* 23 March 1886, 3; ibid., 24 March 1886, 3.

21. *Printers' Circular* (April 1886): 21; *Printers' Circular* (March 1886): 2; *Times,* Philadelphia, 14 March 1886, 8.

22. Barnes, at al., *Fast Typesetting,* 33.

23. McCann, "Old Time 'Swifts.'"

24. *Inland Printer* (April 1885): 319. See also Goble, "Roger's Typograph Versus Mergenthaler's Linotype," 26–44, as well as Goble, "Mark Twain's Nemesis," 2–16.

25. The most recent biography of Reid is Bingham Duncan, *Whitelaw Reid: Journalist, Politician, Diplomat* (Athens, Ga.: University of Georgia Press, 1975). In 1888 Reid was the Republican candidate for the vice presidency on an unsuccessful ticket headed by James G. Blaine. In 1905 Theodore Roosevelt appointed him United States ambassador to the Court of St. James.

26. Duncan, *Whitelaw Reid,* 95–97.

27. Ibid., 97; Moran, *Printing Presses,* 196.

28. Huss, *The Development of Printers' Mechanical Typesetting Methods, 1822–1925,* 83.

29. Ibid., 84. Henry Burr operated the Burr Typesetter (and the Burr Printing House) until his death in 1885. Henry Thrush bought the Burr patents in that year and once again renamed the machine, this time calling it the Empire Composer.

30. Duncan, *Whitelaw Reid,* 97.

31. Ibid.

32. Ibid.

33. Ibid., 99.

34. Ibid.

35. Barnes, McCann, and Duguid, *Fast Typesetting,* 65.

36. Stevens, *New York Typographical Union No. 6,* 326.

37. Ibid., 327.

38. It succeeded through strenuous and committed litigation. The Linotype profited from the backing of a combination of newspaper moguls led by Whitelaw Reid of the *New York Tribune.* The group bought Ottmar Mergenthaler's company, forced him from the company that bore his name, and proceeded to drive out contending machines such as John R. Rogers's Typograph. Rogers's firm took his machine out of the country and later, when patents had expired, rejoined the United States market as Intertype. Goble, "Roger's Typograph Versus Mergenthaler's Linotype," 26–44.

39. Stevens, *New York Typographical Union No. 6,* 327. As of June 3, 1883, such "perfected composing machines" as existed were "of the moveable type variety." Even ten years later, when New York's Local No. 6 first attempted a wage scale for machine work, such typesetters were still the city's typical machine. Southward, *Type-Composing Machines of the Past, the Present, and the Future,* 33.

40. *Printers' Circular* (April 1886): 22.

41. Minutes, Meeting of the Board of Delegates, 9 May 1886. These minutes are part of the Minutes of the Regular Meetings of New York Local No. 6 of the International Typographical Union, 9 May 1886, 326.

42. Barnes, McCann, and Duguid, *Fast Typesetting,* 57.

43. Joseph W. McCann, "Old Time 'Swifts.'"

44. Technological change among printers and the concomitant changing role of women in the workplace has inspired a historical sociology rich in the vocabulary of "demasculinization," "deskilling," and "remasculinization." See Baron, *Work Engendered,* especially Baron's own essay: "An 'Other' Side of Gender Antagonism at Work: Men, Boys, and the Remasculinization of Printers' Work, 1830–1920," 47–69.

45. See Christina Burr, "'That Coming Curse—The Incompetent Compositress': Class and Gender Relations in the Toronto Typographical Union during the Late Nineteenth Century," *Canadian Historical Review* 74, no. 3 (1993): 344–66; see also Baron, "Contested Terrain Revisited," 58–83; Loft, *The Printing Trades,* 48.

46. *Inland Printer* (December 1888): 258; ibid., November 1890, 174.

47. *Union Printer* (30 December 1893), quoted in *Inland Printer* (February 1894): 398.

48. For Monheimer, *Inland Printer* (December 1888): 262; for Reilly, *Inland Printer* (March 1894): 467; *Union Printer* (30 December 1893), quoted in *Inland Printer* (February 1894): 398.

49. *Philadelphia Bulletin,* 4 October 1899, 12. See also *Inland Printer* (December 1899): 384; William Henry Stubbs, *Stubbs Manual: A Practical Treatise on Linotype Keyboard Manipulation* (Baltimore, Md.: William Henry Stubbs, 1902), 2.

50. *Inland Printer* (December 1899): 384.

51. Stubbs, *Stubbs Manual,* 38; *Inland Printer* (January 1900): 584.

52. I suggest here the tendency toward organizational rationality that is a theme of late nineteenth-century modernization, and that characterizes the way we understand much "liberal" change in recent American history. Robert H. Wiebe's *The Search for Order: 1877–1920* (New York: Hill & Wang, 1967) remains a cogent expression of this "discipline."

53. Stevens, *New York Typographical Union No. 6,* 372.

54. *Inland Printer* (October 1899): 82; ibid., April 1897, 45; ibid., April 1897, 45–46.

55. Stubbs, *Stubbs Manual,* 38; Stevens, *New York Typographical Union*

No. 6, 337; Tracy. *History of the Typographical Union,* 638; see also Loft, *The Printing Trades,* 121; and *Inland Printer* (September 1900): 848.

56. *Inland Printer* (January 1900): 584.

57. Barnes, McCann, and Duguid, *Fast Typesetting,* 29.

8. Art and the Swifts

1. Lawson, *The Compositor as Artist, Craftsman, and Tradesman,* 14.

2. See for example the introductory comments of Peter VanWingen to the 1981 Garland Publishing Company edition of Thomas Lynch, *The Printer's Manual: A Practical Guide for Compositors and Pressmen* (Cincinnati, Ohio: Cincinnati Type Foundry, 1859), v–xi. See also Walter Sutton, *The Western Book Trade: Cincinnati as a Nineteenth-Century Publishing and Book-Trade Center* (Columbus, Ohio: Ohio State University Press, 1961).

3. Oscar Harpel, *Harpel's Typograph, or, Book of Specimens* (Cincinnati, Ohio: Oscar Harpel, 1870), 32.

4. Ibid., 24.

5. Maurice Annenberg (ed.), *A Typographic Journey through the Inland Printer* (Baltimore, Md.: Maran Press, 1977), October 1891, 386–87.

6. The English Arts and Crafts Movement, inspired by John Ruskin and led in the late nineteenth century by William Morris, arrived in the United States with many precepts intact, notably a hostility to "cheap and nasty" Victorian mass production. Philip B. Meggs, *A History of Graphic Design* (New York: Van Nostrand Reinhold Company, 1983), 202.

7. Harpel, *Harpel's Typograph,* 244.

8. Ibid., 24, 244 (Harpel's italic).

9. *Printers' Circular* (September 1870): 287.

10. Ibid., December 1870, 426.

11. Ibid., November 1870, 381.

12. Ibid., February 1871, 509.

13. Ibid.

14. Harpel, *Harpel's Typograph,* 4, 3.

15. Actually, prepublication subscription orders cost $5 for the standard version and $10 for the limited edition; subsequently the prices were $5.50 and $10.50. *Printers' Circular* (February 1871): 517. One hundred thirty years later, a *Typograph* fetched $2,000 in the rare book market. Harpel, *Harpel's Typograph,* 4.

16. *Printers' Circular* (December 1870); 426.

17. See, for example, *Printers' Circular* (December 1872): 364.

18. Barnes, McCann, and Duguid, *Fast Typesetting,* 21–22.

19. *Inland Printer* (April 1886); 403; Lawson, *The Compositor as Artist, Craftsmen, and Tradesmen,* 13.

20. Annenberg, *Typographic Journey through the Inland Printer,* 386.

21. Ellen Mazur Thomson, *The Origins of Graphic Design in America, 1870–1920* (New Haven, Conn.: Yale University Press, 1997), 57; *Inland*

Printer (December 1883): 1; ibid., September 1885, 538. See also *Inland Printer* (March 1886), 363.

22. *Inland Printer* (March 1886): 363.

23. Ibid., March 1885, 246; ibid., September 1885, 538; ibid., March 1886, 363; ibid., January 1888, 297.

24. Allexon's wins perhaps were coupled with some embarrassment. The original five-person committee consisted of executives or spokespersons of prominent Chicago printing firms, including B. F. Philbrick of Shepard and Johnson Printing Co., the publishers of *Inland Printer* and employers of Mr. Allexon. *Inland Printer* (September 1885): 538; ibid., October 1886, 54.

25. Ibid., January 1890, 317.

26. Thomson, *Origins of Graphic Design,* 45–49.

27. *Inland Printer* (April 1885): 294.

28. Ibid., April 1884, 11.

29. A. Jay, "Artistic Printing," *Artist Printer* 7 (December 1889): 27, as quoted in Thomson, *Origins of Graphic Design,* 45; *Inland Printer* (December 1892): 213.

30. Thomson, *Origins of Graphic Design,* 64.

31. Ibid.

32. See, for example, Joseph Blumenthal, *The Printed Book in America* (Boston: Godine, 1977), 19. See also Meggs, *History of Graphic Design,* 216–17, and Thomson, *Origins of Graphic Design,* 64.

33. A shopfloor profile of Rogers conforms to Robert H. Wiebe's description of an emerging "new" middle-class man. See Wiebe, *Search for Order,* 111–13.

34. Payroll 1880–1883, fMS Am 2030.1 (26), Riverside Press, Archives of Houghton Mifflin Co., Houghton Library, Harvard University, Cambridge, Massachusetts.

35. Blumenthal, *Printed Book in America,* 11–12.

36. Ellen B. Ballou, *The Building of the House: Houghton Mifflin's Formative Years* (Boston: Houghton Mifflin 1970), 533.

37. Blumenthal, *Printed Book in America,* 16.

38. Bruce Rogers to Thomas Wood Stevens, 4 March 1904, quoted in ibid., 21–22.

39. Ibid., 537; Riverside Press, *A Portrait Catalogue of the Books Published by Houghton, Mifflin & Company* (Cambridge, Mass.: Riverside Press, 1905–06), 218, 240.

9. The Death of a Velocipede

1. *Inland Printer* (October 1884): 42.

2. The best source on printing's occupational diseases is Alice Hamilton and Charles H. Verriel, *Hygiene of the Printing Trades* (Washington, D.C.: Government Printing Office, U.S. Department of Labor, Bureau of Labor Statistics Bulletin No. 209, 1917). Before Hamilton's pathbreaking studies,

in printing and elsewhere, there were no entirely reliable statistics on sickness and death among printers.

3. Hamilton and Verriel, *Hygiene of the Printing Trades,* 11. The famous Swift Joseph McCann and Augusta Lewis, founder of Women's Typographical No. 1, both found paths away from the composing room and thereby escaped their actuarial destinies. McCann left the *New York Herald* in 1888, moving to Washington, D.C., where he became a proofreader at the Government Printing Office and met and married Mary A. McDermott. In time he would invent a training keyboard for Linotype operators. Lewis married Alexander Troup, a printer and former secretary of the International Typographical Union. In 1872 Augusta Lewis Troup moved with her husband to New Haven, Connecticut, where he had founded the *New Haven Union.* Mrs. Troup thereupon assumed leadership of various Italian-American causes, earning abundant local esteem. Both Joseph McCann and Augusta Lewis Troup lived well into the twentieth century.

4. Hamilton and Verriel, *Hygiene of the Printing Trades,* 16.

5. *Inland Printer* (February 1885): 200; ibid., November 1886, 88.

6. Boston Typographical Union. *Leaves of History,* 33.

7. *Printers' Circular* (October 1871): 8.

8. *Inland Printer* (August 1886): 701; ibid., October 1887, 59.

9. Ibid., February 1885, 200; Hamilton and Verriel, *Hygiene of the Printing Trades,* 87–90. See also *American Dictionary of Printing and Bookmaking,* 111.

10. *Inland Printer* (November 1886): 88.

11. Stevens, *New York Typographical Union No. 6,* 502. See also Hamilton and Verriel, *Hygiene of the Printing Trades,* 72–82.

12. Hamilton and Verriel, *Hygiene of the Printing Trades,* 82; ibid., 5–6. Subsequent tests on lead dust found it "sterile as far as tubercle bacilli are concerned." See Frederick Hoffman, *Health Survey of the Printing Trades, 1922–1925* (Washington, D.C.: Government Printing Office, U.S. Department of Labor, Bureau of Labor Statistics Bulletin No. 427, 1927), 122.

13. Hamilton and Verriel, *Hygiene of the Printing Trades,* 90; *Inland Printer* (April 1884): 10–11.

14. Quoted in Stevens, *New York Typographical Union No. 6,* 504.

15. Ibid., 503.

16. *Inland Printer* (November 1886): 88.

17. Stevens, *New York Typographical Union No. 6,* 502, 504.

18. Boston Typographical Union, *Leaves of History,* 33.

19. *Inland Printer* (October 1887): 59.

20. Ibid., August 1886, 701.

21. Hamilton and Verriel, *Hygiene of the Printing Trades,* 95; McCann, "Old Time 'Swifts.'"

22. Hamilton and Verriel, *Hygiene of the Printing Trades,* 96.

23. *Printers' Circular* (May 1886): 42.

24. Annenberg, *Typographic Journey through the Inland Printer,* January 1895, 491.

25. Ibid.

26. *Philadelphia Inquirer,* 15 March 1886, 2; *New York Herald,* 16 December 1885; *Printers' Circular* (August 1886): 105; *Printers' Register* (6 September 1886): 51.

27. Barnes, McCann, and Duguid, *Fast Typesetting,* 39.

Afterword

1. Duffy, *The Skilled Compositor, 1850–1914,* 120.

2. Robert Bringhurst. *The Elements of Typographic Style* (Vancouver, Canada: Hartley & Marks, 1992), 163.

3. Matthew Butterick, "Type Is Dead: Long Live Type," *Texts on Type: Critical Writings on Typography,* eds. Steven Heller and Philip B. Meggs (New York: Allworth Press, 2001), 39.

4. Butterick, "Type Is Dead: Long Live Type," 40.

5. See, for instance, Megan L. Benton, *Beauty and the Book: Fine Editions and Cultural Distinction in America* (New Haven, Conn.: Yale University Press, 2000).

Bibliography

Primary Sources

Manuscript Collections

Dublin Typographical Provident Society, Minute Books, Trinity College Library, Dublin, Ireland.

McCann, Joseph W. The McCann Archives are in the possession of Charles H. Potter, Washington, D.C.

Munsell, Joel. "Printers Scraps: Feats of Fast Typesetting," volume 11 of bound scrapbooks containing newspaper clippings, marginal notes, and assorted ephemera. Rare Books and Manuscripts Collection, Butler Library, Columbia University.

New York Local No. 6 of the International Typographical Union, Minute Books, New York (N.Y.) Public Library.

Riverside Press Archives of Houghton Mifflin Co., Houghton Library, Harvard University, Cambridge, Massachusetts.

Periodical Publications

PRINTING JOURNALS

American Artisan and Patent Record	*Printer's Register*
Inland Printer	*The Proof-Sheet*
Paper & Printing Trades Journal	*Typographical Journal*
Printers' Circular	*Typographical Messenger*

NEWSPAPERS

Boston Advertiser	*Philadelphia Inquirer*
Boston Globe	*Philadelphia Press*
Boston Herald	*Philadelphia Record*
Boston Post	Philadelphia *Times*
Boston Journal	*Providence Journal*
Chicago Tribune	*Revolution*
New York Herald	*Rochester Democrat and Chronicle*
New York Sun	*Rochester Morning Herald*
New York Times	

Nineteenth-Century Printing Literature

Alden Typesetting and Distributing Machine Co. *The Wonderful Type-Setting and Distributing Machine.* New York: Alden Typesetting and Distributing Machine Co., 1863.

American Dictionary of Printing and Bookmaking. New York: Howard Lockwood & Co., 1894.

Annenberg, Maurice, ed. *A Typographic Journey through the Inland Printer.* Baltimore, Md.: Maran Press, 1977.

Barnes, William C., Joseph W. McCann, and Alexander Duguid. *A Collation of Facts Relative to Fast Typesetting.* New York: Concord Cooperative Printing Company, 1887.

Boston Typographical Union, *Illustrated Historical Souvenir.* 1898.

———. *Leaves of History: From the Archives of Boston Typographical Union No. 13.* Boston: Boston Typographical Union, 1923.

DeVinne, Theodore Low. *The Printers' Price List: A Manual for the Use of Clerks and Book-Keepers in Job Printing Offices.* New York: Francis Hart & Company, 1871.

Hamilton, Alice, and Charles H. Verriel. *Hygiene of the Printing Trades.* Washington, D.C.: Government Printing Office, U. S. Department of Labor, Bureau of Labor Statistics Bulletin No. 209, 1917.

Harpel, Oscar. *Harpel's Typograph, or, Book of Specimens.* Cincinnati, Ohio: Oscar Harpel, 1870.

Hoffman, Frederick. *Health Survey of the Printing Trades, 1922–1925.* Washington, D.C.: Government Printing Office, U.S. Department of Labor, Bureau of Labor Statistics Bulletin No. 427, 1927.

International Typographical Union. *A Study of the History of the Interna-*

tional Typographical Union, 1852–1966. Two Volumes. Colorado Springs: International Typographical Union, 1964, 1967.

Lynch, Thomas. *The Printer's Manual: A Practical Guide for Compositors and Pressmen*. Cincinnati, Ohio: Cincinnati Type Foundry, 1859.

McCann, Joseph W. "Old Time 'Swifts.'" In *Convention Souvenir*, publication of the International Typographical Union, 60th Session, Providence, R.I., August 10–15, 1914.

MacKellar, Thomas. *The American Printer: A Manual of Typography*. Philadelphia: MacKellar, Smiths & Jordan, 1885.

McVicar, John. *Origin and Progress of the Typographical Union: Its Proceedings as a National and International Organization, 1850–1891*. Lansing, Mich.: D. D. Thorp, Printer and Binder, 1891.

Providence Typographical Union. *Printers and Printing in Providence, 1762–1907*. Providence, R.I.: Typographical Union No. 33, 1907.

Ringwalt, Luther J., ed. *American Encyclopaedia of Printing*. Philadelphia: Menamin & Ringwalt, 1871.

Riverside Press. *A Portrait Catalogue of the Books Published by Houghton, Mifflin & Company*. Cambridge, Mass.: Riverside Press, 1905–06.

———. *The Riverside Press*. Cambridge, Mass.: Riverside Press, 1911.

Southward, John. *Type-Composing Machines of the Past, the Present, and the Future*. Leicester, U.K.: Raithley, Lawrence & Co., De Montfort Press, 1891.

Stevens, George A. *New York Typographical Union No. 6: A Study of a Modern Trade Union and Its Predecessors*. Albany, N.Y.: J. B. Lyon Company, 1913.

Stubbs, William Henry. *Stubbs Manual: A Practical Treatise on Linotype Keyboard Manipulation*. Baltimore, Md.: William Henry Stubbs, 1902.

Thompson, John S. *History of Composing Machines*. Chicago: Inland Printer Co., 1904.

Tracy, Walter A. *History of the Typographical Union*. Indianapolis, Ind.: International Typographical Union, 1913.

Walker, Edward, and Paul S. Koda. *The Art of Book-Binding: A Descriptive Account of the New York Book-Bindery*. New Castle, Del: Oak Knoll Books, 1984 (New York: E. Walker & Sons, 1850).

Wilson, John. *A Treatise on English Punctuation*. 16th ed. Boston: Crosby & Ainsworth, 1866.

Yeaton, Charles C. *Manual of the Alden Type-Setting and Distributing Machine*. New York: Francis Hart and Company, 1865.

Secondary Sources

Baehr, Harry W., Jr. *The New York Tribune Since the Civil War*. New York: Dodd, Mead & Company, 1936.

Baker, Elizabeth Faulkner. *Printers and Technology: A History of the International Printing Pressmen and Assistants' Union*. New York: Columbia University Press, 1957.

Ballou, Ellen B. *The Building of the House: Houghton Mifflin's Formative Years.* Boston: Houghton Mifflin 1970.

Baron, Ava. "Contested Terrain Revisited: Technology of Gender Definitions of Work in the Printing Industry, 1850–1920." In *Women, Work, and Technology: Transformations,* edited by Barbara Drygulski Wright, 62–65. Ann Arbor, Mich.: University of Michigan, 1987.

———. "Questions of Gender: Deskilling and Demasculinization in the U.S. Printing Industry, 1830–1915." *Gender & History* 1, no. 2 (1989): 178–99.

———. "Women and the Making of the American Working Class: A Study of the Proletarianization of Printers." *The Review of Radical Political Economics* 14 (Fall 1982): 23–42.

———. ed. *Work Engendered: Toward a New History of American Labor.* Ithaca, N.Y.: Cornell University Press, 1991.

Barry, Kathleen. *Susan B. Anthony: A Biography of a Singular Feminist.* New York: New York University Press, 1988.

Benton, Megan L. *Beauty and the Book: Fine Editions and Cultural Distinction in America.* New Haven, Conn.: Yale University Press, 2000.

Biggs, Mary. "Neither Printer's Wife nor Widow: American Women in Typesetting, 1830–1950." *Library Quarterly* 50 (1980): 431–52.

Blumenthal, Joseph. *The Printed Book in America.* Boston: Godine, 1977.

Bringhurst, Robert. *The Elements of Typographic Style.* Vancouver, Canada: Hartley & Marks, 1992.

Burr, Christina. "'That Coming Curse—The Incompetent Compositress': Class and Gender Relations in the Toronto Typographical Union during the Late Nineteenth Century," *Canadian Historical Review* 74, no. 3 (1993): 344–66.

Butterick, Matthew. "Type Is Dead: Long Live Type." In *Texts on Type: Critical Writings on Typography,* edited by Steven Heller and Philip B. Meggs, 39–41. New York: Allworth Press, 2001.

Carey, James W. *Communication as Culture: Essays on Media and Society.* Cambridge, Mass.: Unwin Hyman, Inc., 1988.

Chudacoff, Howard P. *The Age of the Bachelor: Creating an American Subculture.* Princeton, N.J.: Princeton University Press, 1999.

Cobb, Irvin S. *Stickfuls: Compositions of a Newspaper Minion.* New York: George H. Doran Company, 1923.

Cowan, Ruth Schwartz. *A Social History of American Technology.* New York: Oxford University Press, 1997.

Darnton, Robert. *The Great Cat Massacre and Other Episodes in French Cultural History.* New York: Vintage, 1985.

Dennett, Andrea Stulman. *Weird and Wonderful: The Dime Museum in America.* New York: New York University Press, 1997.

DuBois, Ellen Carol. *Feminism and Suffrage: The Emergence of an Independent Women's Movement in America, 1848–1869.* Ithaca, N.Y.: Cornell University Press, 1978.

Duffy, Patrick. *The Skilled Compositor, 1850–1914: An Aristocrat among Working Men.* Aldershot, U.K.: Ashgate Publishing Ltd., 2000.

Duncan, Bingham. *Whitelaw Reid: Journalist, Politician, Diplomat.* Athens, Ga.: University of Georgia Press, 1975.

Fabian, Ann. *Card Sharps, Dream Books, & Bucket Shops: Gambling in 19th-Century America.* Ithaca, N.Y.: Cornell University Press, 1990.

Flexner, Eleanor. *Century of Struggle: The Woman's Rights Movement in the United States.* Cambridge, Mass.: Belknap Press of Harvard University Press, 1959.

———. "Augusta Lewis Troup." In *Notable American Women,* Vol. 2. Edited by Edward T. James, 478. Cambridge, Mass.: Harvard University Press, 1971.

Foner, Philip. *Women and the American Labor Movement: From Colonial Times to the Eve of World War I.* New York: The Free Press, 1979.

Gaskell, Philip. *A New Introduction to Bibliography.* New York: Oxford University Press, 1972 (1974).

Goble, Corban. "Rogers's Typograph Versus Mergenthaler's Linotype: The Push and Shove of Patents and Priorities in the 1890s." *Printing History* 35: 26–44.

———. "Mark Twain's Nemesis: The Paige Compositor," *Printing History* 36: 2–16.

Gorn, Elliott J. *The Manly Art: Bare-Knuckle Prize Fighting in America.* Ithaca, N.Y.: Cornell University Press, 1986.

Gray, Barbara L. "Organizational Struggles of Working Women in the Nineteenth Century." *Labor Studies Journal* 16 (Summer 1991): 16–34.

Harris, Neil. *Humbug: The Art of P. T. Barnum.* Chicago: University of Chicago Press, 1973.

Herron, Belva Mary. "Unionization for Women: The Typographical Union." In *Root of Bitterness: Documents of the Social History of American Women,* edited by Nancy F. Cott, 338–42. New York: Dutton, 1972. (originally Belva Mary Herron, "Labor Organization Among Women," *University of Illinois Bulletin* 2, no. 2 [1905]: 16–24).

Holtzberg-Call, Maggie. *The Lost World of the Craft Printer.* Urbana, Ill.: University of Illinois Press, 1992.

Huss, Richard E. *The Development of Printers' Mechanical Typesetting Methods, 1822–1925.* Charlottesville, Va.: University Press of Virginia, 1973.

———. *Dr. Church's "Hoax": The Inventions of a Yankee Genius.* Lancaster, Pennsylvania, Pa.: Graphic Arts Inc., 1976.

Kelber, Harry, and Carl Schlesinger. *Union Printers and Controlled Automation.* New York: Free Press, 1967.

Kugler, Israel. "The Trade Union Career of Susan B. Anthony." *Labor History* 2 (1961): 90–100.

Laurie, Bruce. *Artisans into Workers: Labor in Nineteenth-Century America.* New York: Noonday Press, 1989.

Lawson, Alexander. *The Compositor as Artist, Craftsman, and Tradesman.* Athens, Ga.: Press of the Nightowl, 1990.

Lazerow, Jama. "'The Workingman's Hour': The 1886 Labor Uprising in Boston." *Labor History* 21 (1980): 200–220.

Lipset, Seymour Martin, Martin Trow, and James Coleman. *Union Democracy: The Internal Politics of the International Typographical Union.* Garden City, N.J.: Doubleday Anchor Books, 1962.

Loft, Jacob. *The Printing Trades.* New York: Farrar & Rinehart, Inc., 1944.

Lum, Khalid. *Augusta Lewis Troup: Elm City Suffragist.* New Haven, Conn.: Independent, 1987.

McNamara, Brooks. "'A Congress of Wonders': The Rise and Fall of the Dime Museum," *Emerson Society Quarterly* 20 (3rd quarter 1974): 216–32.

Meggs, Philip B. *A History of Graphic Design.* New York: Van Nostrand Reinhold Company, 1983.

Mokyr, Joel. *The Lever of Riches: Technological Creativity and Economic Progress.* New York: Oxford University Press, 1990.

Montgomery, David. *Beyond Equality: Labor and the Radical Republicans, 1862–1872.* New York: Random House, 1967.

————. *Workers' Control in America: Studies in the History of Work, Technology, and Labor Struggles* Cambridge, Mass.: Cambridge University Press, 1979.

Moran, James. *Printing Presses: History and Development from the Fifteenth Century to Modern Times.* Berkeley, Calif.: University of California Press, 1973.

Nasaw, David. *Going Out: The Rise and Fall of Public Amusements.* New York: Basic Books, 1993.

Potter, Charles H. *Typeline.* Washington, D.C.: U.S. Government Printing Office Employees newsletter. Summer 1991.

Pretzer, William S. "Tramp Printers: Craft Culture, Trade Unions, and Technology," *Printing History* 6, no. 2 (1984): 3–16.

Rheault, Charles A. *In Retrospect: The Riverside Press, 1852–1971.* Boston: Society of Printers, 1979.

Rorabaugh, W. J. *The Craft Apprentice: From Franklin to the Machine Age in America.* New York: Oxford University Press, 1986.

Rosenzweig, Roy. *Eight Hours for What We Will: Workers and Leisure in an Industrial City, 1870–1920.* Cambridge, Mass.: Cambridge University Press, 1983.

Saxon, A. H. *P. T. Barnum: The Legend and the Man.* New York: Columbia University Press, 1989.

Schlesinger, Carl, ed. *The Biography of Ottmar Mergenthaler, Inventor of the Linotype.* New Castle, Del.: Oak Knoll Books, 1992. (Originally published as *Biography of Ottmar Mergenthaler and History of the Linotype,* Baltimore, Md.: n. p., 1898.)

Schudson, Michael. *Discovering the News: A Social History of American Newspapers.* New York: Basic Books, 1978.

Sutton, Walter. *The Western Book Trade: Cincinnati as a Nineteenth-Century Publishing and Book-Trade Center.* Columbus, Ohio: Ohio State University Press, 1961.

Tebbel, John. *Between Covers: The Rise and Transformation of American Book Publishing.* New York: Oxford University, 1987.

Thomson, Ellen Mazur. *The Origins of Graphic Design in America, 1870–1920.* New Haven, Conn.: Yale University Press, 1997.

Wecter, Dixon. *Sam Clemens of Hannibal.* Boston: Houghton Mifflin Company, 1952.

Weir, Robert E. *Beyond Labor's Veil: The Culture of the Knights of Labor.* University Park, Pa.: Pennsylvania State University Press, 1996.

Wiebe, Robert H. *The Search for Order: 1877–1920.* New York: Hill & Wang, 1967.

Winship, Michael. *American Literary Publishing in the Mid-Nineteenth Century.* Cambridge, Mass.: Cambridge University Press, 1995.

Index

of, 55–59; Linotype and, 145–50; "long revolution" of, 14–16, 51–55; *New York Tribune* and, 141–45; "re-masculinization" of, 150–51; shop-floor reorganization and, 154–56
typesetting races: Arensberg Wager, 37–40; Barnes-McCann match, xiii–xiv, 89–91; Boston tourna-ments, 115–24; Chicago tourna-ment, 98–109; McCann-Somers match, 86, 87–88; Memphis tour-nament, 87; Monheimer-Thienes races, 151; Philadelphia Linotype race, 152–53; Philadelphia tourna-ment, 132–41; Pittsburgh tourna-ment, 87; Providence race, 39; Rochester tournament, 93–94
Typograph (John R. Rogers), 211 n. 38
Typographic Messenger, 41, 169

Ulrich, Al, 42
Union Printer, 152
United States Telegraph, 18
Updike, Daniel Berkeley, 156, 176
U.S. Department of Labor, 178, 181, 184

Van Bibber, W. H., 87
Varitype, xvi

Wall, C. C., 38
Wall, Michael, 85
Wallace, Hugh, 154
Walsh, John, 75
Wang, xvi
Washington, James, 134, 136, 137
Washington Republican, 166
Welch (composing machine tester), 55, 57, 202 n. 8
West, J. H., 117
White, Miss (printer), Boston typeset-ting race and, 119–24
Willard (composing machine tester), 57, 59

Willard, Press, 28
Willard, Thomas, 180
Williams, Jim, 27
Williamstown, Ireland, 84
Wilson, John A., 161, 166
Wilson's Business Directory, 10
Windows operating system, 189
Winship, Michael, 10
Withee (Providence printer), 28
Woburn Advertiser, 122
women printers: Anthony-Lewis de-bates, 67–82; Boston women's race and, 119–30; classic trade and, 7–8, 18; disgust with shopfloor habits, 129–30; gendered composing ma-chines and, 56–59; International Typographical Union apprentice programs and, 53–54; "manly com-petence" and, 71–72; photocompo-sition and, 188; twentieth-century decline of, 188; union displacement and, 129–30, 205 n. 36; union membership and, 111–12
Women's Typographical Union No. 1, 66; collapse of, 82–83, 111, 124, 125, 129; founding of, 69; Interna-tional Typographical Union charter and, 70–71, 76; marriage and, 82; New York book and job strike of 1869 and, 73–74
Wonderful Type-Setting and Distrib-uting Machine, The, 57
Woodhull, Victoria, 81
Woods, Jimmy, 39
Working Women's Association, 66, 67–69, 74, 78
World Wide Web, 189

Yates, Edgar, 25, 27–28
Yeaton, Charles C.: Alden Typesetting Company and, 55; corporate prospectus and, 57–59; marketing strategy of, 56–57
Young, James, 16